GRAPHICS TABLET SOLUTIONS

Iril C. Kolle

Graphics Tablet Solutions

Credits: Cover and interior design, Michelle Frey, Stephanie Japs, Cathie Tibbetts, and John Windhorst, *DOV Graphics*; copy editor, Lori Jareo, *WordTech Communications*; index, Kevin Broccoli, *Broccoli Information Management*.

Library of Congress Catalog Number 2001086929

ISBN 1-929685-14-9

5   4   3   2   1

MUSKA&LIPMAN

Muska & Lipman Publishing
2645 Erie Avenue, Suite 41
Cincinnati, Ohio 45208
www.muskalipman.com
publisher@muskalipman.com

This book is composed in Melior, Columbia, Helvetica, and Courier typefaces using QuarkXpress 4.1.1, Adobe PhotoShop 5.0.2, and Adobe Illustrator 8.0. Created in Cincinnati, Ohio, in the United States of America.

About the Author

Iril C. Kolle
www.iril.no

Iril C. Kolle was born in Oslo, Norway, and was educated in signmaking and decoration before moving on to graphic design and, later, visual arts. She has worked with graphic design since 1986, primarily with magazines and newspapers, and has also done illustrations for various publications in Norway. After a brief detour as a journalist, Iril went back to design, discovering the Internet and HTML in the mid-1990s, when she designed one of the first e-commerce solutions in Norway. Simultaneously, she started using her first graphics tablet with Photoshop. She has worked with Internet solutions ever since; her portfolio contains Web solutions for clients ranging from ship brokers to motorcycle resellers and everything in between. She works 100 percent electronically, using a Wacom Intuos Tablet, and has created a tutorial on using Photoshop masks and Intuos for Wacom Europe. She now has her own company, developing concepts for the Internet and advising clients on Internet solutions.

Iril lives in the country with her fiancé, four cats, a dog, a turtle, and several fish, and she loves gardening.

Dedication

To Jann Owe for nudging me in the right direction and bearing with my many whims and projects, and to my mother, Ragnhild, for always being supportive.

Acknowledgments

Not in my wildest dreams—and they can be pretty wild—did I ever imagine I'd write a book. Thanks to the initiative of Andy Shafran at Muska & Lipman, not only have I written a book, but I've also discovered just how much fun writing really is.

My warmest thanks go to Hope Stephan, the managing editor of Muska & Lipman. Hope has done an outstanding job of coaching, encouraging, and supporting me throughout the entire project. Optimistic, fun, and eye-opening e-mails have arrived from Hope at regular intervals, giving me boosts of confidence when I really needed them. Lori Jareo has been supportive as well, giving me some good advice. I am likewise grateful to the other members of the production team, as they have all done a marvelous job with the book. Finally, a sincere and grateful "thank you" to the excellent graphic artists and designers out there, especially those who generously share their tips, tricks, and ideas. I sincerely hope this book will demystify a few graphic arts tricks as well, be inspirational, and fun to read.

Credits

Adobe—Photoshop, Elements, Illustrator, and Adobe Gamma are registered trademarks of Adobe Inc. Figure 7.17 in Chapter 7 is taken from the Photoshop 5.5 Tutorial CD.

Astrup Fearnley—Chapter 9, Figures 9.4 and 9.5.

Brendmoe & Kirkestuen—Vestbanen photo: Chapter 6, Figures 6.21 to 6.24.

Corel—Painter, CorelDRAW, Corel PHOTO-PAINT, Corel ColorPremium, and so on, are registered trademarks of Corel Inc.

Ecolchem Norway—Chapter 9, Figure 9.20. *Thanks to Jan Erik and Morten!*

Harley-Davidson—Harley-Davidson is a registered trademark.

Harley-Davidson Christiania—Web site illustration and examples in Chapter 6, Figures 6.25-6.30. *Thanks to Thomas and Stian!*

Harley-Davidson Christiania Chapter—Chapter 9, Figure 9.12. *Thanks to Ståle*

Homdrum, Gunnar—Photos in Chapter 6: Figures 6.1 to 6.5, and 6.12 to 6.20. Chapter 10: Figure 10.1, Appendix Figure A.10. *Thanks a lot, Gunnar!*

Legemidler og Samfunn—Illustrations created for its monthly publication: Chapter 7: Figure 7.28 to 7.30. Chapter 8: Figures 8.17 to 8.25. *Thanks to Jan and Anne!*

Pantone—Pantone OfficeColor Assistant, Pantone Digital Color System Guide, Pantone ColorSuite for Businesses, Pantone ColorWeb Pro, and Pantone Matching System Colors are registered trademarks of Pantone Inc. A picture of the Pantone Web site is used in Chapter 6, Figure 6.40.

Wacom GmbH Europe—The Christmas card tutorial and examples in Chapter 7.

Contents

Introduction

Thanks for buying this book! *Graphics Tablet Solutions* is a problem-solving and practical book, filled with hands-on examples to help you learn about graphics tablets and how to use them with various drawing and photo-editing programs. The book is loaded with examples, starting from scratch, that you can follow; and it has tricks and techniques you can apply to your existing artwork or photographs. *Graphics Tablet Solutions* will help you get the most out of your graphics tablet and give you sound advice on buying a tablet if you don't yet have one.

Professionals and amateurs alike can easily follow the examples. At the same time, advanced techniques are presented to give your work a distinctive, professional-looking result. Almost 400 color illustrations will guide you through the secrets of working with a graphics tablet.

What You'll Find in This Book:

You'll find several ways in which information about graphics tablets is delivered to you:

▶ **Tutorials** on drawing vector and bitmap graphics, creating artwork, and editing photographs. You'll also see advanced techniques you can do with a tablet, and you'll explore programs like Adobe Photoshop and Illustrator, as well as Corel's Painter and CorelDRAW.

▶ **Hands-on examples** with color illustrations that show you how to work with graphics, filters, custom brushes, and more with a tablet and various input devices.

▶ **Tips** on how to find the tablet that suits your needs.

▶ **Techniques** on how to create stunning effects, not only with filters, but also by hand.

▶ **In-depth knowledge** on manipulating and editing photos, drawing masks, and creating collages.

▶ **Reviews** of tablets and input devices and the many pressure-sensitive tools in various programs.

▶ **Recommendations** of software, filters, and plug-ins that support pressure-sensitive tablets.

▶ **Time-saving tips** for various programs.

▶ **Customization tips** for your pressure-sensitive tablet and practical advice on using it.

▶ **Companion Web site** with additional tutorials, updated links, and recommendations at **www.iril.no.**

Whom This Book Is for

Graphics Tablet Solutions is for anyone either considering buying a graphics tablet or who already owns one. This book can help the prospective purchaser make an intelligent choice about product features and how well they work. It can also help those who already own a graphics tablet utilize this tool to its fullest potential. This book is for professionals who crave in-depth knowledge and want to learn some new tricks and techniques, but also for ordinary people who enjoy drawing or editing their vacation and holiday photographs. *Graphics Tablet Solutions* will show you how to realize more of your artistic potential.

How This Book Is Organized

Graphics Tablet Solutions is divided into four parts. These parts are further divided into twelve chapters, plus appendices. The appendices have Web links and information about various software packages and filters.

Here are the various parts:

Part 1: Your Tablet and Tools

Chapters 1, 2, and 3—Part One guides you through selecting your tablet with an overview of graphics tablets, including size and compatibility issues. This part continues with installation procedures and reviews various input devices for Wacom tablets. You can use this information to customize your tablet and tools. Part One also has a thorough overview of the many pressure-sensitive tools in applications like Photoshop (6.0, Elements and 5.5), Painter, and Illustrator. You'll also get a few practical tips regarding tablet placement and desk clutter.

Part 2: Objects, Photos, and Color

Chapters 4, 5, and 6—In Part Two, you'll learn everything you need to know to work efficiently with objects, selections, and backgrounds. Various tools and tips used in working with selections are also discussed. You'll learn about layers and how to work with them, creating both quick and advanced masks. Paste-into techniques and other creative procedures are presented, and you'll find out about Photoshop 6.0's layer styles and effects. You can also investigate how to use masks and why a tablet lets you manage masks without plug-ins.

You'll learn to adjust illustrations professionally—editing photographs, retouching images, and improving photo composition. Transformation tricks, adding depth and interest to a photo, and creating perspective are all there. You'll also find out the necessary techniques for creating photo collages and removing red eye with Photoshop Elements' Red Eye Brush.

You'll work with color and explore how to adjust and replace colors in images. You'll also read about color management and color modes.

Part 3: Creating Graphics

Chapters 7, 8, and 9—Part Three starts with basic drawing techniques and drawing with brushes and pens. I'll also show you how to create cartoon characters and compose an illustration. Then, we'll cover understanding and creating vector graphics and bitmapped images; you'll also learn to combine them. There is also a section that covers paths and s. shapes, and applying effects. You'll see how and when to use clip art and icons.

The secrets of optimized Web graphics are likewise revealed in this section. Learn how they look good and load fast. Compression is discussed here, too. You'll read about type on the Web and how to do effective workarounds to get the results you want for the Web pages you create.

Part 4: Special Effects and Filters

Chapters 10, 11, and 12—In Part Four, you'll learn how to draw realistic shadows and cast shadows, create depth and light, and make metal effects like brushed metal or gold. You'll also discover how industrial-looking objects are made, and then you can use the tutorials to create them yourself.

Natural weather effects, such as clouds or stormy weather, are spelled out in detail. You'll create a beach, leaves, grass, and other natural objects. Because you may need your own brushes to create natural effects, we'll create our own brushes.

In the last chapter, we'll walk through the advantages of textures and patterns used correctly. You'll become a pro in editing patterns or creating your own.

Conventions Used in This Book

The following conventions are used in this book:

All Web page URLs mentioned in the book appear in **boldface**, as in **www.wacom.com.**

Besides these terminological and typographic conventions, the book also features the following special displays for different types of important text:

TIP

Text formatted like this offers a helpful tip relevant to the topic being discussed in the main text.

NOTE

Text formatted like this highlights other interesting or useful information that relates to the topic under discussion.

CAUTION

Cautions highlight actions or commands that can make irreversible changes to your files or potentially cause problems in the future. Read them carefully, because they contain important information that can make the difference between keeping your files, software and hardware safe and losing a huge amount of work.

Keeping the Book's Content Current

Everyone involved with this book has worked hard to make it complete and accurate. But as we all know, technology changes rapidly and a small number of errors may have crept in besides. If you find any errors or have suggestions for future editions, please contact Muska & Lipman at this Web site:

www.muskalipman.com/graphicstablet

You can also find updates, corrections, and other information related to the content of the book.

Part I
Objects, Photos and Color

1

An Overview of Graphics Tablets

So you thought graphics tablets were just for professional artists and engineers working on digital masterpieces? Think again. Consumers today have a wide selection of tablets to choose from, ranging from tablets designed especially for young children to hand-held pen tablet computers useful for writing notes in your own handwriting, and professional graphics tablets.

It's true that graphics tablets were once expensive tools used mainly by design professionals. Now, they are much more affordable. With so much variety available, at so many cost levels, how do you know what to buy? That's what this chapter is for. In the following pages, we will:

▶ Explore various graphics tablets and their differences

▶ Discuss why tablet size matters

▶ Take a brief look at the new LCD tablets

▶ Look at a couple of hand-held pen tablets and tablet computers

▶ Look at compatibility issues with various programs

Graphics Tablets Up Close

The tablets that have allowed professional artists, computer-aided design (CAD) engineers, and architects to throw away pencil and paper and work electronically have more advanced functions and higher precision than their consumer cousins—and, in the past, the price tag reflected that. Now companies like Wacom are offering professional-level tablets to the home market in price ranges most people can afford.

Beyond price and size, you'll have to consider what kinds of tools come with the tablet, the level of pressure sensitivity and accuracy it offers, and the amount of resolution it has. In addition, you'll have to decide what kind of connection you need with your computer and whether the software that comes bundled with the tablet will be adequate for your needs (or whether you will have to buy other software packages).

NOTE

The pressure-sensitivity levels in a tablet determine how natural it will feel to use. Pressure sensitivity is also important to accuracy; you'll want the tablet and pen to perform as close as possible to a real-life situation with pen and paper. A tablet of 512 levels or less will do the job, but for those who draw with low pressure on their pencils in real life, a Wacom Intuos with 1,024 levels of pressure sensitivity will perform better. A tablet with no support of pressure-sensitivity will resemble drawing with your mouse in a cheap drawing program—it will give you no control whatsoever over the stroke width or stroke strength, which is what drawing is all about.

Some tablets are especially made to do just one thing—write. The iPen Pro from Cross (manufactured by Addonics) consists of a digital pen and tablet allowing you to mark up and edit documents in your own handwriting on your PC. (It is currently not available for Mac.) You can write comments and notes, make corrections, sign your name, and highlight phrases. It's compatible with Word, which makes it easy to e-mail the documents you've written. Several manufacturers have released hand-held pen tablets and pen tablet computers, which we'll look at later in this chapter.

Tablets targeted for kids in all ages (and up to adults) are also available.

A regular touchscreen lets you point your fingers directly on the screen and press for menu choices and commands. Some touchscreens come with pens attached, which you use to point-and-click directly on the screen. This system is widely used in, for example, the medical industry. The screen itself can be an LCD screen or even a regular computer monitor. Technology from manufacturers like FastPoint lets you place the pen in front of the screen and the cursor appears. Touching the screen with the pen tip, or clicking the side switch, is the same as pressing a mouse button. To configure your computer into a touchscreen system requires a so-called light pen connected to your computer and the light pen interface. The light pen functions on any CRT monitor. You can choose from several light pen styles and models. The light pen interface, which makes this gizmo work, can be installed internally or externally on your computer.

A digitizer, or digitizer tablet, is often used for sketching new images or tracing old ones. You work on the electronic tablet with a pen or puck (sometimes called a mouse), either connected to the tablet or cordless. The puck is often preferred for tracing highly detailed engineering drawings, because its crosshairs let you pinpoint ends and corners precisely. Many tablets allow parts of the tablet surface to be customized (with menu strips), so that they can be tapped to select menus and functions in applications. When drawing or tracing on the tablet, a series of X-Y coordinates (vector graphics) are created, either as a continuous stream of coordinates or as end points. Most digitizers are large, because they're used by architects and other professionals who work with large engineering drawings.

A pen tablet is specialized for handwriting, signatures, and hand marking; they're small and mostly hand-held. Advanced pen tablets are LCD panels than emulate flowing ink as the tip touches the surface and pressure is applied. You can see what you write directly on the LCD screen. This requires handwriting recognition software, often preinstalled in the pen tablet.

A graphics tablet is similar to a digitizer, and often the term digitizer is used for a graphics tablet as well. Many graphics tablets are pressure-sensitive, while many digitizers are not. A pressure-sensitive tablet lets you draw with a pen (or stylus) with precision, varying width and styles on your strokes to simulate real-life drawing. Some tablets, such as the Wacom Intuos, have additional input devices with airbrush and stroke pens for additional drawing and painting styles. Graphics tablets come in various shapes and sizes but are generally smaller than most digitizers. Some are consumer-oriented and others are for professionals, which often is reflected by the price tag and levels of pressure-sensitivity. Most graphics tablets come with a regular mouse and pen and not the digitizer puck with crosshairs, the exception being Wacom Intuos, which offers the 4D-mouse.

For those of us who have gotten beyond doodling away on a tablet just for fun, there are several graphics tablets ranges to choose from. Let's take a look at some manufacturers and their graphics tablets, in alphabetical order, with highlights on some of their products:

Acecad

Acecad makes tablets for the PC platform (Windows, OS/2) and has products that range in size from 5 × 5 inches (127mm × 127mm) to 12 × 18 inches (304 mm × 457 mm). Acecat III is a 5 × 5 tablet that comes with a three-button programmable pen (stylus) and has a resolution of 2540 lines per inch (lpi). With the Acecad driver, the pen and tablet can co-exist with another mouse or trackball. Acecad tablets have cords between the tablet and pen, and the pen is not pressure-sensitive. The programmable 3-button pen includes both "inking" and "non-inking" cartridge tips. The Acecat III is made for the home consumer market and is recommended for home office use, business, and Internet graphics.

GTCO Calcomp

GTCO Calcomp offers several tablets, ranging from small consumer-priced tablets up to large digitizers for CAD professionals. (The company offers the Learn'n'Sketch for kids as well.) The DrawingBoard III (see accompanying photo) is a small-format graphics tablet for CAD and graphic arts applications on a PC with a 2540 lpi resolution. Most of GTCO Calcomp's tablets are offered with a choice of various pointing devices. The DrawingBoard III includes a cordless pressure-sensitive pen with two side buttons and 256 levels of pressure

sensitivity. This product is available in sizes of 12 × 12 and 12 × 18 inches (30.5 × 30.5 and 30.5 × 45.7 cm), and comes with TabletWorks™ software, which is a set of tools used to customize tablet use. Calcomp offers other tablets and digitizers for the Mac platform (see the section entitled "Compatibility Issues" in this chapter). GTCO Calcomp also offers products like DrawingBoard Interactive (Dbi), a kind of "electronic copyboard" for the PC, that captures and prints notes instantly.

KB GEAR

Pablo is a small tablet for home office use and for design, animation, and photo editing. It has a drawing area of 8 × 6 inches (20.3 × 15.2 cm) and a resolution of 1000 pixels per inch (ppi) , a corded pressure-sensitive pen (256 levels), and a choice of universal serial bus (USB) or serial port connection. Pablo is offered with a suite of graphics software that includes Photoshop LE and PageMill from Adobe and WebPainter from Totally Hip Software

KB Gear also offers the "Jam Studio" package, a complete Web graphics tool kit including Web Painter and a 7 × 5-inch tablet. Jam Studio is available for both PC and Mac platforms and has a pressure-sensitive pen (256 levels).

Kurta/Altek

Kurta, a division of Altek Corporation, offers several lines of tablets, from the small PenMouse series to the medium-sized XGT tablets to the large DT-4 digitizers. Kurta's DT-4 series digitizing tablets for the CAD and GIS professional are available in four tablet sizes ranging from 18 × 24 to 42 × 60 inches. The tablets have a resolution of 1000 points/inch (40 points/mm) and a choice of two pointing devices.

Also worth mentioning is the DataFlex II Digitizer (for PC platforms), which can be rolled up for storage or transport. Dataflex II (46 × 37 inches or 1168 × 940 mm) has a cordless stylus and a 16-button cordless mouse. The PenMouse Plus (see accompanying photo) and PenMouse Pro tablets (for PC and Mac platforms) are recommended for home office and professional use. They each have a cordless pen with 512 levels of pressure-sensitivity and an eraser. These tablets come in two sizes: 4 × 5 inches (101 × 127 mm) and 6 × 9 inches (152 × 228 mm) active area, with a resolution of up to 2540 lpi.

The XGT tablets have only 256 levels of pressure sensitivity, but they are available in larger sizes: 12 × 12 inches (305 × 305 mm) and 12 × 18 inches (305 × 457 mm) drawing area. The XGT series tablets have several pointing devices: a cordless pen, a cordless four-button mouse, and a corded sixteen-button mouse. Both sizes have 2540 points/inch resolution. They both also have better accuracy than PenMouse: +/− 0.005 inch (0.127 mm).

KYE

KYE produces its Genius line of small tablets for kids and home office users working on the PC platform. The NewSketch 1212HRIII tablet (see accompanying photo) is worth mentioning for home office use because this 12 × 12-inch (305 × 305 mm) product comes with two pointing devices—a three-button stylus and four-button mouse, both programmable. This tablet has 2540 lpi resolution, a corded mouse, and a stylus that is not pressure-sensitive.

Kid's Designer features a 7 × 5 inch (178 × 127 mm) drawing area which allows children to draw, paint, and sketch. It is offered with the KidPix Studio entertainment and education software.

KYE also offers the e-Pen, which has a working area of 3 × 2 inches (76 × 50 mm) with a resolution of 1000 lpi. You can use it to draw, sketch, add a note, or simply sign your name on an electronic document. The EasyPen Pro is larger, 4 × 3 inches (101 × 76 mm), with 2540 lpi resolution. Easy Pen Pro is recommended as a travel mate to your notebook. Both of these mini-tablets are corded.

UC-Logic

UC-Logic has both a tablet keyboard and small tablets available; the SuperPen Tablet WP series, with a cordless, pressure-sensitive pen, has 512 levels of pressure-sensitivity. The SuperPenTM Tablet WP4030 and WP4030U (see accompanying photo) have an active area of 4 × 3 inches. They work with PCs running Windows 95, 98, NT 3.5, Me, or NT 4 and come with pen utilities to hand-write e-mails, sign documents, and so on.

The UC-Logic Tablet Keyboard integrates both pen and keyboard functions in a single unit for a steady writing surface with minimal cables. It provides freehand drawing, handwriting, signature, and mouse, plus traditional keyboard functions. Its pressure-sensitive pen (512 levels) enables you to draw accurately. If you're looking for a very small tablet area for notes or signatures, this is a very neat product, especially as it's cordless.

Wacom

Wacom, the industry leader, has been offering professional tablets for years for PC, Mac, UNIX, and SGI platforms. According to the company, there are more than 2 million users worldwide using Wacom tablets and tools. The small Graphire tablet for both PC and Mac (including iMac and Power Mac) is priced at the consumer level for home use. This tablet measures 4 × 5 inches (101 × 127 mm), comes in several translucent colors (see photo above), has a 1000 dpi resolution, a cordless mouse (with no mouseball to get dirty), a cordless pressure-sensitive pen (512 levels), and the choice between serial or USB interface. The Wacom control panel lets you set eraser tip functions and double side-switch functions (such as right-clicking, for instance).

Graphire comes bundled with software as well in the Graphire PowerSuite—Photoshop LE, Corel Painter Classic, Sensiva (PC only), ActiveShare (PC only), Paragraph PenOffice 2000 SE (PC only), and Wacom PenTools, which is a free set of Photoshop plug-ins with pressure-sensitive effects and filters.

The Wacom Intuos range gives you five sizes of tablets to choose from: the A6 (4 × 5 inches or 101 × 127 mm); A5 (6 × 8 inches or 152 × 203 mm); A4 (8.2 × 11.4 inches or 210 × 297 mm), both regular and oversized; and the Intuos A3 (11.4 × 16.5 inches or 29.7 × 42 cm). The Intuos range is priced at the professional level, and it is more accurate and advanced than Graphire. The Intuos range is available for PC, Mac, and SGI platforms, with 1024 levels of pressure sensitivity and a choice of six cordless tools. The various tools are described in detail in Chapter 2.

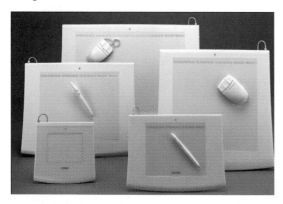

Every Intuos tablet has a programmable menu strip and supports ToolID, a system for recognizing various tools and their customizable functions. The Intuos pens recognize Tilt angles (up to +/–60 degrees), which is great for controlling the tool tip width when you're drawing and need those varying line widths. (Not all software supports this feature, however.) Intuos is clearly the most advanced tablet on the market today, because the menu strip and Wacom Tablet Control Panel give you vast possibilities for customizing the tablet to meet your needs. As with Graphire, you can set eraser tip functions on the pens and double side-switch functions. The Intuos A4 oversize and A3 tablets have an accuracy of 0.15 mm. The smaller tablets have an accuracy of 0.25 mm and resolutions of 2540 dpi. Wacom still offers two tablets in the "old" UltraPad range: an A3 (11.4 × 16.5 inches or 297 × 420 mm) tablet and even an UltraPad A2 (16.5 × 23.6 inches or 420 × 600 mm) tablet. Wacom also offers three liquid crystal display (LCD) tablets.

LCD Tablets

LCD tablets are great for artists who have difficulty achieving precision because of the high degree of hand-eye coordination required when drawing on an ordinary tablet and watching the monitor. If you haven't used a tablet before, I suggest you'd look at LCD tablets before trying ordinary tablets. If you're used to working with hand-held computers, you'll feel at home with an LCD tablet.

Currently, there are just a few LCD tablets to choose from. There are many LCD touchscreens out there, some with light pens you place in front of (not necessarily on) the screen, but few tablets. Wacom offers three LCD tablets: the PL-300, PL-400, and PL-500 (see accompanying photo). The PL-300 LCD Display and Tablet from Wacom has an active area of 8.3 × 6.2 inches (210 × 157 mm). The PL-400 has an active area and display area of 10.6 × 8 inches or 270 × 203 mm), which is a bit smaller than A4 landscape (11.4 × 8.2 inches or 297 × 210 mm). The PL500 has an active area of 11.9 × 8.9 inches (302 × 226 mm). The PL-500 is a LCD monitor with a display quality of 1024 × 768 pixels with a 24-bit color depth (supports up to 16 million colors). The display features a fully integrated graphics tablet, which means that you can draw, sketch, and write with the pen directly onto the surface of the LCD display.

TIP

Some tablets have pens that never will fall on the floor or behind furniture, because they are attached to the tablet by a cord. This is a great solution for kids, but adults want the flexibility of drawing without having a cord getting in the way. Luckily, most tablet tools are cordless nowadays, and if you invest in a cordless keyboard as well, you will see a lot less clutter on your desk. Wacom, Calcomp, and Altek offer cordless pens and pointing devices.

Other Possibilities

Since this book looks at *graphics* tablets, hand-held pen tablet computers and other solutions will mostly fall outside our main tablet category; they are created for writing and not working with advanced graphics. Still, some are worth mentioning, especially for those of you in a line of work that would benefit from portable solutions instead of large, stationary tablets. For more information about the following products, take a look at the Web links in Appendix B.

Let's take a look at a couple of manufacturers and what they have to offer:

Fujitsu

Fujitsu has several hand-held pen tablets, three in the Stylistic series (see photo): Stylistic 3500X, 3500S and 3500R. They all have a 500MHz processor, 15 GB HD, a modem, a choice of 64 to 256 MB SDRAM, and 10.4-inch displays. Choose between Windows 98 Second edition, Windows 2000 Professional, or Windows NT4 operating systems. They come with CIC PenX handwriting recognition software, a microphone, and 256-color XGA (1028 × 768 pixels) or SVGA (800 × 600 pixels) TFT displays. The Stylistic 3500S is indoor/outdoor viewable, which is a great advantage.

Mitsubishi

Mitsubishi Mobile Computing has released a couple of hand-held computer tablets. The Amity CP has a 7.5-inch color VGA LCD (640 × 480 pixels resolution) and integrated Wacom digitizer. A keypad allows fast input of numerical values, and it has handwriting recognition software as well. The software works with most applications. You can add an external keyboard, mouse, headset, microphone, monitor, printer, and other serial devices. The newer model, Amity XP (see photo), has a 8.4-inch TFT active matrix color LCD (800 × 600 pixel SVGA image) with an integrated resistive touch digitizer. It has Windows 98 as its operating system (Windows 2000 was not supported at the time of this writing), and you can add an expansion station to it.

Part I Your Tablet and Tools

Sony

Sony recently released a nicely designed pen tablet computer—a computer, tablet, and LCD-screen rolled into one package. The Sony VAIO Slimtop PCV-LX900 Pen Tablet computer has its LCD pen tablet technology from Wacom and comes complete with a cordless pen. It's pressure-sensitive, naturally. Since this is a computer as well, the price reflects that, selling for $3,000 (which actually is a bit expensive compared to similar products).

For the price of a (small) used car, you get a 1 GHz Pentium III with Windows Me and a long list of pre-installed software, including Adobe Photoshop LE (now somewhat outdated with the release of Photoshop Elements), Adobe GoLive, Microsoft Word, Adobe Premier, and lots more. I was impressed by the software list. Hardware includes a 40 GB hard disk and 128 MB memory. The display stand lets you hold the LCD as you would a pen tablet, at a normal writing angle. The display is 17.1 × 14.1 inches. I would recommend this as a second PC and not a work station for graphics professionals without additional PCs or Macs. The memory is upgradable only to 512 MB, and for Photoshop 6 you should have a *minimum* of 256 MB RAM. In addition, the included hard disk spins at only 5,400 rpm, considerably slower than desired if you're working with 3D applications (or other demanding files and applications) and you are used to disks at 7,200 rpm or faster. If you're considering buying this, add more RAM and get a faster hard disk right away.

Xplore Technologies

If you ever get the urge to drag a pen tablet through mud in the jungle, a model from the Rugged GeneSys System is what you'll want! Designed and manufactured for tough customers "in the field" and outdoors-type professionals, it's made with strong metal housings, industrial-rubber bumper system (!) and internal shock mounting for durability. It is a complete system with a docking station, keyboard, X-pander (port replicators and quick release docks provide connectors, wireless, modem, and PC card expansion options), and lots of accessories (see accompanying photo).

The GeneSys II model is fully resistant to shocks and vibration, as well as dust, dirt, humidity, moisture, and blowing rain—likely to be found in areas from your back yard to the Amazon. It has a good-sized 10.4-inch screen—SVGA (800x600) TFT Ultra Hi-Brite Color, a display that is four to five times brighter than average notebook screens, according to the manufacturer, readable in direct sunlight, dimmed light, and intense fluorescent lighting. The pen interface allows for signatures, handwriting recognition, drawing, or sketching directly onto the display. The hardware is a Intel Pentium III 500 MHz processor, 8 MB on-board video RAM, memory from 64 to 256 MB RAM, with Windows 95, 98, NT, or 2000 operating system.

Choosing the Right Size

As we've seen, graphics tablets come in various shapes and sizes. Shapes and general design are fairly standard from one brand to another, because graphics tablets are naturally square or rectangular (imitating paper sizes). There are some variations such as ergonomically contoured edges, translucent colors, and accessories. The tablets made for kids, often rounded in shape and brightly colored, stand out from the rest in design.

With a small tablet, you can rest it in your lap or hold it in your hand. Smaller tablets and tablet computers are also portable—you can carry them around and work with them outdoors, on trains, and so on. If you're looking at flexibility, take a look at hand-held pen tablets. With an A3-sized tablet (11.4 × 16.5 inches or 297 × 420 mm), you'd naturally keep it on your desk. But choosing the right size of graphics tablet is not like choosing a new keyboard or mouse, and your deciding factor should not be merely the size of your desk and whether it will fit. Rather, what you really want to consider is what you are going to do with it!

If you just need to make quick notes on it, do sketches and small graphics, or perhaps a little photo editing, you probably will do just fine with a tablet in size A4 (8.2 × 11.4 inches or 21 × 29.7 cm) or smaller. If you are concerned about the price, you will want to take a look at the consumer-friendly models (like Graphire) and steer clear from the professional lines like Intuos. This has to do not just with size, but also with functionality and available tools, which I will explain in detail later.

TIP

Choosing the right size is really easy and can be reduced to the following formula: *Big drawings, big tablets*. When you've decided on the size, you're ready to decide how much functionality and customizing you need.

Professionals will look seriously at A4 tablets but will probably opt for an A3 tablet with various tools if money is not an issue. Why? Well, most illustrations will be made in size 1:1, especially if those artists are used to drawing on paper. If artists have very small tablets and would want to make a drawing in size A3 for print with a high resolution, they would really have to adjust their drawing techniques, because what they draw in size 1:1 on the tablet will have to be "scaled" to the right format on screen. Or they would have to get used to see only small parts of their drawings at a time. But if they're drawing very small icons usually measuring 40 × 40 pixels with a 21-inch monitor and an A3 tablet, they are not using their equipment to the fullest. Buying an A3 tablet knowing small icons is what will usually be created would be overkill, and you would probably be better off spending the amount of money that an A3 tablet costs on something else!

So what will you use the tablet for? Having an idea about what you want, such as "I'd like to buy something for my kids so they can make drawings on the PC" is a good start and would probably lead you to a smaller graphics tablet. If you are a doctor, or have a profession where it would be convenient to lean back in your chair with a tablet in your lap taking notes, you also should look at smaller tablets. If you're looking for a device for CAD work, you might want to look at some digitizers as well and not just graphics tablets. Digitizers are often available in large sizes; the Kurda D-4 is available in 42 × 60 inches (1066 × 1524 mm).

When in doubt, ask someone who knows. If you know someone with a tablet, ask him or her what it's used for, if the tablet size works well, and if he or she has discovered that the pen and mouse that once seemed quite adequate pale in comparison to the airbrush on another tablet. Recommendations are a great thing, and you should always lend an ear to another's experiences, because you might hear something you have not even considered. I have an A3 tablet myself, which is just the right size for me, as I do all my work on it (illustrations, design, and everything I use the PC for) and really need a tablet that big. I probably would have been okay with an A4 tablet half the time, but I can guarantee you I would be cursing while having to make do with a smaller tablet than I need.

Choosing the Right Type

Most professional tablets today are available for both PC and Mac platforms, and some also for SGI or UNIX systems. Many home office or consumer tablets are made for the PC only. Your platform decides to some extent what kind of tablet you can buy, and the availability of a USB port also affects your choice. A USB port supports plug-and-play functionality, it's fast, and it can support several external devices. Make sure your computer has a USB port before you buy a tablet made for USB connection.

Do you have certain functions you use frequently that you'd want to program into the tablet? Some tablets, like the Intuos range, have pre-programmed the most widely used commands and functions such as "New," "Open," "Save," and so on, and have more available for you to insert. These tablet shortcuts are conveniently placed on a menu strip, which is a row of small "clickable" fields at the top of the tablet. This is especially useful if you're not used to keyboard shortcuts like Ctrl+S (Command+S on a Mac) or do not use them much.

This is a matter of preference and experience: Some "always" have one hand on the keyboard for shortcuts, while others prefer to program their tablets. Still others do their work using a combination of both, often combined with on-screen functions in the programs they are using, right-clicking with a mouse or pen, or using actions in Photoshop. The Intuos devices are completely user-specific, which means you can dedicate various functions to various tools or programs. Let's say you need the whole tablet area when you work with Painter using a pen, but you'd want to use the Quick Point area when working with a mouse in desktop publishing programs (DTP) programs like PageMaker. No problem. The control panel lets you decide what to use when. See Figure 1.1.

Figure 1.1
Close-up of a tablet
control panel (Wacom
Intuos A3) on a PC (it
looks exactly the same
on a Mac).

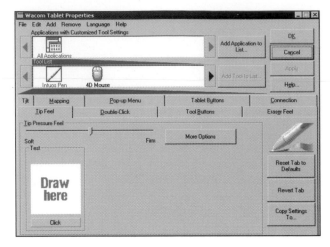

Deciding on which tablet to choose comes down to how much advanced functionality you'll
need and how experienced you are working on your computer. If you're an artist who uses an
airbrush when you work, you'd want to try the Intuos Airbrush. The Intuos tablet has the widest
range of tools (input devices) offered; other tablets have just the pen plus a mouse or two with
various programmable buttons. If you use mostly pens, you have a wider range of tablets to
choose from. For you, the decision will come down to what you need combined with what
you'd want to spend on a tablet.

Compatibility Issues

You will find a compatibility chart in Table 1.1 that lists most tablets (and a few digitizers) and
their compatibility with operating systems. I have left out most of the digitizers and hand-held
pen tablets, mostly because they either are for professional CAD use only (and therefore
available in only large sizes) or hand-held and, therefore, too small for graphics work.

In general, a consumer-oriented tablet works with any program on your PC or Mac, because its
compatibility is similar to that of an ordinary mouse. There are a few exceptions, however, and
those are usually found in some of the smaller tablets which have several bundled software
items or an entire software package of their own. Even then, this seldom is a problem if you're
buying a tablet for the kids, as many tablets support an ordinary mouse in addition to the tablet
tools. I've used Wacom tablets on various PCs and Macs for six years now and I still haven't
found a program that didn't support the pen and mouse input devices. Some variations are
found regarding what input device you're using, but then again, you probably won't use an
airbrush when you're writing a letter in Microsoft Word anyway. On Wacom's homepage, you'll
find a list of supported software: **www.wacom.com**.

Of course, a program without pressure-sensitive functions (such as a word processor) won't let
you take advantage of the tablet's pressure-sensitive options, but most drawing programs today
do, indeed, have pressure-sensitive tools.

Table 1.1

Compatibility Chart for Tablets and Operating Systems

	PC (Windows)	Mac	SGI
Acecad Acecat III, A1212, A1812	Yes (also supports OS/2 and DOS)	No	No
Aiptek HyperPen 5000, HyperPen 6000USB and 8000 USB	Yes	No	No
GTCO CalComp CADPro, DigiCad Plus	Yes	Yes	No
GTCO CalComp Summasketch III Digitzer*	Yes	Yes	No
GTCO CalComp DrawingBoard III, Summagrid V, SuperLSeries	Yes	No	No
Dynalink FreeDraw	Yes	Yes	No
Genius (KYE) NewSketch 1812HR, 1212 HRIII, EasyPen, EasyPen Pro, e-Pen, KidsDesigner	Yes (1212 also DOS)	No	No
KB Gear Pablo and Jam Studio	Yes	Yes (USB only)	No
Kurta PenMouse Plus, PenMouse Pro, XGT	Yes	Yes	No
RM Natural Pen, Wacky Kids Pad	Yes	No	No
UC-Logic SuperPen PP3333, PP6045, PP4030, WP4030, WP5540	Yes (also DOS)	No	No
Wacom Intuos range	Yes	Yes	Yes
Wacom Graphire and PL tablets	Yes	Yes	No
Wacom UltraPad A3, A2	Yes	Yes	Yes
YTG Eagle Pen and SmartPad systems	Yes	No	No

Also supports OS/2, Sun Solaris, and UNIX Systems

Before you make your purchase, ask your local dealer what software you can use with the tablet, and also have a look at the Web resources listed in Appendix B, where you will find links to all of the manufacturers' homepages.

At this point, you should have a good idea about the kind of tablet that would suit your work (or play!) and what size it should be. You might even have bought a tablet already. Turn to the next chapter for installation tips and an overview of the many tablet accessories for the Wacom Intuos tablet.

2

Installing Your Tablet

In this chapter, we'll cover most aspects of installing USB and serial port tablets for the PC and Mac platforms. We'll also look at the various input devices available for the Wacom Intuos range of tablets. These input devices, or *tools* as they're commonly called, give you the opportunity to try almost any drawing technique known under the sun. Whether you're used to drawing with a pen, painting with brushes, or creating airbrush art, there's an input device for the tablet. You'll get practical tips on how to solve problems like where to place your tablet and how to avoid desk clutter.

This chapter shows you:

▶ How to install your tablet, plus some troubleshooting tips

▶ How to pick a tool for the Wacom Intuos tablet and what the different tools do

▶ A few practical user tips

Getting Started

Because you're reading this, chances are you've opened up the carton with your newly acquired tablet and are ready to go. Or, maybe, you're still debating whether to buy a tablet. If you're still wavering, skip to the "Tools" section later in this chapter and read about all the fantastic input devices you can get. If you're already holding a CD-ROM (or floppy) with "tablet drivers" or "tablet software" printed somewhere on it, stay right here.

Whether you have a PC or Mac, installing a tablet nowadays is very easy. A few years ago, it could be a hassle (on Windows NT 3.5 and 4.0, for example), but with the degree of plug-and-play today's operating systems offer, you should be okay. So relax—it's a breeze to install a tablet on most systems. Nevertheless, you should be aware of PCs with built-in modems and also of potential conflicts with the serial port—see the section called "Troubleshooting Windows." Before we begin, and unless you're installing a tablet on a USB port, **turn off your computer**. And you might as well go get a cup of coffee now, because you won't be able to tear yourself away from your new tablet once you have it up and running. Finding your system CD-ROM is also a good idea; always keep it handy when installing new devices.

TIP

USB, or universal serial bus, is the computer standard for easier connection of peripherals to your computer. Pluses with the USB are its speed and the ability to connect numerous devices to your computer at once—technically, more than 100 (but, in practice, less, because many devices need USB bandwidth). More information can be found on the USB Web page: **http://www.usb.org/**.

Serial port or USB—how do I know which one I have? You probably do know, but in case you don't, the tablet cables look different, as you can see in Figures 2.1a and 2.1b.

Figure 2.1a (left)
The serial port connection.

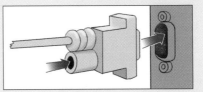
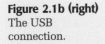

Figure 2.1b (right)
The USB connection.

Wacom has a helpful system for identifying the kind of connection a tablet requires: If your tablet model number ends with an "R," it's a serial device. If it ends with a "U," it's a USB device. If it ends with an "A," it can be connected only to an Apple desktop bus (ADB) device. Did you know that if you have a serial tablet from Wacom, you could use it not only on your PC, but on a Mac or an SGI platform as well? If you have a USB tablet, you can use it on both a PC and a Mac (providing you have a USB port, of course). Remember to get the correct drivers before you swap platforms.

Installation with a Serial Port Connection under Windows

1. With your computer turned off, connect the tablet cable to the serial (communication) port and the power cable to the tablet cable as shown in Figure 2.1a. Connect the power adapter to a power strip or an AC outlet.

2. Depending on what kind of tablet you have, there may be a power switch on the tablet—if there is, turn it on. The tablet LED indicates that your tablet has power and is ready.

3. Turn your computer back on.

4. If you have any virus protection programs running, such as Norton or McAfee, disable them until you've finished installing the tablet. Close other programs as well before installing tablet software.

Part I Your Tablet and Tools

5. Put the CD-ROM with your tablet drivers in the CD-ROM drive (or the floppy in your floppy drive).

6. Plug-and-play versions of Windows (such as 2000 or Me) will give you a dialog box saying "New Hardware Found" when you start Windows. If this happens, choose "Driver from Disk Provided by Hardware Manufacturer," press the Enter key and select your CD-ROM drive. Press Enter again and follow the screen prompts.

7. If you don't see the "New Hardware Found" dialog box, open Windows Explorer (or My Computer) and select your CD-ROM drive. Double-click the Setup icon on the CD-ROM and follow the screen prompts.

8. Now reboot. You should be up and running. You can now install any bundled software that came along with your tablet, such as Adobe Photoshop LE, Painter, or other goodies.

Installation with a USB Port Connection under Windows

1. With your PC turned on, connect the tablet cable to the USB port. (USB supports so-called "hot-plugging," so you can install or uninstall hardware without turning the computer on and off).

2. Depending on what kind of tablet you have, there may be a power switch on the tablet—if there is, turn it on. The tablet LED indicates that your tablet has power and is ready.

3. If you have any virus protection programs running, such as Norton or McAfee, disable them until you've finished installing the tablet. Close other programs as well before installing tablet software.

4. Put the CD-ROM with your tablet drivers in the CD-ROM drive (or the floppy in your floppy drive).

5. Plug-and-play versions of Windows (such as 2000 or Me) will give you a dialog box with "New Hardware Found" when you start Windows. Then the Hardware Wizard starts. If this happens, choose "Search for the best driver…," select your CD-ROM drive, and click Next. Follow the screen prompts.

6. If the drivers aren't found by the Wizard, recheck your CD-ROM drive and try to select the driver manually. The Wizard may ask for a file from your Windows CD-ROM as well, so have it ready.

7. At the end of the setup process, you'll probably be asked for the driver CD-ROM again. Complete the steps and then you should be able to move the tool (mouse or pen) on the tablet and see the screen cursor behave accordingly.

8. Now you may install any bundled software that came with your tablet, such as Adobe Photoshop LE, Painter, or other goodies. And your coffee is probably getting cold.

NOTE

Troubleshooting Windows

The serial port—First, check that everything is connected and has power. If you have a computer with a built-in modem, you may experience a conflict with the serial port and tablet. If you don't have a serial port available, you need to configure your modem's port, add a serial port, or remove an existing device before installing the tablet.

To change the COM (communications) port for a modem in Windows, open Phone and Modem Options in the Control Panel. On the Modems tab, click the modem you have installed and then click Properties. On the Advanced tab, click Advanced Port Settings. In Com Port Number, click the port number you want to use.

In Windows 2000, new devices are detected and an Install Wizard for Hardware starts automatically. If not, you should look in Add/Remove Hardware in the Control Panel and Add/Troubleshoot a device.

If you replaced your mouse with the tablet, you must navigate with the keyboard when installing the tablet. This might be awkward if you're not used to doing this. Use Ctrl+Esc to select the Start menu, and scroll up and down in it by using the arrow keys. Press Enter to select a choice or open submenus.

If you still have problems, turn your computer off again, disconnect the tablet, and plug your mouse back in. Go online to the tablet manufacturer's Web page (addresses are in Appendix B) and look at the support or driver updates pages. Often you'll find new information, new drivers, and, most likely, a solution to your problem. Note what driver version you installed and check if there's a more recent one available for your tablet and operating system.

The USB port—If the tablet does not respond after you have installed the drivers, browse to your CD-ROM drive and run Setup or Install manually.

Installation with a Serial Port Connection on a Mac

1. With your computer turned off, connect the serial adapter cable to the tablet cable, then connect the AC power cable.

2. Connect the adapter cable to the serial port and the power adapter to an AC outlet.

3. If your tablet has a power switch, turn it on. The tablet LED indicates that your tablet has power.

4. Start your computer. If you have any virus protection programs running, disable them until you've finished installing the tablet. Close other programs as well before installing tablet software.

5. Put the CD-ROM with your tablet drivers in the CD-ROM drive; click the Install icon and follow the prompts.

6. Now you may install any bundled software that came with your tablet.

Part I Your Tablet and Tools

CAUTION

iMacs and USB tablets will not work unless you have the correct Mac OS version, so you might have to install an iMac firmware update or an iMac update first. Check your Mac OS and ROM versions before you install the tablet and compare them to the tablet requirements. If you click "About this computer," you should see the OS version displayed in the upper right corner in the dialog box. The Wacom Intuos, for example, requires Mac OS 8.5 or greater, plus OS ROM 1.2.1 or greater. See your iMac manual on how to perform the upgrades.

Installation with a USB Port Connection on a Mac

1. With your computer turned on, connect the tablet cable to the USB port on your computer. USB supports so-called "hot-plugging," so you can install or uninstall hardware without turning the computer on and off.

2. If your tablet has an LED indicator, it should indicate that your tablet is now powered up.

3. If everything is working, you should be able to use your tablet tool now. If you have pressure-sensitive tools, you have to install the software for them. Place the CD-ROM with the software in your CD-ROM drive and locate the Setup or Install icon. Follow the screen prompts.

4. Reboot the computer and you should have a working tablet.

Installation on the Apple Desktop Bus

1. With your computer turned off, connect the tablet cable to the ADB port.

2. If your tablet has a power switch, turn it on. The tablet LED indicates that your tablet has power.

3. Start your computer. If you have any virus protection programs running, disable them until you've finished installing the tablet. Close other programs as well before installing tablet software.

4. Put the CD-ROM with your software (for instance, for pressure-sensitive tablets you must install the software for them) in your CD-ROM drive, click the Install icon, and follow the prompts.

5. Then you may install any bundled software that came along with your tablet.

NOTE

Troubleshooting Macs

The serial port—First, check that everything is connected and has power. Check the serial connection by opening the Connection tab in the Control Panel. The Tablet Driver On checkbox should be selected. If your system has an internal modem installed, this could cause the external port to be disabled.

The USB port—Check that everything is connected and has power. Try plugging the cable to another USB port. If your tablet has an LED indicator, see if it's on. If you installed a USB interface card, make sure you've installed the software to support the card. You may need to download the Apple USB Card updates from Apple if your USB card does not recognize the tablet. If your Mac already has one or more USB ports, it's USB ready. You can check the USB port by plugging another USB device into it and verifying that the USB port itself is working properly.

The ADB port—Make sure everything is connected and has power. If your computer does not have a free ADB port, you must connect the keyboard to the tablet cable's pass-through connector while your computer is turned off.

When your tablet is up and running, you may want to familiarize yourself with your new toy before trying some real work. The tablet and its tools will load with their default settings, which is adequate for experimenting with the basic tasks on your computer. Try moving a few icons around, and use the pen and mouse as you ordinarily would. We will look into the finer arts of tool and tablet customizing later. If you have Painter, Photoshop, or other programs that support pressure-sensitivity, play around with their tools and see how great pressure-sensitivity really is.

Tools (Input Devices)

If you have ever tried to crop a person's head in a picture using an ordinary mouse, you know what an impossible task I'm talking about. Not only does it take hours to complete, but the result will never be perfect. You are guaranteed to fail, simply because you don't have the right tools. Just as a carpenter will never use a stone instead of a hammer to get those nails in place, you should never use a mouse to do the tasks of a tablet pen. Most tablet manufacturers bundle their tablets with two tools—a customizable mouse, with two, three, or more buttons, and a pen. The pen itself may have a button or two, enabling you to right-click or do other fun things with it. Pens from Wacom have an eraser at the end, so that just as with an ordinary pencil, you can flip them around and erase what you just did. The pen (and tablet) may be pressure-sensitive as well, and if you're now grinning happily because that's what you've just bought, you are in for a real treat. The advantages of a pressure-sensitive pen are enormous and must be experienced to be believed. Imagine tying your arm up so that the pencil barely touches the paper and you never can get a variation in pressure—that's how much fun a pen without pressure sensitivity is.

An Intuos tablet from Wacom will recognize a new tool when you use it. It opens a dialog box so you can customize it right away, or you can use default settings. We will look into the various options in the Control Panel later and concentrate now on the tools and what they can do.

Wacom Input Devices for the Intuos Tablet

Wacom is the market leader because of its continuous improvement and development of new tools. Wacom also offers the most tools for its tablets, including the much appreciated Intuos Airbrush (a device which Wacom alone offers at the moment). Wacom's pen and mouse can, to some degree, be compared with other brands, but its ToolID system is unique. The company's Intuos tablets also have the highest level of pressure-sensitivity available. Let's take a closer look at the tools in Wacom's Intuos range:

NOTE

Here are some terms and expressions related to Wacom Intuos tools:

ToolID—This feature lets you customize each tool, and the Intuos tablet recognizes which tool you're using and loads the proper settings for it.

Tracking Speed—Use this feature to adjust the speed of your cursor when using the tool in Mouse Mode.

Mouse Mode—This term is also known as relative positioning, which means you can navigate the screen cursor as you would with a mouse.

Fingerwheel—This device is the control wheel on the Airbrush tool.

Pressure sensitive—This term means the tablet recognizes the amount of pressure you use, so that when drawing with pressure-sensitive tools, you may vary line width, ink flow, or similar attributes.

Intuos Pen

The Intuos pen is ergonomically shaped and somewhat narrower where your fingers hold it, so that it resembles a smooth, modern pen. But the resemblance to a ballpoint pen is only skin deep.

Unlike some input devices, the Intuos pen has no cord that gets in the way. It also has no batteries, and it's pressure sensitive just like an ordinary pen or pencil. With the Intuos Pen, you can do basic stuff like clicking, pointing, and dragging just like you would with a mouse. But hey, that's not why you will love it. With a Pen, you can make accurate selections, draw detailed masks in photo editing programs (which I will show you how to do in a later chapter), and, finally, you can draw with it. And I don't mean a jagged, unprecise line like with a mouse, but a steady, accurate line with a result that looks like you have drawn it on paper. You can adjust the tip feel of the pen (see Chapter 3), which means that if you want to create broad, soft, or "blurred" strokes and you're clicking lightly on the tablet, a Soft setting will work for you. When drawing thin and crisp lines, use a Firm setting. You may change this in the tablet's Control Panel or use the Tablet Menu Strip.

The tablet has a transparent sheet overlay so you may still draw sketches on paper and trace them on the tablet, but as you get used to the pen and tablet surface, you will draw directly on the tablet and see the miracle onscreen. The pen works with the tablet even if you don't hold it against the tablet surface. The tablet recognizes it up to 1 centimeter above the surface, which is a great advantage when moving around in applications, because you can see the cursor.

You hold it like you would any other pen, but you have to get used to its DuoSwitch. The DuoSwitch is a two-way button that can be programmed with your favorite commands or functions, such as right-clicking, and you use your thumb or forefinger to press the two active areas on the DuoSwitch. I hold my pen so the DuoSwitch is placed outward between my thumb and forefinger. When I use the DuoSwitch, I scroll the pen with my index finger so I access the areas with my forefinger. Find a technique that works for you; the point is to access the button easily without changing the grip on the pen or accidentally pressing the DuoSwitch when drawing. The pen comes with replaceable pen tips, so you can replace them as you wear them out. They last for months, so you won't need new ones soon. The Intuos Pen also has Tilt support. When you hold the pen in various angles, the tablet senses the angle and projects ink accordingly. Unfortunately, tilt is not supported in all applications.

Intuos Stroke Pen

The Intuos Stroke Pen hasn't much in common with the Intuos Pen. It hasn't got the DuoSwitch, and its main function is to imitate a brush. The tip is much softer than the Pen, and its 1,024 levels of pressure-sensitivity enable you to draw perfect brush strokes of varying strength and width. This is a typical drawing tool, as its soft tip is very awkward to use when navigating around in programs trying to click or drag-and-drop items. (This is easier to do with the firm-tipped regular Intuos Pen.) The Stroke Pen's tip "retracts" when you apply more than a soft pressure. The surface of the Intuos Stroke Pen is not as smooth as the regular pen, and it's much lighter in weight. The latter helps when you think about comparison to an ordinary brush, which doesn't weigh much.

To familiarize yourself with the Stroke Pen, try it in a program such as Painter, CorelDRAW, or Photoshop, which have pressure-sensitive brushes and tools. In Photoshop, for instance, try the various tools like Paintbrush and Airbrush with the Stroke Pen, and use different brush sizes as well. You will notice that the Paintbrush is the most accurate tool to use when imitating real brush strokes. It responds to pressure, intensity, stroke width (if you have set the Stylus to control Size in the Brush Options dialog box), and performs like a paintbrush should. The Pen tool will give you the best result when drawing very thin lines perhaps, but I'll bet you will stick with the Paintbrush and Airbrush tools. The Airbrush tool does not have the Size option available, so you will get strokes of the same width but with varying intensity. Its pressure settings give you the best results when painting really soft, almost invisible strokes. To get the best results when creating drawings, you need to know the different tools and their specialties, both regarding what input devices you choose and the software tools. The rest is training and experience. See Figure 2.2.

Figure 2.2
The Intuos Stroke Pen has three different Photoshop 5.5 Tools. The Paintbrush is in pink, the Airbrush is in blue, and the Pencil is in green. Note the differences in stroke widths and intensity in these doodles.

Part I Your Tablet and Tools

Intuos Inking Pen

The Intuos Inking pen is a real ballpoint pen. It is created for hand-writing text, writing your signature on documents, or illustrating original artwork. The Inking pen, like the Stroke Pen, does not have the eraser tip or the DuoSwitch. It comes with replaceable plastic tips which let you write, sketch, or trace like you would with ordinary pen and paper. The transparent overlay on the tablet lets you trace your artwork securely. The metal ballpoint refills are to be used on real paper put on top of the tablet, because they contain real ink! Remember the paper! It took me just a couple of minutes to

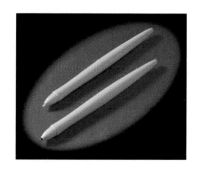

forget I had put the ink refill in instead of the plastic tips I normally use, and the next time I looked at my tablet, it was covered in blue doodles! You get plastic refills, plus three metal-tipped ballpoint refills with the pen. I tested the different tips in Photoshop (see Figure 2.3) with various tools set to 3 pixels in diameter, and although you may not spot the difference, it's there.

Figure 2.3
The Intuos Inking Pen tested with various tools in Photoshop. The first three lines were written with the plastic tip and the last three were written with the ballpoint tip.

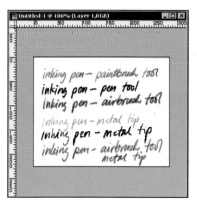

The ballpoint tip is far more precise, tracing more accurately and behaving like a conventional ballpoint pen. The tip is more "inky"—not just in the float but also in the feeling of it against the tablet when you write or trace. Naturally, it's easier to use the ballpoint tip when writing your signature, because you can see what you're writing on the paper and don't have to look at the screen! When switching from paper to a tablet, that's the hardest part—getting used to looking at the screen and not the tablet when you're drawing. I find that I keep a line better with the ballpoint tip in the Inking Pen, and it's easier to keep in control. When writing (or scribbling) with the Inking Pen, the lines are clearly "inked" to look at when you apply varying pressure. You can try this with the Paintbrush tool in Photoshop, or you can try the many pen-and-pencil tools in Painter for both great effects and pen options. You have to replace the tips manually when switching from the plastic tip to the ballpoint tip or vice versa. May I suggest an Inking Pen with a plastic tip in one end and a ballpoint tip at the other?

Intuos Airbrush

Wacom is currently alone in offering a digital airbrush tool. The Intuos Airbrush performs similarly to the Intuos Pen in some ways but has a few special features. The fingerwheel on the Airbrush can be used to control the spray intensity. There are three choices for the wheel in the Tablet Control Panel; the settings of Minimum, Intermediate, and Maximum relate to how much movement is needed to acquire the maximum effect you want. Not all applications support the Airbrush, so look at Wacom's homepage for updated information about which applications you can use it with. The Airbrush also has a side switch that you can program to right-click, left-click, or to utilize smart functions such as pressure hold or modifier keys (Alt, Shift, and so on).

The Airbrush works perfectly with Wacom's own PenTools—a plug-in you can use with programs such as Photoshop, Painter, and Imageready for PC or Mac. PenTools can be downloaded for free at Wacom's homepage. In PenTools, you can choose the Virtual Airbrush, which has settings for Tool Control. There you can choose that the Size and Ink flow be controlled by either the fingerwheel, the pressure, or a fixed mode. You can change the brush size and ink flow density, based on the amount of pressure you apply to the pen, or you can keep it "fixed" using the settings for this. You can use PenTools with other input devices, but you won't benefit from the fingerwheel control settings. We will take a closer look at using PenTools in Chapter 7 and the other PenTools options you have in addition to the Virtual Airbrush. See Figure 2.4.

Figure 2.4
The Wacom PenTools Virtual Airbrush options dialog box.

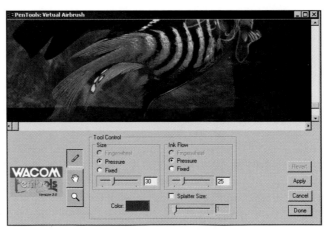

Intuos Lens Cursor

The Intuos Lens Cursor has a cross-hair lens that can be adjusted 50 degrees left or right. It has five programmable buttons to suit your needs for commands. Left- and right-clicking functions are just the beginning. Just as with the other Intuos tools, the Lens Cursor has its own ToolID so you can customize it for different programs. It's battery-free and very lightweight, with an impressive accuracy of +/–0.15mm—perfect for CAD applications. It is especially useful for tracing drawings. A very nifty function of this device is that two buttons can work simultaneously. If you program one button as a so-called Modifier key, such as the Ctrl (Command) key, you can program a second button with an S stroke. Pressing the two buttons at the same time gives you Ctrl+S (Command + S), in other words, Save. Make a mental note of the commands you use most frequently and program the Lens Cursor with them.

The five default button settings of the Lens Cursor are left-click, right-click, left double-click, middle-click, and left-click lock. Here's a quick Windows 98/2000 tip: Instead of wasting one of the buttons of the Lens Cursor with the left double-click, open the Windows Control Panel and select the Mouse dialog box. Select "Single-Click to open an item" on the Buttons tab. You can now program the button on your lens cursor to do something other than left double-clicking! And you never have to double-click to select an item again!

Intuos 4D Mouse

A mouse is not just a mouse anymore. The 4D mouse has five programmable buttons plus a thumbwheel. As with the Lens Cursor, the 4D mouse can work two buttons simultaneously. The 4D mouse supports axial rotation, so you can use it with applications that support device rotation. The thumbwheel is great for browsing through Web pages or documents, because a single nudge scrolls the page just a little. Moving the thumbwheel backwards (or forwards) without letting go of the thumbwheel lets you scroll through several pages without stopping. In the Control Panel, you can select the option of using the mouse as a fifteen-button device. This means each button can be programmed with three different functions that can be selected depending on the position of the thumbwheel. (This takes some practice before you use the mouse efficiently and remember all the positions.) Take a look at Chapter 3 and the section called "Customizing the 4D Mouse and Lens Cursor" for a thorough walk-through on how to program your 4D-mouse properly.

TIP

DualTrack can persuade your mouse that it's a keyboard. Every Intuos tablet from size A5 and up supports something called DualTrack. This is a clever system that lets you use two different Intuos tools on the tablet at the same time. For example, you can use the Pen plus the 4D mouse simultaneously. You can program the mouse as a Button Box (in the tablet Control Panel) that lets you use the mouse as a keyboard. You will not be able to use the mouse to navigate in the Button Box mode, but you have great control when drawing. You use the pen to draw and the mouse buttons to perform keystrokes—such as holding the Shift key down to draw straight lines in Photoshop using the Paintbrush tool.

A Few User Tips

The next paragraphs are meant to help you with a few annoying problems, such as where to place your tablet, how to avoid desk clutter, and how to get used to the unfamiliar tablet surface.

Tablet Placement and Desk Clutter

You might think this is a totally unnecessary explanation—you just place the tablet on your desk and you're ready to go, right? Life should be that simple. With a small tablet, you just put it to the right or left of your keyboard and you're happily drawing away on your new tablet. Try that with an A3-sized tablet and you'll be wondering why your arms were not made of rubber and why your spine is now at a very weird angle. The tablet is just too big! And unless you have excellent vision, you won't be able to read the menu strip items from so far away.

I use both the tablet and the keyboard simultaneously when working. I'm right-handed, so I have my left hand at the keyboard for shortcuts. At first, I wondered if a really clever solution was to have a small plate for the keyboard which I could pull out from under the desk, but reaching over this plate to the tablet was not a good idea—the top of the tablet became unreachable. I ended up with the tablet right in front of the monitor, and with the keyboard to the left of it, slightly angled. Now I have a cordless keyboard, which is wonderful, because I can either place this in my lap or on top of the tablet when writing and not just typing software shortcuts. There's now tablet software called Sensiva available which lets you draw letters and symbols instead of using keyboard shortcuts. Read more about Sensiva in Appendix A.

While we're on the subject of placement, I might as well give you a tip regarding how to avoid desk clutter. One word: Cordless. Get a cordless keyboard and a cordless mouse if you want to keep an ordinary mouse in addition to the tablet tools. And buy a clever pen holder for your tablet tools! If you have a large Intuos, you get a tool holder with it. Use it—don't let the tools lie around on your desk where the sensitive tool tips may become damaged or dirty.

From Plastic to Paper

When you first start using your tablet, its surface might feel unfamiliar to you. Paper has a surface that—even if it's really smooth paper—gives you a certain amount of "resistance" against the pen. A tablet, on the other hand, has a plastic overlay sheet that makes the tools slide a bit, much the same way as writing with a felt-tipped pen on overhead transparencies. I was surprised at how hard it was to get even, perfect lines into an image editing program when tracing a sketch that is lying protected by the overlay sheet. Wacom insists the overlay sheet has a paper-like feel to it, but I don't agree, because the surface is far too smooth. When I started out with a tablet, I found the surface so annoying that I cheated. I used a very fine sketching paper or watercolor paper on top of the tablet, held in place by a strip of Scotch tape in each corner. The benefit of this is obvious—you get the pen-on-paper feeling back until you learn to use the tablet tools with the software and draw and look at the screen like you've done nothing else for years. Do not use a paper that's too thin, because it will wrinkle under the pen's pressure.

TIP

Don't try to learn everything at once, and don't get lost in the Control Panel settings. A tablet like the Wacom Intuos has lots of great customizable settings, but if you start out customizing all your tools right away, you're more likely to be confused than impressed. Start with customizing your tools with the same settings for all programs. That way you can easily compare how the input device works with different software tools. When you know which program you prefer with which tools and settings, you can start customizing.

Cleaning Your Tablet

Do not use strong soap and water solutions on your tablet, and stay away from other cleaning aids like window cleaners, anti-static sprays, and so on. For dusting off, use a paper towel or wipe off the tablet surface with a dry cloth. If you spill something on your tablet, dry it off immediately with a paper towel or clean cloth. Then use a cloth dipped in a lukewarm, mild soap solution (use something like dishwashing liquid, but in less concentration) and remove any sticky residue from your spill. Make sure you dry off the tablet afterwards with a dry towel or paper towel. Clean your input devices the same way. For the input devices, it's sufficient to dry them off with the type of dry cloths that remove fat and grease without the use of any soap or water. Just rubbing the cloth over the tools will do the trick.

This concludes our overview of the tablets and tools that are available and with installing them on your computer. In the next chapter, we'll look at how you can customize your tablets and tools and how to use the tools with various programs.

3

Customizing Your Tablet and Tools

Many people buy accessories for their computers and start using them right away after installing them. There's nothing wrong with that, because default settings will get you started. But to discover the full potential of the accessories, you should take a thorough look at what they can do. To discover your graphics tablet's possibilities, you must become familiar with its Control Panel. Did you know that you can customize the settings for a tool with different settings for each program you use? This chapter will guide you through the options in a typical tablet Control Panel, with step-by-step examples on how to customize the different settings to suit your needs. We'll also take a look at settings for the various input devices and how you add them into the Control Panel. This chapter will guide you through:

▶ All the options in a typical tablet Control Panel

▶ Adding pressure-sensitive input devices and customizing their settings for various programs

▶ How to use the pressure-sensitive tools in Photoshop 6.0, Photoshop Elements and Photoshop 5.5, Corel Painter 6, and Illustrator 9

Tablet Control Panel Settings

This section will cover all aspects of the tablet Control Panel. We'll go through all of its settings one by one, discussing every customization possible for your tablet and tools, using a Wacom Intuos and various input devices. Many tablets will share some of the settings, so even if you don't have a Wacom Intuos tablet, you can pick up valuable tips from this section. However, some functions and choices are relevant to the Intuos product line only. We'll also take a look at how to add new tools to your tablet and how to utilize the various settings for them. After you customize your tools, you'll see how to add numerous applications, each with different tools.

Don't faint when opening the tablet Control Panel (located in the Tablet Properties box) the first time, even when you read unfamiliar choices like Positioning Mode and Tilt. We will use this section to safely guide you through every customization possible for your tablet and tools. Before we dive into the various tabs in the Control Panel, though, you might want to take a look at the Control Panel menu bar. If you choose Edit > Preferences here, you have the option of selecting Right Handed or Left Handed for the 4D mouse and Lens Cursor.

We'll start with just one tool, a regular Pen. In good time, we'll explore the customized settings for various applications—but you may wish to use the All applications choice (the default). Don't feel you have to change any settings just to say you've changed them. It's not *illegal* to use your tool with the default settings, but I guarantee you'll want to change the pressure settings in the Tip Feel tab.

Figure 3.1
The Wacom Tablet
Control Panel with just
one tool, a Pen,
installed.

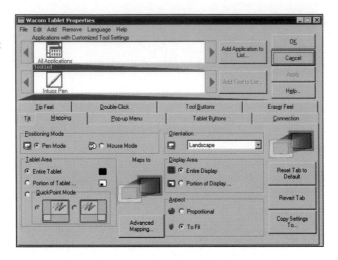

Tip Feel Tab and Eraser Feel Tab

The Tip Feel tab (see Figure 3.2) lets you set the pressure with a slider to suit your drawing style. Use the test area a few times and draw naturally. If you draw very soft, you won't see anything in the test area if the slider is positioned all the way to the Firm setting. Clicking the More Options button will give you the Advanced Options dialog box, which enables you to independently change the click pressure and pressure curve settings. The pressure slider will override what you do in Advanced Options, so if you complete settings in Advanced Options first and then change the slider, your advanced settings will be lost.

Use the Automatic area in Advanced Options to help you set the value for maximum force. When you've done that, you see the curves in the middle change. The curve displays the relationship between pressure reported to an application and the force you have applied to the tool. Changing the values manually is not something you'd start with, so leave them alone and use the Automatic option first. You can type values in the red field (in percent) to adjust click force—in other words, the amount of pressure required to make a button click. Wacom recommends you set both the click force and minimum tip force to the same value.

Changing the blue pressure curve (or the values in the blue fields) will modify the tip feel. If your touch is soft, you might agree with a setting between 50 and 80 percent, so you don't have to use maximum force to get the full pressure effects.

When you are happy with the settings, you'll see a blue checkmark next to the Options button. This will still be visible when you close the advanced settings and go back to the Tip Feel dialog box. Remember not to move the slider, unless you want to override what you just did.

The Eraser Feel tab look precisely the same as the Tip Feel tab, but it adjusts the settings of the eraser end of the Pen.

Figure 3.2
The Tip Feel tab.

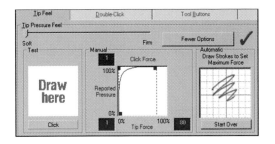

TIP
 If you've made an error in your Control Panel settings, don't despair. There are three buttons to the right in each tab; the first one, Reset Tab to Defaults, is all you need. Clicking it will restore the tab to its default settings—click Apply and you've corrected your mistake. Clicking the Revert Tab button will load the previously saved settings.

Double-Click Tab

The Double-Click tab also has an automatic area that lets you double-click as you're used to for speed and distance. (See Figure 3.3.) The value in the distance area changes automatically to reflect this. A setting of 3 or 4 pixels should be adequate, with the speed slider approximately in the middle. If you set the distance to high values and/or the speed to slow, it may disturb your drawing, because the tablet will think you'll want to double-click instead. Remember, you can use the DuoSwitch button on your Pen to double-click.

Figure 3.3
The Double-Click tab.

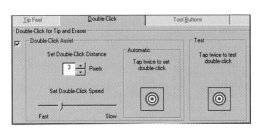

Part I Your Tablet and Tools

Tool Buttons Tab

The Tool Buttons tab changes its appearance depending on which tool you're customizing. We're still using the Pen Tool, so the dialog box will look like Figure 3.4. Here you can change the functions assigned to the DuoSwitch button and the Eraser, using drop-down menus to select your choice. Right-Clicking and Pressure hold are the most obvious—and popular— choices, as well as left double-click (unless you have set single-click in Windows). Choose Modifier from the pull-down menu to set modifier keys like Shift, Alt or Ctrl (Command, Option, and so on).

The eraser is not reachable without changing your grip on the Pen, so don't use the eraser button for functions you use often. I must admit I'm not very adventurous regarding my tool buttons settings, as I use the default settings.

Figure 3.4
The Tool Buttons tab.

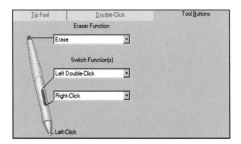

Tilt Tab

Not all applications support tilt sensitivity, but those that do can help you control brush orientation. You adjust tilt sensitivity for your Pen and Airbrush simultaneously—for both the tip and the eraser—and you see the graphical display change as you move your pen sideways, forwards, and backwards. If you set the tilt at high sensitivity, you'll need to tilt your pen just a little to get full tilt response in your application. When you hold the pen in various angles, the tablet senses the angle and projects ink accordingly. The Tilt tab is shown in Figure 3.5.

Figure 3.5
The Tilt tab.

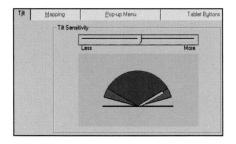

Part I Your Tablet and Tools

Mapping Tab

The Mapping tab in Figure 3.6 is the toughest tab to understand right away, but it's the most important one to get right, because it adjusts the things you do on your tablet in relation to your display. We'll do the easiest bit first: The Orientation setting is found in the upper right corner. You'll want the Landscape or Portrait setting from the drop-down menu. If you like working a bit weird, you also have the options of Flipped Landscape or Portrait—if you like a 180-degree rotation.

Figure 3.6
The Mapping tab. Hold onto your hat when changing settings here.

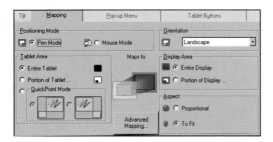

Next, choose the Display Area settings. There are two choices: Entire Display or Portion of Display. Choose Entire Display if you want to use the tablet against the whole screen area, and not just parts of it. Aspect defines the relationship between your tablet and the screen. Proportional means that what you draw will be 100 percent correct vertically and horizontally, where To Fit will scale to fit and not maintain proportions. To Fit is a bad setting if you're tracing drawings a lot. Using the tablet with the To Fit setting resembles using an ordinary mouse, because you may reach your whole display area from a small mouse pad. If you have a small tablet and a 21-inch monitor, you might want to set either the Portion of Display setting and the Proportional aspect or you can use Entire Display and To Fit settings. If you have an A3 tablet and a 21-inch monitor, you'd be happier with Entire Display and the Proportional aspect. See the difference between settings in Figure 3.7.

Figure 3.7
The difference as it would be seen on your screen in Proportional (left image) and To Fit settings.

We move on to the Tablet Area settings. This should be adjusted in relation to the Display Area settings and allows you to select the tablet area that will be mapped to the display area. The default setting is Entire Tablet, which probably is what you should start with. You can define different tablet areas for different tools as well. You can also choose Portion of Tablet, which opens a dialog box. Here you may drag the handles to set the tablet area in relation to the screen (shown in orange in Figure 3.8; the display is marked in gray), enter the proper coordinates, or click to define tablet area—which is what I recommend you try. Follow the instructions on the screen and click the tablet corners (inside the active area) as instructed.

The last choice in Tablet Area settings is the QuickPoint Mode. It divides the tablet into a drawing area and a QuickPoint area used for navigation. This is pointless if you want to use your whole tablet and screen for drawing and navigating at the same time without changing tools. I've tried to use this setting a couple of times, but I never remember what area I should be clicking on for navigating, and I panic when I lose control over the cursor—total access is my motto. But I'm making this a bit more complicated than it really is, because you will have total control if you select a portion of the tablet to use with the pen and the whole tablet to use with the mouse. Just remember you have to switch between the tools; in other words, use the mouse if you want access to the whole display area. I replaced the ordinary mouse with my Pen a long time ago, so naturally I use Entire Tablet display settings and right-click with the DuoSwitch.

When you've really gotten the grasp of mapping, try the Advanced Mapping functions. In this dialog box, you may create several tablet-to-screen mappings by setting the tablet and screen areas, plus Aspect.

Figure 3.8
Tablet area (here shown in orange) and display area (in gray).

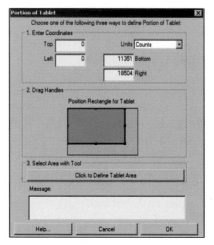

Pop-up Menu Tab

The Pop-up Menu is great for adding your own favorite keyboard shortcuts and commands, such as Cut, Paste, New, Save, Open, and so on.

To access your customized Pop-up Menu when using your tools, you have to assign to it a button on your tool on the Tool Buttons tab. As shown in Figure 3.9, you can choose the Add Keystroke button and then type the keystroke you want. Next, you can name it, click OK, and you have saved it. You may also rearrange the order on the Pop-up Menu. You can also add mapping options to your pop-up menu and, of course, remove items from the menu.

Figure 3.9
The Pop-up Menu lets you add your own keystrokes.

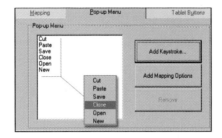

Part I Your Tablet and Tools

The Tablet Buttons Tab

Finally, you're ready to customize the menu strip on top of your tablet. Go to the Tablet Buttons menu. The first eleven choices are by default set to New, Open, Close, Save, Print, and so on. From a drop-down menu, you can change these by selecting the various items, or you can add your own commands—up to twenty-seven choices. Selecting Keystroke from the drop-down menu will open a small dialog box like the one in Pop-up Menu. See Figure 3.10. The menu strip has a removable section where you can type the names of your choices with a pencil. You have to carefully lift the left corner of the tablet overlay to access the menu strip, which then can be pulled out. Use the tablet menu for keystrokes that are tricky to do without looking at the keyboard, such as Shift+Ctrl+K (Shift+Command+K), which loads the Color settings in Photoshop 6.

Figure 3.10
The pulldown menu in Tablet Buttons lets you add your own keystrokes and commands to your tablet menu strip.

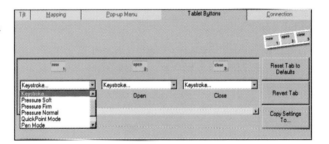

The Connection Tab (Serial) or Tablet Mode Tab (USB)

If you have a tablet connected to your serial port, you'll have a Connection tab. If your tablet is connected to a USB port, you'll have a Tablet Mode tab. In the Connection tab, you'll see which COM port is used, plus you'll have settings for Mode (Standard, Recognition Data, Single Mode). The Single Mode is for No Dual-track, which some applications prefer. The Standard Mode, for both serial and USB, is Dual-track.

Adding and Customizing Tools

We'll take a look at how to add new tools to your tablet and at the various settings for them that are not covered in the previous section. Remember than when you hold a new tool to the tablet, the Intuos tablet recognizes it immediately; displays a message saying, "A new tool has been detected"; and uses the default settings for it. You have to then open the Tablet Control Panel to customize your tool. The previous section showed you the various settings you can use with the Pen Tool, so we'll take a look at the different settings available for the other tools. When installing a new tool, you basically have three choices: Starting fresh with customized settings for the tool (described above); copying settings from a tool with which you're satisfied and/or customizing the tool to a specific application.

TIP

Copying your settings from one tool to another is not difficult.

Let's say you're really happy with the settings you have made for the Pen Tool. No need to go through the settings for pressure and tilt all over again with the Stroke Pen. The tablet has recognized the Stroke Pen, and you are ready to copy your settings from the ordinary Pen to it. This is what you do:

1. Go to the Copy Settings dialog box.

2. Select the Pen Tool icon in the Tool list.

3. Click the Copy To button.

4. In the dialog box, you can choose which applications and/or tools you want to copy to. The tool you have selected will be the default choice in the Copy From part of the dialog box.

5. We have not added any applications yet, so All Applications is selected by default. In the Copy To part, the Stroke Pen will be the default choice (if you had more tools available, you would have had to select it). You also have the option of copying only some of the tab settings in the Copy From part of the dialog box—see Figure 3.11.

6. Make sure your selections are the way you want them and click OK. You have now copied the settings from your Pen to the Stroke Pen.

7. To check if the settings are copied properly, you can click the Tip Feel tab, note the values, then switch to the Pen Tool, and see if the values are the same.

Figure 3.11
The Copy To button opens up a new dialog box where you can choose what tools, applications, and settings you copy from—and to.

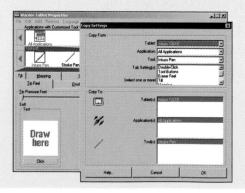

Customizing the Stroke Pen

With the Stroke Pen, you have the same options available as the Intuos Pen except for the Tool Buttons, because there are no tool buttons on the Stroke Pen. For some strange reason, you have the Tool Buttons tab and the Pop-up Menu tab available all the same in the Control Panel, but this is probably just to confuse you. If you use the Pen Tool much like a mouse, with medium to firm Tip Feel settings, you might want softer pressure settings with the stroke pen to benefit from the nuances in stroke width in applications like Painter and Photoshop.

Customizing the Airbrush

The Intuos Airbrush has tab options similar to the Pen, with the exception of the Tool Buttons tab options, which you see in Figure 3.12. You can customize the settings for:

▶ **The eraser**—The options here are exactly the same as for the other tools with an eraser.

▶ **The fingerwheel**—This tool controls the ink flow, opacity, and brush size. There are three choices for the wheel; a setting of Minimum, Intermediate, or Maximum relates to how much movement on the wheel is needed to acquire the maximum effect you want. Maximum is the default setting. You move the wheel towards the tip of the Airbrush for less of an effect and backwards towards the eraser for more effect. Doing this and keeping the Airbrush steady takes some practice, especially for those who have never used a real Airbrush before, so I suggest you start with the settings on default. When using Photoshop 6.0 and the Airbrush Tool from the Tool palette, you have Brush Dynamics settings which let you choose Size, Pressure, and Color. These are controlled by the Stylus (which in this case means the Airbrush). Experiment with these settings and the fingerwheel. If you want to keep the brush size, but adjust the intensity and ink flow of a color with the fingerwheel, you choose Off on both Size and Pressure but Stylus on Color.

In Wacom PenTools, you have more options. You can select the Virtual Airbrush, which has settings for Tool Control where you can choose the Size and Ink Flow to be controlled by either the fingerwheel, the pressure, or fixed mode. You can change the brush size and ink flow density, based on the amount of pressure you apply to the pen, or you can keep it "fixed," using the settings for this.

▶ **The Switch button**—Like the DuoSwitch button, the Switch button lets you set keystrokes or modifier keys, pressure hold, right-click, and so on.

Figure 3.12
The Fingerwheel Range on the Tool Buttons tab is offered only for the Airbrush.

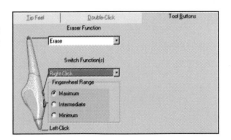

Customizing the Inking Pen

With the Intuos Inking Pen, you have almost the same tab options as the Intuos Pen and Stroke Pen, but there are no eraser or other buttons on it. The settings in the Control Panel are not where you'll get the most out of it, as it will be the application of your choice which will let you "customize" it. In Photoshop 6.0, the application recognizes what input device you use and automatically selects the proper tool for you—in this case, the Paintbrush Tool.

Customizing the 4D Mouse and Lens Cursor

The 4D mouse can be customized physically for left-handed persons. If you pull the two (upper and lower) parts of the mouse gently apart, you can rock the parts back and forth until the other (hidden) thumbwheel is displayed on the right side of the mouse. Snap it into position and you have a left-handed mouse. The 4D mouse has five programmable buttons plus a thumbwheel, and the Lens Cursor has no thumbwheel. Both can work two buttons simultaneously. They support axial rotation, so you can use them with applications that support device rotation. In the Mapping tab, if you select Pen Mode, the mouse adapts the settings you have for the Pen, so if you have chosen the Entire Tablet and Entire Display settings plus Proportional aspect settings, your mouse moves very slowly on the display. Selecting Mouse Mode instead makes it behave more like your common mouse, dashing around more or less uncontrollably, where the smallest movements let you skip from one corner of the display to another. To test the various settings, remember to click Apply in the Control Panel (you don't have to close it) before you try another setting. As seen in Figure 3.13, you can also choose the tracking speed of the screen cursor.

Figure 3.13
Let your screen cursor be a fast rabbit or a slow turtle with your 4D Mouse.

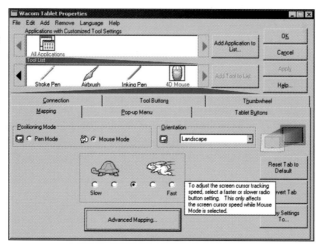

The Tool Buttons tab lets you allocate whatever keystroke or command you want to the various mouse buttons, and don't forget the Pop-up Menu options (which I explained earlier—refer back to Figure 3.9), which you can use on one of the mouse buttons for your own customizable menu. In this tab, you can also tick the Button Box option, which lets you use the mouse as a keyboard. Remember, you can't navigate the screen cursor with it if you choose this option, so you'll have to use another tool simultaneously. See Figure 3.14.

Figure 3.14
Tool Buttons tab for the
4D Mouse and Lens
Cursor.

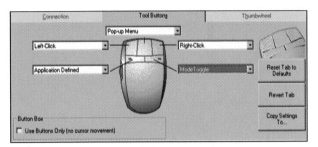

The Thumbwheel tab on the 4D mouse lets you do lots of weird stuff. You may choose between:

▶ **IntelliMouse emulation**—With this option selected, not only does the mouse pretend to be an IntelliMouse, but you may zoom in/out with the thumbwheel in programs like Photoshop 6.0—very handy.

▶ **Fifteen-button 4D mouse**—In this setting, the combination of each button plus the *mode* of the thumbwheel (forward, center, back) creates a total of fifteen choices. If you select this, the choices for forward, center, and back automatically show up in the Tool Buttons tab.

▶ **Application defined**—This is for applications that support this. The default is zoom in/out in Photoshop 6.0.

▶ **Pressure**—Use this feature so back and forward movements simulate pressure.

You can also choose the thumbwheel range in the Thumbwheel tab. There are three alternatives—Minimum, Intermediate, and Maximum—that relate to how much movement on the wheel you need to get the effect you want.

TIP
You can give your tools new names in the Control Panel. This is a very good idea, especially if you have customized your tools to certain functions or tasks or share the tablet with someone at work. You might want to call them, for example, "Paintbrush" or "2B Pencil" or something similar. To change the tool name, you simply select Rename Tool from the Edit menu. In the following dialog box, you choose which tool you want to rename from the menu and type the new name. Click OK, and you'll see it displayed with its new name on the Tool list.

Adding Applications

We're not finished with the Control Panel just yet. After customizing tools from here to eternity, you may add numerous applications, each with different tools. As shown in Figure 3.15, this is what it looks like with Photoshop, Illustrator, Painter, and CorelDRAW added. Photoshop is selected, and three tools are dedicated to it—the Pen, Stroke Pen, and the Airbrush. So forget the All Applications setting for now, which is the default setting.

Figure 3.15
We have added several applications to the Control Panel.

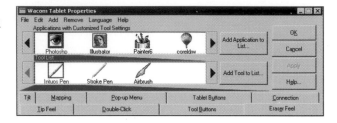

How to Add an Application

You can add an application by either selecting Add from the Control Panel menu and then selecting Application for Custom Settings or by simply clicking the Add Application to List button. Both bring you the dialog box for adding applications.

Here is an example of how to add Photoshop to the Control Panel:

1. Open the Add Application dialog box as explained above. Any application you have open will be visible in the applications list. If you want to add another application, simply click the Browse button.

2. Select your application by clicking the Browse button and choose the Program file for your application, in this case, Photoshp.exe. After you have clicked it, you'll see the path to the application displayed below the Browse button.

3. Select your tablet from the list in Add to:—in most cases, you have just one tablet and that will be selected by default.

4. Click OK.

5. A new dialog box pops up. Here you select the tools you want to customize with Photoshop. Select the Pen and click OK. If you want to select more tools, just click the choices (without holding down the Ctrl key—it's not necessary here) and then OK.

6. You are now back in the main dialog box, and you can customize the settings you want for the Pen in Photoshop.

After you have customized a tool with an application, you'll notice the tab settings are set to default for that application and tool. If some of the settings you have made for the tool in All Applications mode are desirable to use with Photoshop, you can copy them. With All other Apps and Pen selected, click Copy Settings To, and choose Intuos Pen in the Copy From fields and Photoshop in the Copy To applications field. Click OK and you are ready to go.

TIP
Your All other Applications icon may disappear. Don't panic. This is because the All Applications icon changes its name when you add applications. The icon will then display All Other Apps instead.

Removing the Application

If you uninstall an application or want to remove the settings for it for any other reason, getting rid of it in the Control Panel is fairly easy:

1. Select Remove from the Control Panel menu.
2. Select Custom Settings for Application from the drop-down menu.
3. In the dialog box, mark the application for which you want to remove the settings.
4. Click OK.
5. Close the Control Panel.

Pressure-sensitive Tools in Applications

There are many applications where you benefit from having a pressure-sensitive tablet and input devices. If you're not familiar with the various pressure-sensitive tools in Photoshop versions 6.0, 5.5, and Elements, Corel Painter 6, and Illustrator 9, I suggest you read the following paragraphs carefully—the information will be useful when you are reading the examples and tutorials in the next chapters.

Pressure-sensitive Tools in Adobe Photoshop 6.0, 5.5, and Elements

There are nineteen pressure-sensitive tools in Photoshop 6.0 and eighteen in Photoshop 5.5; you can use them with a variety of input devices. Photoshop Elements has many of the same tools, plus a couple of new ones (see Note on page 48). We'll take a look at them and what they do in the same order as they are on the tool menu in Photoshop 6.0. You may observe the difference in the menus in Figure 3.16. We skip the first six main tools—the Marquee Tools, the Move Tool, the Lasso Tools, the Magic Wand Tool, the Crop Tool, and the Slice Tool—they are not pressure-sensitive. The Slice Tool is a new tool, and I will mention it and other new tools in 6.0. Most of the tools in the toolbox will have an option of Mode, which means Blending mode (Normal, Dissolve, Darken, and so on), but I will not get into them here. All the examples mentioned will be with the Mode set to Normal.

Figure 3.16
The toolbox in
Photoshop 6.0 (left) and
Photoshop 5.5 (right).

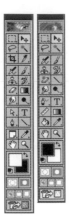

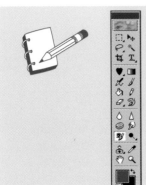

NOTE

In addition to the well-known selection tools, blur, sharpen tools, erasers and so on in previous Photoshop versions, Photoshop Elements contains a few new tools and functions. Among those you'll find the Custom Shape Tool—select a predefined shape from the pop-up palette and click and drag to create a shape. You'll enjoy the pressure-sensitive Red Eye Brush as well, which lets you correct red eyes in photographs. The new Impressionist Brush is neat for quick blurry effects. Photoshop Elements has a Hints palette that displays hints and tips for any tool or function you're considering, so it's easy to get started using this software.

The Airbrush Tool

This tool was one of Photoshop's first pressure-sensitive tools, and it can be used both to create Airbrush effects and to draw blurred lines. (By "blurred," I mean the edges of the stroke are more diffuse than those created with the Paintbrush or Pencil Tools. This is useful when creating masks, as I will demonstrate in a later chapter.) In Photoshop 5.5, you can double-click the Airbrush and you'll see the corresponding Airbrush options displayed. Here you have pressure settings in percent, as well as options to have the stylus control the pressure and/or color and also fading. In Photoshop 6.0 and Photoshop Elements, you have the same options, but in the new Options bar, it's called Brush dynamics and has almost the same choices. You can choose from Size, Pressure, and Color, and all three choices can be in three modes: Off, Fade, and Stylus. This gives you immense control over how you want the tool to behave with your input device. Remember, as the input device itself is pressure-sensitive, you can set the Pressure to 100 percent in Photoshop and tick off Stylus in the Pressure settings to control the amount of ink with the pressure you use. If you use an input device that is not pressure-sensitive, you can use the pressure settings with the Airbrush, but you will not benefit from having varying ink amounts when drawing a line, just the percentage that you choose.

The Paintbrush Tool

 This tool now shares the same place in the Toolbox with the Pencil Tool in Photoshop 6.0. You left-click and hold to display a small pop-up menu with the two choices. In 6.0 and Elements, you will have the same options as the Airbrush plus Wet Edges; in 5.5 you have Opacity, Fading, Wet Edges (which is a darker edge on your line that resembles watercolor), and options to have the stylus control the size, color, and fading. Of course, you use the Paintbrush to paint as you would with a brush! With a medium-sized brush selected (about 12 or 13 pixels), you can set the size and opacity to be controlled by the Stylus. This means that if you draw very softly, you have a thin line, and more pressure will give you a line that's widening as you increase the pressure—up to the brush size you've chosen. If you choose Wet Edges, you'll see the whole stroke gets a more watercolor feeling, plus transparency where strokes are crossing.

TIP

Take advantage of pressure-sensitivity and let the Stylus control size and opacity when drawing with a Paintbrush in Photoshop. This is great when you need to draw things with a natural fade and want to avoid crisp endings on your strokes. In the example in Figure 3.17, you see what it looks like when drawing some seaside or underwater grass. Note that the tips of the grass seem to disappear into thin air. I began with the tips, increasing pressure as I drew them, reaching almost maximum pressure and size at the end of each blade of grass. Simultaneously, you get the effect that the grass is floating away from you.

Figure 3.17
This underwater view of seaside-type grass was made with the Intuos Pen in Photoshop. The settings let the Stylus control both opacity and size.

The Pencil Tool

 This old tool now shares the same place in the Toolbox with the Paintbrush Tool in Photoshop 6.0, instead of the Line tool, its old companion in 5.5. You use it to draw crisp-edged strokes and lines. The option to Auto-erase is still there. Many never use the Pencil Tool much, because the lines always seem jagged due to the missing anti-aliasing. This will be obvious when you look at the Brush palette and see all the brushes jagged as well. The choices are the same as for the other tools mentioned above. The Pencil Tool is at its best when holding Shift down to create straight lines. If you point and click repeatedly, you can draw a shape of straight lines. The Pencil Tool can also be useful when filling in small areas with one pixel of color at a time, especially on those occasions where you simply don't want anti-aliasing—like when you're drawing icons. Setting the Opacity to be controlled by the Stylus will let you draw more subtle lines, and you always have the opportunity to do something about the jagged lines if you apply a filter or two, such as Blur.

The Clone Stamp Tool and the Pattern Stamp Tool

a.

b.

The Clone Stamp Tool *(a.)* is an old, familiar friend; it's great for retouching photographs and duplicating parts of a photo or drawing. In both program versions, you have the option of letting the Stylus control the size and opacity of the Clone Stamp Tool. This tool is great for painting with a (selected) part of an image you already have. New in 6.0 and Elements is the Pattern Stamp Tool *(b.)*. This is the tool you'd want when painting with patterns (you'd never guess that, now would you?), which we'll take a look at in Chapter 12. This tool is a good addition to painting patterns using your own customized brush. You choose a pattern from a pop-up menu in the Options bar or create your own pattern to use. By setting the options of Opacity to the Stylus, you can paint patterns of varying transparency depending on how much pressure you use. This is wonderful for more natural-looking effects and fading.

History Brush and Art History Brush

a.

b.

The History Brush *(a.)* is familiar from Photoshop 5.5 and is great for correcting mistakes in your artwork. You can control Size and Opacity with the Stylus, but the Art History Brush is more advanced. The new Art History Brush tool *(b.)* in 6.0 lets you paint strokes by using the source data from a snapshot or specified history state. You can simulate the texture of painting with different colors and artistic styles, with several options available: Styles (Tight, Loose, or Medium Curl), Fidelity in percent, Area, and Spacing. The difference between the two brushes is that while the History Brush paints by recreating a specific part of data, the Art History Brush does the same, but in addition, lets you manipulate that data using different artistic styles and colors. You can control Size and Opacity with the Stylus, which is recommended for taking advantage of pressure sensitivity. When you use these tools, remember that you have to create a state for them to work with; just opening artwork or a photo to edit with the History Brush will give you nothing, because there's no data to work with yet.

For smoothing out edges or editing photographs, add a filter (like Blur, Smart Blur, or Motion Blur) and paint back the details you want to be really sharp with the brush. Use Opacity to be controlled by the Stylus to get the smoothest transitions. The two brushes are not included in Photoshop Elements.

TIP

Use the History Brush to erase a filter effect. Photoshop and Painter filters have generous settings, and the EyeCandy Waterdrops filter is no exception when it comes to things like Opacity and Amount. The problem was that I wanted raindrops only in *parts* of the photo in Figure 3.18. An unusual way of erasing, perhaps, but I applied the filter and then grabbed the History Brush to erase the parts I did not want. I could, of course, have made a selection of the areas I wanted the filter applied to, but this is a great way of doing it. I used the History Brush with various brush sizes and experimented with Stylus-controlled Size and Opacity as well. I could then erase some raindrops completely or just diffuse others.

Figure 3.18
Erasing some of the applied water drops by using the History Brush. The original photo is to the left and the result is to the right.

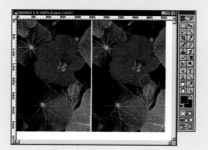

Eraser Tools

a.

b.

c.

There are three eraser tools in both the 6.0, Elements and 5.5 versions: the Eraser Tool *(a.)*, the Background Eraser Tool *(b.)*, and the Magic Eraser Tool *(c.)*. The first two are pressure-sensitive, but the Magic Eraser is not—it works like a Magic Wand by deleting what you select instead of just selecting it. With the Eraser, you can set the Stylus to control Size and Opacity as well as Erase to History and Wet Edges. If you Erase to History, you can achieve the same effects as in Figure 3.18 above, and the result will be the same. Check off Erase to History before you begin, apply the effects you want, and use the Eraser with the Stylus controlling opacity, which allows you to fade in or out between the two versions with precision. To erase backgrounds quickly and easily, choose the Background Eraser Tool. Set Tolerance to be controlled by the Stylus and Find Edges if you have a clean object you want to remove the background from. Note the small crosshairs which show you where the sample to erase comes from—it's important that you don't stray into the parts of the image that you want to keep, or the tool will think that you want those erased as well.

Blur, Sharpen, and Smudge Tools

a.

b.

c.

These three tools are familiar to us from previous versions of Photoshop, and they all have settings for the Stylus to control Size and Pressure. You should always use the Pressure settings to Stylus with these tools, because that will give you the best precision. The Blur Tool *(a.)* is excellent for "fading" objects or people in a photo so they are less dominant or to simply soften edges in an image. The Sharpen Tool *(b.)* is great for sharpening edges in an image. The Smudge *(c.)* Tool smudges the areas of the image you want and can help you create small movement effects or natural endings of strokes. If you look at the turtle in Figure 3.19, you'll see the Blur and Smudge Tools in practice. By applying various amounts of pressure, you can control the degree of blurring very precisely.

Figure 3.19
The sharpness of the image on the left makes the turtle seem to stand still in the water. By using the Blur Tool on some of the edges, plus the Smudge Tool on the back and neck, the turtle seems to be moving.

Dodge, Burn, and Sponge Tools

a.

b.

c.

The Dodge *(a.)* and Burn *(b.)* tools are included in the Photoshop toning tools. As familiar as these names might be, they originate from professional photography. The Sponge Tool *(c.)* changes the saturation (color strength) of an area, making it a great tool for fixing photos where the colors are too bland. These tools are also familiar to us from previous versions of Photoshop, and they're excellent for adjusting images— whether you want parts of your image darker or brighter or want to change the color saturation. They have different modes and ranges, and all three have settings for the Stylus to control both Size and Pressure. We'll look at how you can use these tools in an example in Chapter 5.

Pressure-sensitive Tools in Corel Painter 6

Corel Painter 6, commonly known as Painter, has an excellent selection of pens, brushes, and other tools to choose from, as you can see in Figure 3.20. You can make your own brushes as well or adjust the ones available so they fit your needs exactly. Each tool has various options for Opacity as well as for different effects. The Expression Settings in the Brush Controls give you numerous choices for choosing settings for Pressure, Direction, and so on, to control everything from Size and Opacity to Angle, Jitter, Grain, and Color. This means that you can tie a Brush feature like Size to Stylus data, and if you set Min Size a lot smaller than the brush size, you can paint strokes with great variety of widths, depending on the pressure you use. Painter supports Tilt, so be aware of how you hold the Stylus to get the results you want when drawing.

Figure 3.20
Brushes: Pencils, Brush Controls, and Controls: Brush palettes as they appear in Painter 6.

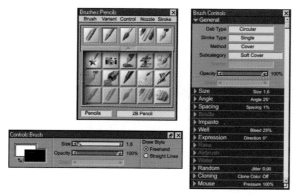

Painter has Brush Tracking Preferences that let you adjust Painter to match your stroke strength. Unfortunately, this information is not saved, so you have to set Brush Tracking each time you start Painter.

To set the Brush Tracking in Painter:

1. On Painter's menu strip, Click Edit > Preferences > Brush Tracking.
2. Use the pressure and speed as you normally would on the scratch pad. You can move the sliders yourself for specific adjustments.
3. Click OK when you're done.

Let's take a look at all the options you have when choosing the Brush Tool in the Tools Box in Painter 6.

Pencils

 If you select the Pencils icon in Painter, you'll see an expandable menu hidden behind a small triangle in the Brushes: Pencils options toolbox (in Figure 3.20, the 2B Pencil is selected from the menu). The menu has these tools: 2B Pencil, Colored Pencil, Flattened Pencil, Sharp Pencil, and Thick and Thin Pencil. The settings in the Brush Control box automatically change when you choose different tools. Most of the pencils respond to pressure, either by the stroke width, opacity, or both.

Brushes

There are fifteen default brushes to choose from, with brushes like Dry Ink, Graphic Paintbrush, Round Camelhair, and the Smeary Round brush. All the brushes are pressure sensitive, and you also have options for each brush in Brush Controls to set Spacing, Bleed, and so forth. The Expression Settings give you numerous options for choosing settings for Pressure, Direction, and the like to control everything from Size and Opacity to Angle, Grain, and Color. See Figure 3.21.

Figure 3.21
Some of Painter's
Brushes and Pencils.
Top row, from left to
right: Captured Bristle,
Graphic Paintbrush,
Opaque Bristle Spray,
Round Camelhair, and
Smeary Flat. Bottom
row: Variable Round,
Dry Ink Brush, Colored
Pencil, 2B Pencil, and
Loaded Palette Knife.

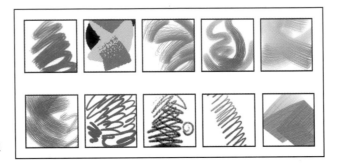

CAUTION

Now, about Painter's Pen and Mouse Mode settings: Always use the Pen Mode setting in the Wacom Control Panel when working with Painter. Painter does not support the Mouse Mode setting in the Control Panel, which causes the Stylus to behave like a mouse.

Dry Media

The Dry Media choices in Painter are great when you want to simulate dry chalk, charcoal, pastels, or crayons. You'll see an example of Basic Crayon in Figure 3.22, where the effect of pressure sensitivity is obvious. Applying various pressure levels will achieve the same effects as on paper. You have ten Dry Media options in the submenu.

Impasto

There are no fewer than thirty-two options in the Impasto submenu. Impasto means that paint is applied to canvas in generous quantities that make it stand out from the surface. Impasto is a technique dating back to the 17th century, and it was used by famous painters including Rembrandt and Velázquez. It was also used by Van Gogh, and if you look at his sunflower paintings, you'll see the deep lines in the paint that emphasize the shape and structure of the sunflower petals. There's no surprise that most options in the Impasto submenu are for creating depth and structure. Fiber is one of them, as shown in Figure 3.22.

Pens

The Pens menu includes tools like Calligraphy and Scratchboard Rake. This menu is your favorite choice when drawing Japanese signs and calligraphic-looking symbols and letters. In the Expressions menu, the default settings are not set to pressure, because drawing with these tools will typically be without edges fading in and out of the strokes. Try changing the Opacity settings to Pressure or use Direction or Velocity with the various submenu choices.

Felt Pens

Three choices are available on the submenu for drawing with felt pen effects. Dirty Marker with the Opacity set to Pressure is shown in Figure 3.22. You can also choose Felt Marker and Medium-tip Felt Pens. These are great for drawing without having to sniff the horrible fumes of some markers!

Airbrushes

You have nine choices in the Airbrushes submenu. Here you'll enjoy graffiti and spatter effects and have the option to set Size and Opacity to Pressure (as controlled by the Stylus). I find that the size set to pressure doesn't work as well with some Airbrush tools in Painter, so you're better off using Wacom's PenTools for this.

Figure 3.22
Some of Painter's brushes and effects: Top row, from left to right: Basic Crayon, Acid Etch, Fiber, Dirty Marker, and Graffiti Airbrush. Bottom row: Pepper Spray Airbrush, Variable Spatter, Furry Brush F/X, Fairy Dust F/X, and Graphic Paintbrush.

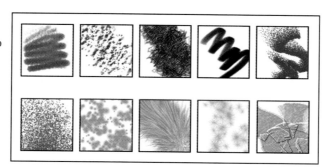

There are even more drawing and painting effects in Painter, including Photo Effects, Image Hose, Artists (applies effects like Impressionist, Van Gogh, and so on), Cloners, Liquid, and Water Color. The F/X submenu is also extensive, with Furry Brush and Fairy Dust (see Figure 3.23 for examples), plus eight more choices. There's no Blur Tool in Painter, but you can apply Blur effects from the Effects menu. To achieve Blur effects, you can try some of the tools in the Liquid menu, but be careful.

Painter's erasers are also pressure sensitive, but I must admit I find these less precise, especially regarding pressure sensitivity, than Photoshop's eraser. When creating artwork, I suggest using Painter for some drawing effects but switching to Photoshop for correcting mistakes or retouching photographs.

Figure 3.23
This screen shot of Illustrator's toolbox has the Paintbrush Tool selected and the Brushes and Attributes tabs showing.

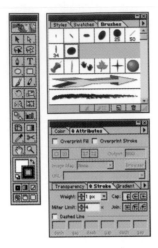

Pressure-Sensitive Tools in Adobe Illustrator 9

Illustrator creates vector graphics, and drawing strokes and lines in Illustrator means *paths*. A path is made up of various segments, each of which contains anchor points. The anchor points can be adjusted so that you can change the shape of the path. When you want to draw and edit freeform paths, use the Pencil tool. You may use the Erase Tool afterward, which lets you remove a portion of an existing path or stroke created with the Pencil or Brush tools. When drawing in Illustrator 9, you can use either the pressure-sensitive Brush or Pencil tools, but you also have the option of creating your very own brushes. Let's take a quick look at Illustrator's pressure-sensitive tools:

Pencil Tool

The pencil is great for quick sketching because it renders a line that looks much like a ballpoint pen. To set the preferences for the Pencil tool, you simply double-click the Pencil Tool icon. The dialog box that pops up gives you the option to set Fidelity in pixels plus Smoothness in percent. The lower the Smoothness value, the coarser the path appears—the higher the value, the smoother the path. To avoid disturbance from seeing the anchor points when you draw, deselect the Keep Selected option, which is chosen by default.

Paintbrush Tool

There are different types of brushes: calligraphic, scatter, art, and pattern. Combined with a pressure-sensitive stylus, you can get great results even if you're doing vector graphics. The Paintbrush Tool creates paths painted with a brush selected in the Brushes Palette. You must select a brush in the Brushes Palette (see Figure 3.24) to use the Paintbrush tool. You set the preferences for the Paintbrush tool the same way as the Pencil tool. To edit a path you've drawn with the Paintbrush tool, you select it with the selection tool or Ctrl-click (Command-click) the path.

Figure 3.24
The Brushes Palette in Illustrator. Set the preferences the same way as for the Pencil tool.

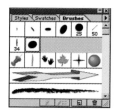

NOTE

Swapping between programs will give you the best results when you're working. You may think that you can do everything in just one application, but this often proves to be wrong. Even though Illustrator now supports layers and transparency, you still may benefit from Photoshop's larger selection of pressure-sensitive tools. You can export art made in Illustrator to Photoshop instead of the other way around. Remember, instead of working up a sweat in one program, try to think if there's another program that will perform just what you want more easily. Import and export your artwork as needed to create the best results.

Now that your tablet and tools are customized and ready to go, we'll move on to the really fun parts of working with the tablet and tools. In the next chapters, you'll learn the basics of working with objects and selections, create nifty masks, and other exciting stuff.

Part II
Objects, Photos and Color

4
Working with Objects

This chapter will cover the fundamental techniques in Painter and Photoshop for selecting objects, modifying selections, and removing unwanted backgrounds from objects. We'll also look at objects and layers, how to avoid fringe pixels, and other essential tricks. Last but not least, we'll use pressure-sensitive tools to create *masks*, which are an absolute must when creating a photomontage.

After you finish this chapter, you will have the necessary insight and confidence to work with objects and layers in almost any program, as the techniques are universal and the tools used are common in many programs. You will have learned paste-into techniques in Photoshop, which create "instant masks," and also how to paint your own masks on objects and layers.

This chapter will show you how to:

▶ Work with objects and selections, including how to modify and adjust selections
▶ Work with objects and layers
▶ Realize the possibilities when working with layers
▶ Remove unwanted areas and backgrounds
▶ Paint freehand masks, use channels as masks, and use plug-ins for masks

Objects and Selections

This section will cover the basic aspects of object and background selection, including adding to and subtracting pixels from a selection. We'll use the common Magic Wand Tool, found in programs like Painter and Photoshop, plus the three Marquee tools and the Lasso Tool. The Rectangular Marquee Tool and Elliptical Marquee Tool are quite common in applications nowadays, so we won't spend time talking about them. We'll cover the importance of using the correct tolerance settings when making a selection, plus look at how to remove fringe pixels, which result from anti-aliasing with objects.

Selecting Objects

In many programs, the selection tools are the same. For example, Painter and Photoshop (versions 5.5, 6.0, and Elements) both have the Magic Wand Tool and various Marquee tools. None of these is pressure-sensitive. For all tool selections, you can use input devices such as the mouse or the pen; when working with masks or difficult selections using, for example, the Lasso Tool, you'll use only the pen for precision. Let's take a look at the basics of object selection.

Selections Using the Magic Wand Tool

 The Magic Wand Tool lets you select areas of adjacent (or neighboring) pixels in a picture, based on their color. The Magic Wand Tool is great for making quick and easy selections of objects where the color contrast (or color difference) between the object and its surrounding pixels is high—like black and white. A good rule is as follows: **The** *less* **contrast between what you want selected and what you don't want means you'll have increased difficulty making a precise selection**. The Magic Wand Tool will select many pixels of *similar* colors, with no regard to which ones you really want, even with low tolerance settings. The area you'll want to select may also be of varying color intensity or nuances and not a solid color. When using the Magic Wand Tool, you'll select only *parts* of the background when the background varies in color. The picture itself decides what selection tool or method you'll have to use. To demonstrate this, let's take a look at a few examples from Corel Painter 6 that show the differences between Tolerance settings that are too low and too high:

In Figure 4.1, I've used the Magic Wand in Painter with a Tolerance setting of 4 and with Destination set to Selection. Tolerance equals the sensitivity concerning color nuances in the neighboring pixels. A Tolerance setting of 4 is too low, so only parts of the background are selected. The brighter areas to the bottom right, plus the cheese's shadow, are not selected at all. Obviously, we'll have to do something about the Tolerance setting, because a higher Tolerance setting will give you a selection that covers more of the color nuances in the background.

Figure 4.1
Notice that only parts of the background are selected in this image.

In Figure 4.2, we've increased the Tolerance (or sensitivity) to 28, which is too high. Now most of the cheese is selected as well, which was not our intention. You don't have to type in various numbers for the Tolerance settings; simply keep the selection active while using the Tolerance slider until you're happy with the result. In this example, the correct Tolerance setting proved to be 18.

Figure 4.2
In this image, the whole background is selected, but so is most of the cheese.

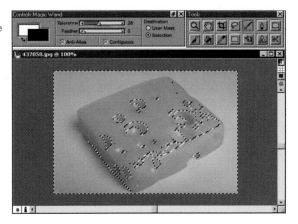

In Figure 4.3, we're as close as we'll get using the Magic Wand Tool. Observe that we have a small part of the shadow selected, which we don't want. Instead, we'll have to use the Lasso Tool and a pen to remove the shadow completely and get a clean selection.

Figure 4.3
We get a nearly perfect selection with the right Tolerance setting.

Adding and Subtracting

When you use the Magic Wand Tool (or other selection tools) to make selections, you'll often have to adjust your selection by adding or subtracting a few pixels. We'll demonstrate this by continuing with our cheese selection in Painter. We'll use a pen for this task.

With the background selection still active, select the Lasso Tool. While pressing the Shift key, trace the edge of the cheese which will be *added* to the selection, as shown in Figure 4.4. If you hold Ctrl (Command) down instead, you'll *subtract* the area you draw from the selection. The same technique can be used in Photoshop. When you're happy with the selection, you invert it by choosing the Invert command (Inverse in Photoshop 6) from the Select menu.

Then the cheese can be cut away from the background or effects can be added to it. In Photoshop, you could save the selection for later as a channel or make a layer mask of it. In Painter, you have to choose between Mask and Selection in the Destination settings *before* you begin selecting, as we did previously when starting on the cheese background.

Part II Objects, Photos and Colors

Figure 4.4
Switching to the Lasso
Tool, we'll remove the
last unwanted pixels by
adding the shadow
pixels to our
background selection.
Be careful to move the
Lasso Tool within your
selection (as shown
with the blue dashed
line) when releasing the
tool after you've made
the adjustments.

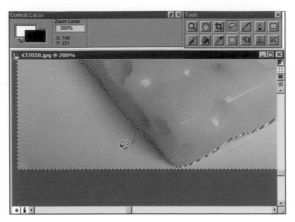

TIP

You'll usually want to select the background instead of the object itself. In
this example, there are too many color nuances and too much contrast in the
cheese for an easy selection with the wand. The background is quite the
opposite—low in contrast and an even color, so you'll know it will be easier
to select. Because we want the cheese selected in the end, and not the
background, we will invert the background selection later to select the cheese.

Selections with the Lasso Tools

a.

b.

c.

In Photoshop, you have three different Lasso tools available: the Lasso Tool *(a.)*, the
Polygonal Lasso Tool *(b.)*, and the Magnetic Lasso Tool *(c.)*. All three are great for
selecting objects with straight edges, and the Lasso and Magnetic Lasso tools can be
used for objects with curves as well. Let's take a look at some playing cards in Figure
4.5. Here we'll use the Magnetic Lasso Tool with an Edge Contrast setting of 5. The
setting is so low because the black background and white card edges are high in
contrast, so there's little risk of selecting the wrong pixels. As you can see, the
Magnetic Lasso traces the card edges perfectly to make a precise selection without
much effort on your part.

Figure 4.5
Making selections with
Photoshop's Magnetic
Lasso Tool is so easy
you can do it in your
sleep.

The Lasso Tool is great for freehand selections when you want both curves and straight lines. In Figure 4.6, we'll select the toothbrush. We begin with the toothpaste, tracing the curved edge carefully with the Lasso Tool. When we reach the toothbrush, press the Alt (Option) key down to create straight selection lines by clicking instead of tracing. Alt (Option) switches from the Lasso Tool to the Polygonal Lasso Tool. It's difficult to freehand trace with precision along straight edges, so we cheat by doing this. In this picture, the other selection tools would be no good, as the lower edge of the toothbrush blends into the background. Simply imagine where the edge is and click your way through the selection while holding Alt (Option) down.

Figure 4.6
Observe where you'll want to switch from the Lasso Tool to the Polygonal Lasso Tool in selecting this toothbrush. The orange line is for the Lasso Tool, and the red line is for the Polygonal Lasso Tool.

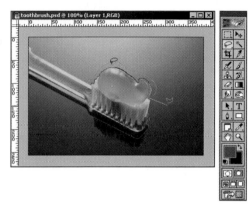

Adjusting Your Selections

If you want to make quick and easy selections, it's great to know a few methods that allow you to adjust your selection to fit the object you want to select—and there are several ways to adjust your selection. In Photoshop, go to the Select menu and choose Modify when you have an active selection. Choose Contract or Expand to decrease or increase your selection in pixels. If you want to move a selection, switch to the Lasso tool and drag the selection where you want it. Here's a tutorial for selecting elliptical objects—in this case a melon—in Photoshop 6.0:

1. Select the Elliptical Marquee Tool and draw an ellipse roughly around the object you want selected. As shown in Figure 4.7, you don't need to be precise.

Figure 4.7
Draw a rough selection with the Elliptical Marquee Tool.

2. From the Select menu, choose Transform Selection (no keyboard shortcuts). You now have a rectangle surrounding your selection, as shown in Figure 4.8, with numerous handles you can drag to modify it.

Figure 4.8
You may adjust the selection as you please, choosing Select > Transform Selection.

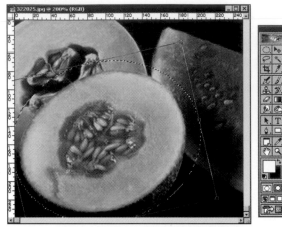

3. You can now scale or rotate your selection as you please, without changing the picture contents. You move the selection by placing the cursor inside the active selection and dragging the selection to fit the object. When you want to resize the selection (making it smaller, for example), use one of the corner handles while holding down Shift. This way, you resize the whole selection proportionally—not holding Shift down lets you adjust height or width independently.

4. After you apply your adjustments, you still have the selection active, so you can rotate or scale it as many times as you'd like without losing your selection. In the end, you'll have a selection looking similar to Figure 4.9. When you want to rotate your selection, place the cursor slightly outside the square and you'll see a small arrow. You may rotate left or right manually, or use Edit > Transform and then select the appropriate option.

Figure 4.9
Your elliptical selection may look something like this.

TIP

If changing the object was what you *really* wanted, you have to do this: From the Edit menu, choose Free Transform (Ctrl+T or Command+T). You can now scale or rotate your selection as you please. To rotate, you need to place your cursor slightly *outside* the selection, where you'll see it'll turn into a small arrow.

You can also use *paths* to create selections, but paths can be used to create very advanced stuff, so we'll cover paths more in chapters 7 and 8.

Removing Backgrounds and Objects

By now, you've seen that backgrounds and objects go hand-in-hand. Sometimes you'll work directly with the object, other times you'll work with the background to get to the object. The following will explore the background options further.

Removing Backgrounds in Photoshop

We'll pick up our cheese picture again, now in Photoshop.

1. Make sure you have the Layers palette visible. If not, in the menu, choose Windows > Show Layers.

2. Make a background selection as we did previously. While it's active, select the Move Tool. When placing your cursor within the selection, you'll see the cursor gets a small pair of scissors next to it. If you press Delete or Backspace now, you'll fill the background with the background color presently in your Toolbox, as shown in Figure 4.10. The same happens if you try to cut out the selection using Cut from the Edit menu (Ctrl+X or Command+X). This happens because, when you're working on a picture, that default becomes a Background Layer when opened in Photoshop. If the picture were on a separate layer, you would simply erase the selection from the layer.

Figure 4.10
The background won't go away no matter how hard you press the Delete key.

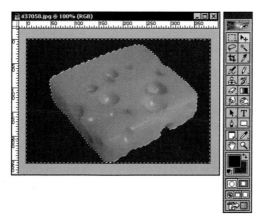

3. To remove the background, keep the selection active while renaming the background layer. Add a new layer by clicking the Layers palette arrow > New Layer. The new layer will be transparent by default.

4. Drag the cheese layer above the new layer in the Layers palette, as shown in Figure 4.11. When you press Delete now, with your selection layer active, the selected area will be transparent.

5. You may now use a pressure-sensitive tool for final adjustments to the cheese, such as blurring or smoothing out the edges.

You can then adjust the new layer you made in any way you wish. You can change its color or export the object as a transparent GIF to be used on a Web page. We'll take a closer look at Layers in the next section, and you can turn to Chapter 9 to learn about Web graphics.

Figure 4.11
Drag the object (cheese) layer on top in the Layers palette. By pressing Delete, you get a transparent background that allows you to do all sorts of fun stuff.

TIP

There's another trick to get rid of unwanted backgrounds in Photoshop 6. Hidden behind the Eraser Tool is the Background Eraser Tool. You can use it directly on your picture to remove the background; you don't need to create a new layer. When you start drawing with the Background Eraser Tool, the layer is renamed automatically to Layer 0. By specifying different Tolerance options, you can control the amount of opacity. The eraser samples the color in the center of the brush, which is seen as a small cross in Figure 4.12. The brush center is also called a *hot spot* and deletes that (sample) color wherever it appears *inside* the brush circle. Consequently, choosing the right brush size is important to achieve precise edges.

Figure 4.12
Erase the background by using the Background Eraser Tool.

Removing Objects

The observant reader will have guessed that we've already removed an object (the cheese) from our previous example and placed it on a separate layer. This shows that there are several ways to reach a goal when it comes to objects. You may, of course, use the previous examples to get rid of objects. You may also use the masking techniques that we'll look at later in this chapter. Another method is simply to *erase the object*, using the pressure-sensitive erasers in Painter or Photoshop. Experiment with the opacity settings for the erasers, because they can give you smooth transitions between the object and the background.

Fringe Pixels and Anti-aliasing

When you select an object—such as the peach in Figure 4.13—and paste it onto a new layer or into a new document, you will sometimes get an edge that contains some of the background pixels in your original picture. These are called fringe pixels, which appear because of anti-aliasing. Anti-aliasing smoothes the edges of a selection by softening the color transition between edge pixels and background pixels, but at the same time, you get annoying fringe pixels. Sometimes, the fringe pixels won't be visible, such as when your original background color is very similar to your new background color. When you look at your selection magnified to 200 percent or more, though, you'll see them clearly.

Figure 4.13
Fringe pixels are everywhere! At the edge of the peach in the picture to the right, you'll see a lot of pixels from the original background.

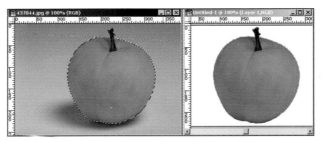

In Figure 4.14, I've pasted an anti-aliased selection of a blue glass bottle in Photoshop. Some of the pixels surrounding the selection border are included. This results in a fringe, or sometimes a "halo," around the edges of the selection. You can see this clearly because I've pasted the bottle on a black background.

Figure 4.14
I've used a black background so you'll see the fringe pixels easily.

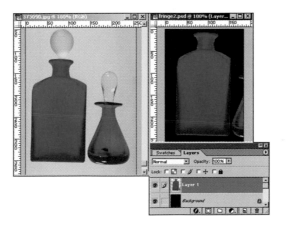

This is how we get rid of fringe pixels:

1. Select the layer with your object (in this case, the blue bottle).
2. From the Layer menu, choose Matting > Defringe.
3. Choose a setting of 1, 2, or 3 pixels in the small Defringe dialog box, as seen in Figure 4.15.
4. Click OK.

Figure 4.15
No more fringe pixels!

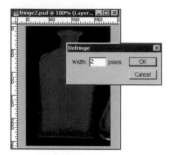

Note that you can also use masks to get rid of fringe pixels, by simply painting them away on the mask. But the above example is the fastest approach. We'll take a look at masks later in this chapter.

Objects and Layers

This section will cover the basics of working with objects and layers. We'll take a look at a handy Paste-Into technique, and other object-related tricks. We'll also take a look at the various Layer styles in Photoshop 6, which has more advanced options than ever.

Moving and Duplicating Objects

Moving objects around isn't hard at all. If they're on separate layers, you can simply drag them around with the Move Tool. You can duplicate an object by copying it and pasting it. Or you can just copy the layer itself and you'll have two objects on their own layers. Can you guess why you'd want to do that?

The whole point of duplicating objects is to make life easier. Here is an example: I got an assignment to make several illustrations for an anti-smoking campaign. One of the illustrations was to be a female heavy smoker "drowning" in an ashtray filled to the rim with cigarette butts. The idea of drawing hundreds of cigarette butts made my head spin. So, it was time for duplication. As you'll see in Figure 4.16 and Figure 4.18, there are plenty of cigarette butts in the finished drawing, but in reality, I drew only four or five of them!

This is the trick: I began by drawing a few different cigarette butts, each on a separate layer. By duplicating the layer, I got more butts.

Figure 4.16
Handy duplication:
Draw one or two
cigarette butts, duplicate
them, rotate each a bit,
and you have different-
looking cigarette butts.

Duplicating a layer is very easy: You simply select and drag the layer you want to duplicate to the bottom of the Layers palette and drop it onto the small Create New Layer icon next to the Trashcan icon in Figure 4.17. As you can see, the Layers Palette has several options at the bottom.

Figure 4.17
The Layers palette in
Photoshop 6.

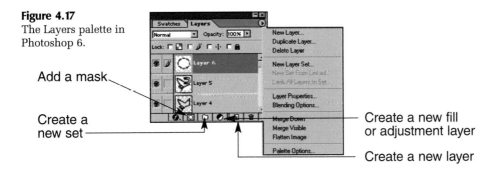

Add a mask

Create a
new set

Create a new fill
or adjustment layer

Create a new layer

Rotating and flipping the layers horizontally and vertically created variations, so I needed just a few to give the appearance of many different-looking cigarette butts. I placed some butts here and there, and I merged some layers so I had an entire group of butts to move around. I then duplicated this layer (with the group of butts) several times, thereby covering large pieces of the ashtray efficiently. The final touch was adding shadows and highlights using a pressure-sensitive pen and Brush tools in Photoshop. You can see the finished result in Figure 4.18.

Part II   Objects, Photos and Colors

This is an illustration for a leaflet about the hazards of cigarette smoking. The target was doctors, who were going to be inspired to help their patients to stop smoking; therefore the doctor should see himself/herself as an 'angel' to the rescue.

Figure 4.18
The end result—lots of cigarette butts and little work.

Selecting an Object on a Layer

When you have an object on a transparent layer, there's a quick way to select it. You don't have to do it manually or go through the "select background" procedure. Simply press the Ctrl (Command) key and click the layer with your pen or mouse. You'll see the cursor turn into a pointer with a rectangle above the Layer thumbnail, and the object is selected. To select the whole layer, and not just the object, use the Ctrl+A (Command+A) shortcut.

Figure 4.19
This figure shows how to select an object on a layer.

Selection Shortcuts

Table 4.1 below shows selection shortcuts that work with applications like Painter 6, Photoshop 6, and Illustrator 9. The most common ones, such as Cut, Paste, and Undo (Ctrl+Z or Command+Z) also work in Microsoft Word and Excel as well as in similar office applications. It's efficient to use shortcuts, because the commands themselves are often hidden in different menus, depending on the application. So instead of wasting your time trying to find them, memorize the shortcuts instead. If you're right-handed, you'll probably use your left hand on the keyboard for the shortcuts, leaving your right hand free to draw on your tablet.

Remember that many of the shortcuts can be programmed on the Wacom Intuos tablet menu strip, as described in Chapter 3.

Table 4.1
Selection shortcuts.

Result	Windows shortcut	Mac shortcut
Select all	Ctrl+A	Command+A
Deselect *	Ctrl+D	Command+D
Constrain marquee (to square or circle)	Shift + *drag*	Shift + *drag*
Draw marquee from center	Alt + *drag*	Option + *drag*
Move selection 1 pixel (active selection *or* the Move Tool selected)	Any Arrow key	Any Arrow key
Free transform of selected object	Ctrl+T	Command+T
Selects object on transparent layer	Ctrl+ *click layer*	Command + *click layer*
Cut selected object	Ctrl+X	Command+X
Paste selected object	Ctrl+V	Command+V
Paste clipboard into a selection (creates a mask in Photoshop)	Shift+Ctrl+V	Shift+Command+V

*Photoshop has finally joined the other applications in this, as Ctrl+D in older versions duplicated an object instead of deselecting it. Note that Microsoft's PowerPoint duplicates an object or text box with this command.

The Paste-Into Technique

We're going to take a closer look at masks later in this chapter, but first, we'll take a peek at a very useful trick that involves masks in Photoshop. It's an advantage to be able to restrain your object to a selected area. This can be useful when working with type—for example, when you want to fill your type with a picture or a texture, when you have a frame you want to paste a picture into, and similar tasks.

The Paste-Into command can be used for pasting objects into any selection, such as a circle, but we'll do something a bit more advanced here. Let's turn a simple typeface into something more exciting. As you see in Figure 4.20, we start with a blue background. The letters *ROCK* (Arial Black, 140 points) are set in white on a separate layer. We also have a picture of an interesting rock surface we'll paste into the type. Duplicate the type layer by dragging it onto the New Layer icon and hide it afterwards by clicking the layer visibility icon (the small eye). We'll use the copy later.

Figure 4.20
We're ready to rock and roll with a type layer and a nice picture of a rock surface.

Select your rock structure. Because we don't know which part of the rock structure will be the prettiest, we'll select it all with the Ctrl+A (Command+A) shortcut. This is now in your clipboard. Switch to your type layer and, with the Move Tool selected, press Ctrl+ click the type thumbnail in the Layers palette to load the letters separately as a selection.

Go to the Edit menu and select Paste Into (or use Shift+Ctrl+V or Shift+Command+V). Your result should look like Figure 4.21. Note the new layer above your type layer, where you'll see the structure with a *mask layer* to the right (where the letters ROCK are visible). The Move Tool is still active, so with the Layer thumbnail selected, you may drag the contents as you please until you're happy with the parts of the structure visible in the letters.

Figure 4.21
The rock surface is now residing on its own layer, with a mask added.

Note that you must always have the structure layer selected (and not the mask itself) when manipulating the content. You can stretch it, rotate it, or do absolutely anything with it, including adjusting the layer opacity so you can view the Type layer below. I'll just adjust the image content and apply the mask.

Now, take a look at Figure 4.22. We'll add some effects to the type:

Figure 4.22
You now have a layer with the letters ROCK made from your rock surface picture.

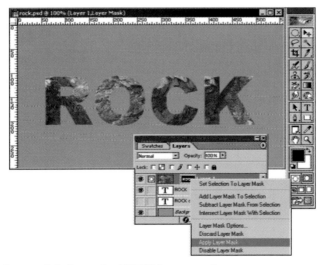

1. Click the mask (where the ROCK letters are).
2. Right-click to bring up a menu.
3. Choose Apply Layer Mask. You'll see the layer has the letters ROCK made up from your selection (visible as the top layer in Figure 4.23).

4. Move the original text layer (which is white) to the left and up, to create a highlight as shown in Figure 4.23.

5. Choose the text copy layer, fill the text with black color, and move it down and to the right to create a black shadow. Add Blur if you want smoother edges to the shadow, and adjust Layer opacity if you want a softer shadow.

6. As the structure selection is still on the clipboard, paste it above the background layer and set the Opacity of the layer to 33 percent.

Figure 4.23
This image results from adding a couple of effects like highlighting and shadow (using the text layers) and adding the texture again above the background.

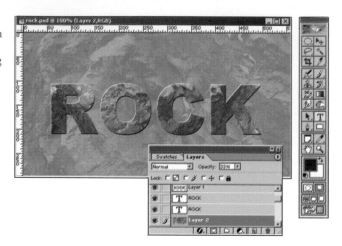

Layer Styles and Effects

Previously, layer effects had to be done manually by duplicating layers and adding filters. Then Photoshop 6 added a lot of exciting layer styles and effects, some of which are great for color adjustments while others are just cool effects you'll see everywhere on the Internet and in print today. Programs like Painter 6, Illustrator 9, and Paint Shop Pro 7 also have layers now, although the options are somewhat different than Photoshop's. You'll find these in Chapter 6.

Layer Styles Defined

Layer Styles affect how one layer interacts with other layers, including the opacity of the layers. You apply layer styles in Photoshop 6.0 using the Styles palette or with Layers menu > Layer Styles. When you apply a layer effect to a layer, you have created a custom layer style made up of that single effect. You can't apply layer styles directly to a background (you have to rename the background as a layer first) or to a locked layer. You can apply several layer styles to a layer, however.

Layer Styles Effects

You have numerous options for customizing and fine-tuning Layer styles. Here are the various Layer Styles in Photoshop and some of their options:

▶ **Drop Shadow**—This effect adds a shadow to the contents on the layer, as shown in Figure 4.24. You can, for example, adjust the intensity of the shadow, the angle (where you'll like it to fall), color, distance (from your object), and width. Older versions of Photoshop did not have Drop Shadow effects, which made filter packages that had it, such as Eye Candy from Alien Skin, very popular. Now less expensive programs like Paint Shop Pro 7 also have Drop Shadow effects, although the adjustment options are few. You can also create your own shadows for the most natural shadow effects, so don't miss the shadow walk-throughs in Chapter 10.

Figure 4.24
This figure shows ROCK with a drop shadow and the Layer Styles dialog box with Drop Shadow selected. Note all the Layer Style options on the left-hand side.

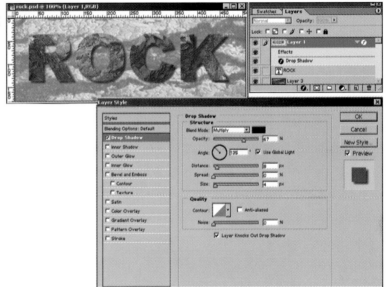

▶ **Inner Shadow**—This feature adds a shadow that falls just *inside the edges* of the contents, giving it a recessed appearance. You have the same adjustment options as for Drop Shadow. Note that the Choke option shrinks the boundaries of the Inner Shadow prior to blurring.

▶ **Outer Glow** or **Inner Glow**—These add glows (or halos) on the outside or inside edges of the contents, both shown in Figure 4.25.

Figure 4.25
Our ROCK letters have the Outer Glow (top) and Inner Glow (bottom) Layer Styles added to them.

Part II Objects, Photos and Colors

▶ **Bevel and Emboss**—This feature adds various combinations of highlights and shadows to a layer, with varying intensity and width that creates the beveled (or embossed) effects. You have two more choices here, Contour and Texture. Texture lets you add a Pattern from a drop-down menu. This could be your own Pattern, which you'll learn to create in Chapter 12. Bevel effects are available also in Paint Shop Pro 7.

▶ **Color, Gradient, and Pattern Overlay**—This is designed to overlay a color, gradient, or pattern on a layer. You may edit color or opacity in the Gradient Overlay panel just like in the Gradient Editor. Reverse will flip the gradient's orientation.

If you're working with a document containing several layers and want the same Layer Style (for example, exactly the same Drop Shadow effect) on two or more layers, you can copy the Layer Style onto another layer. Right-click the Layer Style icon on the layer you want to copy *from* (the icon is a black circle with an F). From the Layer palette menu, select Copy Layer Style as seen in Figure 4.26. Select the layer you want the effect *copied to*. Right-click again and choose Paste Layer Style from the Layer palette menu.

NOTE

Avoid these Layer palette obstacles: You must place your cursor to the right of the Layer thumbnail in the Layers Palette when you right-click to display the correct menu choices for Layer styles. If you right-click on the Layer thumbnail, you'll see only choices like Layer Properties and Blending modes.

Figure 4.26
This figure shows how to copy a Layer Style.

Choose 'Copy Layer Style' from the right-click menu. Move to the layer you want to add the effect on, right-click again, and choose 'Paste Layer Style'.

CAUTION

Note that the Layer opacity settings also affect the Layer Style. If you set the opacity to 30 percent, you'll also set the opacity of the style to 30 percent. Because the Layer Style will interact with other layers, you can run into trouble when merging layers with or without other effects. To avoid this, you have to convert the style to layers. When you've done that, you can no longer adjust the Layer Style, so you have to be certain you've got the result you want before converting. Right-click at the Layer Style icon, and from the menu, choose Create Layer. With the Drop Shadow as an example, you'd get a new layer with your original object and a new layer below it with the Drop Shadow style converted to a layer, as shown in Figure 4.27.

Figure 4.27
This figure shows Layer Style (Drop Shadow) and object converted to layers.

Creating Masks

In this section, we'll continue to look at masks, which we took a peek at previously in the Paste-Into tutorial. A mask lets you protect areas of an image as you apply color changes, filters, or other effects to the unmasked part of the image. You can also use masks for advanced image editing techniques such as gradually applying color or filter effects to an image. A mask also lets you erase edges or parts of an image with great accuracy—using, for example, the pressure-sensitive pen.

Painting Freehand Masks

Painting on a mask lets you manipulate pictures or objects precisely, a necessity when working on a photomontage. Infamous pictures of celebrities on the Internet are often fakes—photos manipulated with masks. If the surrealist artist Magritte had worked digitally, his paintings of men with no heads would have been created with masks! Masks are great for creating the perfect picture, such as when you have one picture of a scene and need an object blended seamlessly into it. You need not worry about fringe pixels when working with masks.

Let's say you have a job for a clothing company, and you are to produce their new catalog for the winter season. You have two pictures: A winter landscape and a picture of a girl, as in Figure 4.28. When you merge two pictures, as we're about to do now, remember that the colors in the two pictures should match. A very dark picture (or an object with dark shades) will seldom work well if blended with a picture of snow (or other pictures with large, white areas). Even if you make adjustments to the pictures regarding contrast and color, your originals must be well suited to one another to begin with.

Figure 4.28
Our two originals are a
landscape and a picture
of a girl.

1. Begin by pasting the girl into the landscape document, selecting the picture with Ctrl+A (Command+A). Keep Ctrl down and drag the selection above the landscape layer and release.

2. In the Layers palette, click the Add Mask icon to add a mask to the layer with the girl. We now want to place the girl exactly where we want her in relation to the background. Because we have trouble seeing the landscape through "her" background, adjust the opacity of the layer with the girl (make sure the thumbnail is selected and not the mask when you do this) to view the landscape layer below. You can resize the girl as well, as shown in Figure 4.29.

Figure 4.29
This picture of a girl has
layer opacity adjusted
and resizing active.

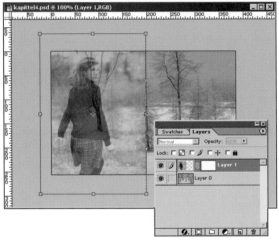

3. Set the layer opacity back to 100 percent. Click the mask layer. In your Toolbox, set the foreground color to black.

4. Because we don't want to do more work than we must, use the Rectangular Marquee Tool to select large areas of the girl's background and fill the selections with black. The quickest way to do this is to right-click over the selection and choose Fill from the menu as seen in Figure 4.30. Fill the selection with 100 percent black.

Figure 4.30
Make rough selections with the Rectangular Marquee Tool and fill with black.

5. Deselect any selection(s) with Ctrl+D (Command+D). It's now time to take advantage of that pressure-sensitive pen! Because black color masks (hides) the unwanted areas of your object, you simply paint with black color on your mask to hide what's left of the girl's background. Photoshop's Airbrush Tool or Paintbrush Tool is excellent for this combined with your stylus. Set the Brush opacity to 20 percent or lower when working close to the girl's edges. This creates smooth transitions between her and the underlying landscape layer. Set the pressure-sensitivity to be controlled by the Stylus in the Brush Dynamics palette. When painting the mask, zoom in to 200 or 300 percent so you'll see what you're doing.

    If you make a mistake and remove parts of the girl, set white as the foreground color and paint her back in! Remember: White adds, black removes on a mask. See Figure 4.31.

Figure 4.31
While working on difficult edges like hair, always use low pressure to create smooth transitions.

6. When you think you're done, it's a good idea to check your result. By temporarily hiding the landscape layer, any mistakes you've made will be visible against the transparent background. As shown in Figure 4.32, I've not been thorough enough around her face.

Figure 4.32
Some of the background is still there, but I didn't see it until hiding the landscape layer.

7. All that's left to do is to make minor adjustments to the color in our girl. The winter landscape is much cooler in color, so we need to get the two layers better matched. By using the Image > Adjust > Color Balance options, increase Cyan and Blue in the midtones. I also adjusted the Levels in the image and experimented with the Replace Color options, which we'll look at more closely in Chapter 6. You'll see the difference before and after my adjustments in Figure 4.33.

Figure 4.33
You can easily see the difference in the color adjustments before (left) and after (right).

TIP

Masks can be created in a flash in Photoshop: Using a selection tool like the Lasso, select roughly (or precisely) the part of the image you want to keep. (Remember to rename the background layer first if you're editing a picture!) Click the Add a Mask icon in your Layers palette, and you have a mask ready to be edited (painted) with your favorite pressure-sensitive tool!

Channels As Masks

You can create permanent masks in Photoshop by storing them in *alpha channels*. This allows you to use a mask again and again in the same image or in a different one.

Remember to rename the background layer first if you're editing a picture. Let's say you want to merge two pictures as we did above. Start with two layers. The bottom layer is a forest stream and the top layer a door. We'd like to see the forest through the door. Select the door by using, for example, the Lasso Tool. Open your Channel palette and create a new channel by clicking the New Channel icon. As you can see in Figure 4.34, your selection is now saved in a channel called Alpha 1. It does not matter if you involuntarily deselect your selection now, because you can easily bring it back from the channel. Move the forest layer above your door layer. For the sake of this example, deselect if you have a selection still active.

Figure 4.34
This figure shows how to add a selection to an alpha channel.

While having the forest layer chosen, go to the Select menu, click Load Selection, and choose Alpha 1 in the Channels dialog box. You now have the selection active again—and this would have been no fun if you'd kept your selection active. Now go to the Layers menu > Add Layer Mask > Reveal Selection. You see a forest in a door opening, as in Figure 4.35.

Part II Objects, Photos and Colors

Figure 4.35
Loading the selection
and adding a mask to
the layer gives you this
result.

Because you have the selection on a channel, you can choose another picture to be seen through the door. Simply go through the procedure as described previously.

To Edit an Alpha Channel

You can use a painting or editing tool to edit an alpha channel: Paint with black to add to the channel, paint with white to remove areas from the channel, or paint with a lower opacity or a color to add to the channel with lower opacities. To see what you're doing, make sure all the channels are visible, as in Figure 4.36. The mask is the default red color, and you can change this color (and its opacity) in Channel options. Click the small arrow on the Channels palette and select Channel options.

Figure 4.36
You may edit the channel mask at any time, then load it as a selection.

Using Plug-Ins for Masks

There are several plug-ins available for creating masks. If you struggle with masks, plug-ins can be helpful tools. Let's take a look at a couple of them and what they do.

Extensis Mask Pro 2.0

The Extensis Mask Pro 2.0 bills itself as a robust collection of tools that greatly reduces the time it takes to mask and select complex objects. The product uses "Exclusive Color Matching" technology and is the only one on the market that provides fast, professional tools for high-quality results. It works with Photoshop (for both Mac and Windows) and Corel PhotoPaint (with Windows). Extensis' own tutorial walks you through a hefty lion mask job, which is one of the worst objects you can choose to mask because of the mane.

Many of the tools are available in Photoshop under different names, but one advantage with Mask Pro is that you have the option of selecting *several* colors for "keep" or "drop" when masking, instead of Photoshop's Sample color and the Protect Foreground Color option. Extensis was selling at about $200 at the time of this writing.

Figure 4.37
The workspace of
Extensis Mask Pro 2.0.

Chromagraphics Magic Mask 2.2

Magic Mask supports Photoshop 5.0 and later, Corel Photopaint 8.0 and later, and other applications that support Photoshop's plug-in standards. The company states that the product is quick and easy to use even for novices.

Magic Mask is not pressure-sensitive, but the program does have a Density Mask tool that lets you create a density mask based on the color (or colors) selected in an image. Density masks are commonly used for color correction purposes. The Density Mask Tool creates a variable "deep mask" and mask gradients such as skin tones for selective color correction. You can create a quick-density mask with one click, use a variety of density mask pre-sets for common color ranges or to knock out backgrounds. You can also create and/or save a new setting using Hue, Saturation, and Value settings.

Figure 4.38
The workspace of
Chromagraphics Magic
Mask 2.2.

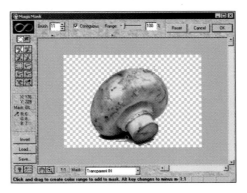

You should now have the necessary confidence to work with masks and selections in your artwork or in photomontages. I hope you will take the time to experiment with difficult tasks, which may prove to be not so difficult at all when you come to know the technique. We'll continue to work with masks in the next chapter as well, where you'll learn photo editing techniques.

5
Photo Editing

This chapter will guide you through the various options for correcting and editing photos, using both built-in color correction and brightness/contrast tools. I'll also discuss freehand editing with various tools on your tablet. When you have finished, you will have learned the necessary techniques to salvage dull vacation photographs, as well as do basic photo editing in Photoshop 6.0 and Elements. We'll also use the techniques you learned in Chapter 4 to create professional-looking photo collages.

This chapter will show you how to:

▶ Adjust images to get a good result from a poor original photo

▶ Add simple effects to create motion or interest in a picture

▶ Remove "red eye," unwanted areas, objects, or other items from photographs

▶ Improve photocomposition by adjusting backgrounds, manipulating perspective, and using other nifty tricks

▶ Create exciting photomontages of varying difficulty, with professional-looking results

Photo Correction

This section will cover the basic aspects of photo correction, including adjusting contrast and brightness in a picture with applications like Photoshop and Paint Shop Pro. We'll take a look at the built-in correction tools of various applications and how you can adjust *parts* of an image using an alpha channel in Photoshop.

Adjusting Images

There are a number of options available for photo correction in various applications. If you're already familiar with brightness/contrast settings, blurring, and sharpening tools, and you know your way around a histogram, flip to the next section, "Adjusting Brightness in Parts of An Image," for some adjustment tips. If you don't, or you want to refresh your knowledge, read on.

CAUTION

Calibrating your monitor is essential. Your pictures may be great, but if your monitor is set too dark or has the wrong contrast, your pictures may look terrible—even if they're not. Before you start adjusting images, use monitor-profiling utilities, such as Adobe Gamma, to calibrate your monitor to a color-display standard suited to your working needs. Otherwise, the image on your monitor may look very different from the same image when it's printed. Correct color calibration is essential with Web graphics, which will be displayed on different monitors around the world.

Contrast, Brightness, and Levels

The Brightness/Contrast command lets you make simple adjustments to the tonal range of an image. This command lightens or darkens the entire image (or just a selection you've made). It is often used to lighten scanned pictures that are too dark. A perfect picture has a good tonal range, with dark tones, middle tones, and bright tones evenly distributed throughout the image. The tonal range is displayed as a histogram in Photoshop's Image Levels dialog box (see Figure 5.1). The Brightness/Contrast command makes the same adjustment to *every pixel* in the image. (This is different than the Levels adjustments in Photoshop.) The Brightness/Contrast command does not work with individual channels, and making heavy adjustments can result in a loss of detail in the image.

Brightness and contrast adjustments are easy tools to start with. You can make pictures brighter, darker, and with varied contrast without too much hassle. In Photoshop 6, you'll find these tools by going to Image menu > Adjust > Brightness/Contrast (see Figure 5.2). Paint Shop Pro 7 has the same adjustments through Color menu > Adjust > Brightness/Contrast. The differences between the two applications are that Paint Shop Pro has two small windows in the dialog box where you can see the image before and after the adjustments (see Figure 5.2). In Photoshop, you drag the sliders until you have the desired result; in Paint Shop Pro, you can click in steps. Personally, I prefer to view the (whole) original image while I make adjustments, even though it can be an advantage to see your original image for comparison. Painter 6 has Brightness and Contrast adjustments through Effects menu > Tonal Control > Brightness/Contrast. The dialog box is similar to Photoshop's, with a preview of the adjustments in the original image.

Figure 5.1
Before (left) and after (right) RGB level adjustments in Photoshop 6. Note the positions of the midtones and highlighted triangular sliders.

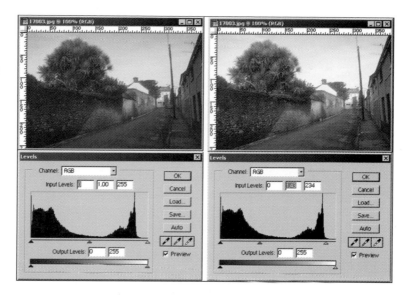

You can use Photoshop's Image adjustment levels to set highlights, shadows, and midtones. (In Photoshop Elements, use Enhance > Brightness/Contrast > Levels.) You may adjust the highlights and shadows in an image by dragging the Input Sliders to the first group of pixels on both ends of the Levels histogram, as shown in Figure 5.1. This adjusts the lightest and darkest pixels towards black and white, increasing the tonal range of the image. You can use the middle Input Slider to change the values of the midtones and leave the two others alone. For example, dragging the middle slider a little to the left increases brightness in the midtones, without altering the highlights and shadows. This is a fast and easy way for correcting pictures that seem too dark with a loss of detail in the midtones, but where both the brightest and darkest parts of the image are correct.

Figure 5.2
Notice the differences between the Brightness/Contrast adjustment dialog boxes in Photoshop 6 (left) and Paint Shop Pro 7 (right).

Part II Objects, Photos and Colors

TIP

A histogram, found in Photoshop 6's Levels dialog box (see Figure 5.1), illustrates how the pixels of an image are distributed. This can tell you whether the image contains enough detail in the shadows (left), the midtones (middle), and the highlights (right) to create a good correction. The histogram also displays the tonal range of the image. An image with full tonal range has an evenly distributed number of pixels in all areas. Identifying the tonal range helps determine appropriate corrections. If you'll look at Figure 5.3, you'll see three different histograms for the same picture. The first (to the left) will be the best to work with, because it contains a lot of pixels in the shadows and midtones.

Figure 5.3
Three different histograms of the same picture. Note that none of the pictures is correctly adjusted.

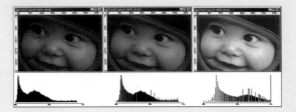

Brightness in Parts of an Image

By saving a selection as an alpha channel (see Chapter 4) in Photoshop 6, you can make adjustments to parts of an image. This is a great trick when you want parts of the image darkened or highlighted and want to bring attention to special parts of an image. In Figure 5.4, I've made a rough selection of the roses in the foreground, saving the selection as an alpha channel. Using a Pen and a pressure-sensitive Airbrush tool, I made corrections to the mask.

If you save your selection in an alpha channel, you can then load the selection onto an Adjustment Layer, which lets you adjust brightness, contrast, colors, hue/saturation, and so on. (We'll take a closer look at some of the wonders of adjustment layers in Chapter 6.) Simply go to Select > Load selection, choose Alpha 1 from Channels, and click OK. The selection is active. From the Layer menu, choose New Adjustment Layer > Brightness/Contrast, and you'll get a new layer in your layer palette plus the Brightness/Contrast dialog box, as shown in Figure 5.4. You can see I have adjusted the brightness too high for the sake of this example. The original picture is shown in Figure 5.5.

Figure 5.4
Making adjustments to
parts of an image, with
the help of an
adjustment layer for
Brightness/Contrast in
Photoshop.

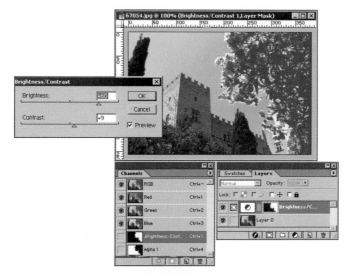

Figure 5.5
The original image,
without any
adjustments.

Painting Blur on an Image

You may wonder why on earth we'd want to blur an image, when many struggle to get their
photos sharp enough. Well, blur is a great effect you can use to add interest to a photograph. You
can use it to "highlight" areas by blurring the surroundings or add blur to the edges of an object
to simulate motion. Many applications, including Photoshop, Painter, and Paint Shop Pro, have
built-in filters for blurring or sharpening images. The blur filters soften a selection or an image
and are useful for retouching, because they smooth transitions between crisply lined areas. Most
of them work very well. You may, however, encounter situations where you'll want to do your
blurring by hand, either because you want special effects in a photo (such as blurring a
background) or because blurring can be great for making small corrections in portraits, for
example.

Part II Objects, Photos and Colors

With the Blur Photo Brush in Painter, you can utilize a blur effect with great accuracy. Using a stylus (pen), you can blur just parts of an image. By dragging the Brush along the girl's contour, as shown in Figure 5.6, as well as blurring other areas of the photo, you'll create an effect that makes the viewer focus more sharply on the girl's face. There's also some blur painted onto her hair, neck, and hands. In Figure 5.7, you can see the picture of the girl before and after the blurring. Use blurring effects to create an illusion of movement and speed in photographs. Always work in at least 200 percent magnification when making adjustments to pictures, because you need to be very precise to get the best result.

Figure 5.6
This image shows the Blur effect using the Blur Photo Brush in Painter.

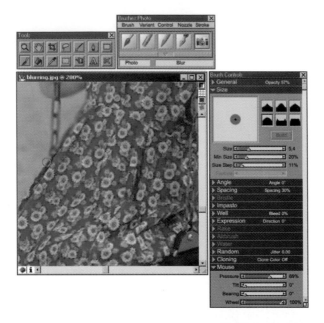

Figure 5.7
Notice the difference between the images before (left) and after a Blur effect is applied.

Focus Tools in Photoshop 6 and Elements

a.

b.

Photoshop's "focus tools" consist of the Blur Tool *(a.)* and the Sharpen Tool *(b.)*. The Blur Tool softens hard edges or softens areas in an image to reduce detail. The Sharpen tool focuses soft edges to increase focus or clarity. The focus tools are widely used for correcting or manipulating images. Popular uses includes softening backgrounds and adding sharp edges.

This is how you use the Sharpen Tool (or the Blur Tool) with Photoshop 6 or Elements:

1. Select the Sharpen Tool.

2. Set the pressure to be controlled by the pen (stylus) in Brush Dynamics.

3. Select the mode. Choose Normal if you simply want to sharpen edges, or you can choose Darken, Lighten, and so on, depending on what you want to achieve. As shown in Figure 5.8, I've set the Mode to Lighten.

Figure 5.8
The original image is on the left. The result with Sharpen Tool is to the right, and the blurred version is below. Note that I've overdone the sharpening, as you can see white pixels in the light areas of the image.

Improving Edges with the Unsharp Mask Filter

Photoshop (versions 5.5, 6.0, and Elements) has a filter called Unsharp Mask, which is found in Filters > Sharpen > Unsharp Mask. Unsharp masking is originally a film compositing technique for sharpening edges in an image. The Unsharp Mask filter corrects the *unwanted* blurring you may get when photographing or scanning. The Unsharp Mask filter locates pixels that differ from surrounding pixels by the *threshold* you specify. It then increases the contrast of the pixels by the *amount* you specify. Consider using Unsharp Mask when you want to adjust *all edges* in an image. When you want only some parts of an image sharpened, you're better off adjusting edges manually with the Sharpen Tool.

Part II Objects, Photos and Colors

Smudge: Another Way to Blur

 Although the Smudge Tool in Photoshop is meant to create wet paint effects, it can also be used to create blur effects if used with a light hand and the proper tablet input device.

The Smudge Tool simulates the action of dragging your finger through wet paint. The tool picks up color where you begin the stroke and pushes the color in the direction you drag. The effect is often seen as a blur. Because the Smudge Tool drags the color *where you want it*, you can achieve some fun effects when purposely overdoing it. Figure 5.9 shows you how a pretty woman can get a more mischievous look by smudging areas of her eye and mouth. We'll take a closer look at more practical ways of using the Smudge Tool in the next section.

Figure 5.9
Using the Smudge Tool in Photoshop (or one of Painter's brushes) can change the expression in a face.

Retouching Images

Nothing is more annoying than having *almost* the perfect picture. The motif is great, but the picture is too dark, or the imperfections in your beloved's skin are too visible. If you've used a cheap film in your camera, you may discover the colors were too bland after developing the film. In the following pages, we'll take a look at some options for retouching images using, among other things, the Smudge, Dodge, and Burn tools in Photoshop 6 and Elements. We'll also remove unwanted items and create a new background for a vacation picture.

TIP

Photoshop Elements is targeted for the home user but with many of the same clever options as 6.0. In many ways, it's a "light" version of Photoshop 6, but it still has plenty of cool effects and options, especially regarding digital picture corrections and enhancements. One of the neat additions in Photoshop Elements is the Red Eye Brush. Choose the brush size you want, preferably close to the area you want to correct. From the Sampling menu, choose First Click. Use the default colors button in the Options bar, or select your own colors (Current color and Replacement color). Position the crosshair in the brush over the red area in the eye, and click and drag to remove it.

Photo Preparation

Imagine you want to make your own Christmas cards or Web page illustrations from a photo of your family or your beloved pet. Before starting, you'll have to decide the scan quality of your image. If you want to use your image on the Web, you'll need a 72 dpi setting. For print, you'll need a minimum of 300 dpi. To get the best results, you have to decide this *before* scanning, because resizing a scanned image will create some loss in quality. (If this confuses you, take a glimpse at Chapter 9 and read about Web and print resolutions.)

If your image was scanned slightly askew, rotate the canvas, as shown in Figure 5.10. In Photoshop 6 and Elements, you may use the Free Transform command: Select your image with Select All (Ctrl+A or Command+A), then press CRTL+T (Command+T) to get it right. If your scanned image was not cropped during the scan processing, crop it using a cropping tool (available in most programs) to remove unwanted background areas.

Now it's time for the final adjustments to your image. Adjust the brightness/contrast if necessary, as described in the previous section. If your picture is too bland in some colors, depending on the film you've used, your camera, or the film processing, you can make further adjustments digitally. In Photoshop 6 and Elements, you may take advantage of the clever Sponge Tool or toning tools. Make sure your image mode is set to RGB, or many of the tools will be unavailable to you. Select Image > Mode > RGB Color if your open document doesn't say "(RGB)" after the image name. (You can read more about color modes in Chapter 6.)

Figure 5.10
1. The scanned picture, slightly askew.
2. Rotated.
3. Cropped for final selection.
4. The result.
The Sponge Tool was used to change the color saturation, or color strength, of an area

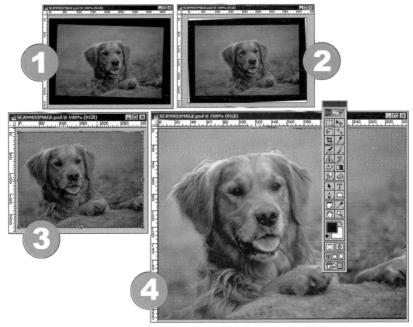

Part II Objects, Photos and Colors

Using the Sponge Tool

 The Sponge Tool changes the *saturation* (color strength) of an area, making it a great tool for fixing photos where the colors are too bland. As you see from illustrations 1, 2, and 3 in Figure 5.10, the dog's fur is not as colorful as it could be. In illustration 4, the Sponge Tool has been used.

Click the Sponge Tool in your toolbox and choose Saturate from the Mode menu. If you had areas of color that were too intense, you would need the Desaturate setting. You can adjust the settings for how intense you'll like the effect to be by dragging the Pressure Slider to, for example, 50 percent. Make sure the Pressure in Brush Dynamics is set to be controlled by the stylus (pen). Choose the brush size you want; the perfect size will depend on the areas you'll want to work on. You may now paint with the Sponge Tool by dragging it back and forth over the desired areas.

Using the Dodge and Burn Tools

 The Dodge and Burn tools are included in the Photoshop toning tools. As unfamiliar as these names might be, they originate from professional photography. When developing prints, photographers limit light exposure to lighten an area on the print (dodging) or increase the exposure to darken an area (burning).

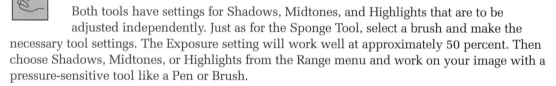 Both tools have settings for Shadows, Midtones, and Highlights that are to be adjusted independently. Just as for the Sponge Tool, select a brush and make the necessary tool settings. The Exposure setting will work well at approximately 50 percent. Then choose Shadows, Midtones, or Highlights from the Range menu and work on your image with a pressure-sensitive tool like a Pen or Brush.

In Figure 5.11, you'll see the effects after the application of both tools. The image to the left is the original. In the middle image, the Burn Tool has been used lightly on the right side of the face to add more shadow, while the Dodge Tool has been used with heavy pressure on the hair and clothes. To the far right is the same picture but with just the Sponge Tool used all over, in Saturated mode, and with a pressure set to 60 percent. Note the unnatural orange shine to the forehead and the intense lipstick color.

Why bother with the pressure settings when the tool is pressure-sensitive? Actually, it's to make sure you don't apply the effect too heavily to your image until you are comfortable using this tool. With some training and a light touch on your pen, you can use the pressure settings up to 100 percent, but this is not recommended when first starting out.

Figure 5.11
The original image is on the left, the middle image saw use of the Dodge and Burn tools, and the Sponge Tool was used in the right image.

Using the Clone Stamp Tool to Remove Unwanted Objects

You may, of course, erase objects when they're in a background without too much variation in color. But when working with photographs, you'll most likely come across difficult backgrounds where you'll need another approach. The Clone Stamp Tool in Photoshop takes a *sample* of an area in your image (the same size as the brush you use), which you then can apply over *another* area in your image to erase unwanted objects or stains. When using the tool, you'll see cross hairs that mark the original sampling point (source).

In Figure 5.12, we'll use the Clone Stamp Tool to erase the diver in this underwater scene. Because we don't want the turtle to be affected by our retouching techniques, we select the parts of the turtle that are close to the area we'll be working on and invert the selection, as shown in 5.13. Zoom in to clearly view the area you'll be working on.

Select the Clone Stamp Tool, set Opacity to 100 percent, and make sure Mode is set to Normal. If Aligned is selected in the Options palette, deselect it. Choose a brush size that's appropriate for the area you'll be working on. In this case, a size 35 brush will do nicely. Move the cursor to a part of the water that you want to use as a sample source. In most cases, sample an area that's close to where you'll use the tool, as this will be best matched in color and texture. Hold down Alt (Option) and click to create a sample point. Drag the tool over the area you want to adjust. Note that the crosshairs show you the sample point at all times, so if you move around a lot, you may sample from an unwanted part of the image. A good idea is to work your way *into* the area you want to correct or adjust your sampling point as you go along. If your brush size is set too small, you'll often get unwanted effects such as patterns when you drag the tool. Adjust this by changing to a larger brush and make a new sample point. When you've gotten the hang of it, your result might look like Figure 5.14.

Similar to the Clone Stamp Tool is the Pattern Stamp Tool. A way of putting the Pattern Stamp Tool to good use is to paint in a pattern in a background or other parts of your picture. Use the patterns supplied in Photoshop or make your own. With the Pattern Stamp Tool selected, choose your favorite pattern and paint it into the background, on a separate layer, or into a selection.

Part II Objects, Photos and Colors

Figure 5.12
The original image has a
diver waiting to be
erased.

Figure 5.13
Working with the Clone
Stamp Tool. Note that
some parts of the turtle
are not selected.

Figure 5.14
The finished result.
Where did that diver
go?

Vacation Photos: A Sandbox for Your Mind

Some images might be almost perfect, like a vacation photograph of an interesting scene. This
scene might have a great building out in front, but it might also have a dull background like a
gray sky. No one expects you to wait for hours for the clouds to change, especially because you
can create the most interesting pictures on your computer.

Let's take an example: You meet these nice girls on your vacation and take their picture. You also photograph some nice sunsets. At home, you wonder why you didn't photograph the girls with a sunset background. (After all, you spent a lot of time together at the beach.) Pick your favorite sunset picture, plus the portrait of the girls, and start working in Photoshop 6. See Figure 5.15.

Figure 5.15
Girls and sunset, soon to be joined.

1. Use the Magic Wand Tool to select the blue sky background in the picture of the girls. Use a tolerance setting of about 20 for this kind of background. Hold Shift down to select more of the sky, if not all of it is selected at your first click. Also select the sky seen through the girl's hair—switch to the Lasso Tool if necessary.

2. Select your sunset picture by using Ctrl+A (Command+A) to select all and then Copy (Ctrl+C or Command+C). Switch to the picture of the girls, go to the Edit menu and choose Paste-Into. You now have a sunset layer with a mask above the layer of the girls.

3. Adjust the mask by painting with white or black color (to add or remove areas) on the mask, as described in Chapter 4. Use little pressure when working on edges, and be careful when working around the hair. When you're happy with the mask, click the layer thumbnail and adjust the sunset by moving it around with the Move Tool until you are happy with the composition. Make sure the layer thumbnail and not the mask is selected, or you'll move the mask around. You may also resize the sunset, to get a smaller or larger part of it visible. The point is to achieve a great composition. As you'll realize when looking at Figure 5.16, your vacation pictures will never be the same again!

Figure 5.16
Girls plus sunset. You will know it's two different pictures, but who will guess it's not one?

Note that to get a good and natural-looking result when merging two photos like this, you need the photos to match in colors. If you have to adjust the color in your photos, do it afterwards when all unwanted areas are gone.

NOTE

Even though Photoshop is considered the expert's choice regarding photo correction, there are other applications you might consider:

Retouching Images with Paint Shop Pro 7

Paint Shop Pro 7 will take you a long way towards good image corrections, and for a better price than Photoshop. In addition to several filters, Paint Shop Pro 7 has a Retouch Brush that's great for retouching your pictures. For example, as shown in Figure 5.17, it's easy to give someone whiter teeth! Remember to set the Pressure Sensitive Tablet Controls and use Vary Opacity to get full control when working with images in Paint Shop Pro.

Retouching Images with Painter 6

Although Painter is primarily a paint program, there are quite a few touchup tools available for salvaging those not-so-great vacation photos. Painter has several filters for tonal control in images, as well as all the customizable and pressure-sensitive brushes you'll ever need. Painter has a set of Photo brushes, shown in Figure 5.18. You can use these for such effects as Add Grain, Blur, or Sharpen, that will work on parts of your image. You can also click Saturation Add and more. If you're mainly looking for a package to create drawings, but need some basic photo adjustment tools as well, Painter is a good choice.

Figure 5.17
No problems with coffee-stained or yellowish teeth when using Paint Shop Pro's Retouch brush.

Figure 5.18
Painter has several Photo brushes to adjust your image.

Improving Photocomposition

We can do a lot of creative work with photographs, even after all the necessary basic adjustments have been made. We can make pictures look older with artificial aging techniques and use creative blur effects. We can also add depth and interest to a picture using the Airbrush Tool or paint in shadows and light to create depth where it's needed.

Adding Interest

How often have you had a great photograph spoiled by intrusions into the background? Do you have people popping up from nowhere just as you take the shot, a foot where you wouldn't want it, or other objects you'd like to remove completely? You may, of course, replace the background altogether as we did in previous examples, but we'll look at some other methods for creating good results.

Creative Blurring

As seen in the section entitled "Painting Blur on an Image," you can use blur to create effects. Blur can also be used in other ways to enhance a picture; for example, you can tone down areas to bring forward the really interesting parts of your picture. In the following example, we'll look at a picture of a dog, Conny, my family's Riesenschnauzer. She was photographed outdoors in the summer, in good lighting conditions. The picture was taken with my 15-year-old Minolta camera and Kodak film. It was processed at my local film developing shop and delivered to me on a CD-ROM. Unfortunately, there are items in the background I don't want there, such as the blue dog run, which appears as a blurred area behind Conny's ear. There are also a few scratches I'd like to remove. See Figure 5.19.

Figure 5.19
This is the original picture of Conny. Note the scratches in the image as well as the unwanted dog run in the background.

1. Download the free picture of Conny from **www.iril.no.**
2. Open the picture of Conny in Photoshop 6, and then open the Layers palette if it's not visible already. Rename the Background Layer to "Blurred." Duplicate this layer by selecting the Layer thumbnail and drag it onto the New Layer icon

Part II Objects, Photos and Colors

in the Layers palette. You now have a layer named "Blurred copy." Rename this layer to "Sharp." Hide this layer by clicking the eye to the left of the Layer thumbnail.

TIP

Naming layers is a good idea when working with several layers in Photoshop, Illustrator, or Painter. You'll often want to copy layers before applying effects, and even though selecting layers isn't difficult, you'll soon lose track of what you're doing if you have several similar-looking layers that block one another from view.

Those of you who are familiar with Photoshop's History palette may wonder why I insist on making layer copies all the time. It's easier and faster to have a copy available than browse through the History states. It's also memory-saving when working with high-resolution pictures, because you'll need a History option set well beyond the default of 20 steps when painting in effects!

3. Select the "blurred" layer. Go to the Filter menu, choose Blur > Gaussian Blur. A small dialog box for Gaussian Blur options pops up, as shown in Figure 5.20. Make sure the Preview option is selected, and adjust the ratio if you want see parts of your image clearly. Select a Radius between 30 and 50 (we'll use 40 here). Click OK when you're happy with the effect.

While the ordinary Blur filter creates smooth transitions between pixels, the Gaussian Blur quickly blurs a selection (or a whole layer) by an *adjustable* amount shown as the Radius. The term "Gaussian" refers to a curve that is generated when Photoshop applies an average to the pixels. The Gaussian Blur filter is often used to add a hazy effect to your pictures and is also great for shadows.

Figure 5.20
This is the Gaussian Blur dialog box. The Radius can be adjusted from 0 to 250 pixels. The higher the number, the blurrier your effect will be.

As discussed previously in this chapter, you may also add texture or paint in effects with the Pattern Stamp Tool for a completely new background. We'll settle for the Gaussian Blur here.

4. Click the eye of your "Sharp" layer to make it visible again and select its thumbnail.

5. Add a Layer mask to this layer by clicking the Add a Mask icon in the Layers Palette. You now have a choice between several tools. You can use your tablet's Stroke Pen or you can use the Pen with Photoshop's Airbrush Tool or Paintbrush Tool.

6. In this example, you'll use your Stroke Pen or Pen with the Airbrush Tool. Use an opacity setting of 30 or so, and select a medium-sized brush. Set the Mode to Normal. In Brush Dynamics (called Brush Options in previous versions of Photoshop), you'll set the Opacity to be controlled by the stylus. Set your foreground color to Black.

7. Zoom in on your picture to see what you're doing and select the Mask. Start painting the background areas of you image with black, as in Figure 5.21. Remember you can also fill large parts of your background by making selections with the Lasso Tool and filling them with 100 percent black.

Figure 5.21
Working on the mask, use black color to airbrush away the background in the "Sharp" layer. This makes the bottom layer visible through the areas you paint.

As you'll see, the background layer "Blurred" comes through in the areas you're painting. You may want to adjust both the pressure settings and brush sizes as you work. For the smoothest transitions between your object and the background, use a small brush and an opacity setting of 20 or 30. If you choose a setting of 100 percent, you will get "harder" and sharper edges, and you'll have great difficulty in precisely masking hairs, fur, and similar complicated details.

8. When you're finished painting the mask, you can apply it to the "Sharp" layer. Right-click over the Mask thumbnail and, from the drop-down menu, choose Apply Layer Mask. Now the dog is residing on her own layer, and you can add additional effects to her or to the background layer. A good idea is to make a

copy of the layer she's on and hide it. This way, you can simply click the layer back if you're not happy with the result.

Often, you may have a mask that looks good to the naked eye but is actually full of errors. You'll discover your mistakes when applying a filter. These mask imperfections will be visible if you hide the background layer or fill a new layer with a contrasting color. An example of mask imperfections is shown in the previous chapter, in Figure 4.32.

9. For the final touches to the picture, add shade and light to create some depth. Make two new layers between the two we already have. Name them Light and Shade, respectively. Use a large Airbrush, such as a size between 45 and 100, with the opacity set to about 40 percent. With a light hand, paint in light using white color on your Light layer, at the left side of the picture. From the existing light on the dog's fur, you'll see the actual light coming from the left, so that's why we'll work on that side. Select the Shade layer and use black to paint in some shade to her immediate right. For a nicer background, select a dark green from the background and paint in some green color to the bottom right corner as well.

If you have problems getting the shade layer light enough, you can adjust a shade painted too darkly by changing the Layer transparency. I've set the Layer transparency to 42 percent. Don't worry about transitions between the dog and the areas you'll be painting—you'll be working on layers beneath her.

The dog is on a separate layer, "blocking" out the layer parts that are exactly underneath her. If you weren't working with layers, you'd have to make selections and worry about smooth transitions in the edges. See Figure 5.22.

Figure 5.22
The finished result of creative blurring. I've cropped the image as well. Compare to Figure 5.19.

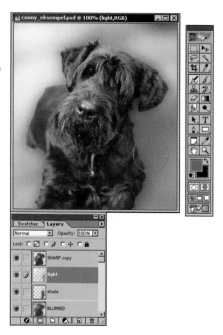

Antiqued Photographs in a Flash

Do you have a photograph of, say, your great-grandparents on their wedding day? Do you like the way its slight sepia tone gives it character? The quickest way to get the same look from a new photograph is to use Photoshop's Hue/Saturation adjustments with the Colorize option selected. You can create wonderful photographs using duotones and other fine-tuned color adjustments, which we'll take a look at in Chapter 6.

Open your image in either RGB or CMYK mode (RGB in Photoshop Elements) and select a medium brown, warm color for your foreground (try RGB 175, 117, 74 or CMYK 27, 56, 78, 9.) From the Image menu, select Adjust > Hue/Saturation (In Elements, choose Enhance > Color > Hue/Saturation). You can also use the shortcut Ctrl+U (Command+U) to bring up this dialog box. Check off the Colorize option and preview the result. You may adjust the sliders for saturation (color strength) and lightness until you're happy with the effect. As shown in Figure 5.23, the last image (bottom right) has lightness adjusted as well. The colors used are RGB values 172, 115, 1 (bottom left), RGB 172, 74, 1 (upper right) and RGB 175, 117, 74 (bottom right).

Figure 5.23
Examples of the Hue/Saturation > Colorize effect. The original photo is upper left, with examples of three various colors used for colorizing the image.

Part II Objects, Photos and Colors

A Deeply Held Interest

You can paint in shadows and light to add interest to a picture, thereby guiding the viewer's eye to the point of interest. Take a look at the picture in Figure 5.24. By adding two layers for light and shade in programs like Photoshop 6 and Elements, Painter, or Paint Shop Pro, we can adjust the foreground in the picture to enhance the steps visible through the door opening. We'll show you how to do this in all those programs.

 In Photoshop 6 or Elements, create the two layers in your Layers palette by clicking the Add Layer icon. Make a selection of the door and door opening and Invert the selection. Choose Select > Inverse. On the shade layer, use a Pen with the Airbrush Tool to paint shade in the foreground. Use black as a color, and use a large brush with Opacity set to about 30. The Mode is set to Normal. When you're happy with the shade, as in Figure 5.25, switch to the light layer (with your selection still active) and Invert the selection again. Use a white color to paint in more light on the wall at the stairway steps and the background wall. You may, of course, also create a new selection for just these parts of the image. (The point with these selections is to avoid painting onto areas you're happy with.) When you're finished, the picture will look like Figure 5.26. You now get the feeling of being drawn towards the open door.

Figure 5.24
This is our original picture. (above)

Figure 5.25
I've added shadows to the foreground. (right)

Figure 5.26
The resulting image (below) has added light and shade. I've used shadows to hide unwanted areas, and I've used light to bring forward the interesting areas. This simple technique can be applied to many photographs.

In Corel Painter 6, create the two layers by opening your Objects Palette: Window > Show Objects, as shown in Figure 5.35. Select Layers and click the small arrow to the right, Add New Layer. Make a selection of the door and door opening with the Lasso Tool. From the menu, choose Select > Invert to invert your selection. On the shade layer, use a pen with the Airbrush brush > Digital Airbrush to paint shade in the foreground. Use black as a color, with a brush setting in Brush Controls of about 20. When you're happy with the shade (as in Figure 5.27), switch to the light layer (with your selection still active) and Invert the selection again. Use a white color to paint in more light on the wall at the stairway steps and the background wall.

Figure 5.27
This is Painter's Layers palette, in the Objects window.

In Paint Shop Pro 7, create the two layers by selecting your Layers menu > New Raster Layer. Make a selection of the door and door opening using the Lasso (Freehand) Tool. In the Tool Options palette, select Point To Point from the menu to make a fast and simple selection of the area. When you've made your selection, choose Selections > Invert to invert it. From the Layers menu, select the shade layer. Use a Pen with the Brush Tool to paint shade in the foreground. Use black color, with the following brush settings in Tool options: Size at approximately 30, Opacity at 20, and Shape set to Round. Hardness should be 0. When you're happy with the shade as in Figure 5.25, switch to the light layer from the Layers menu (with your selection still active) and Invert the selection again as described above. Use a white color with almost the same brush settings as before, but with a smaller brush size, to paint in more light on the wall at the stairway steps and on the background wall. See Figure 5.28.

Part II   Objects, Photos and Colors

Figure 5.28
In Paint Shop Pro 7, swap between your layers using the Layers menu item.

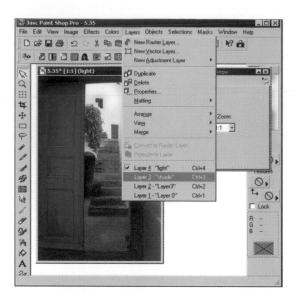

Transformations and Other Tricks

In this section, we'll look at other ways to create interesting images besides adjusting colors and shade. We'll look at how to take advantage of some transformation options available.

A New Perspective

Sometimes, adjustments to shadow and light alone aren't enough to make a picture exciting. Adjusting the perspective of an object can be the right approach to avoid dull photographs. To prove this point, I have selected an incredibly dull object for the next example. I'll show you how to add a little perspective—a little more interest—to an image by transforming an object to create depth. Let's take a look at a very uninteresting roll of twine, as shown in Figure 5.29. In Photoshop 6, select Edit > Transform > Perspective (In Elements, choose Image > Transform > Perspective). Drag the handles in one of the upper corners to make the upper part of the image go away from you, as seen in the first example in Figure 5.30.

Figure 5.29
This picture is pretty dull.

Figure 5.30
Changing the
Perspective can improve
the picture dramatically.

Dragging one of the bottom handles changes the perspective. Thus, it seems the twine is coming towards you, as seen in the bottom example in Figure 5.38.

Create Depth—Fast!

You can add depth by creating a shadow for your object. We'll look at precise shadows in Chapter 10, but for now, we'll look at a fast way to create shadows in Photoshop using Layer Styles. Make an exact selection of your object and copy the selection. Use Ctrl+P (Command+P) to paste the selection, automatically creating a new layer with just the roll of twine on it. You may now add a shadow by clicking Layer > Layer Style > Drop Shadow. Adjust the angle to –138 degrees, set the distance to 40 pixels or more, and tinker with the spread settings until you're happy with the preview.

Make It Disappear

You can make an object disappear completely, fade parts of it, or create shadows by using layer masks in Photoshop 6. In this example, we'll use the roll of twine on a separate layer above a black background.

1. With the object on a separate layer above a dark background, make a mask by clicking the Add a Mask icon.

2. Select black as the foreground color and choose the Gradient Tool. Use a setting of Gradient/Linear with the linear set from your foreground color to Transparent.

3. Select the Mask and drag the tool from right to left, thereby masking the right side of the object, making it seem to fade into darkness on the right side. If you use a low opacity setting for the Gradient/Linear tool, you can make parts of the object seem to be in a deeper shade, as shown in Figure 5.31. You can also paint on the mask as we've done previously, but in this example it's faster (and easier), because we'll want a gradient effect.

4. For final touches, add light (or highlights) on separate layers. Instead of using the Outer Glow Layer effect, make a new layer between the object and the dark background. Choose a bright yellow color (such as RGB 249, 251, 199) and use the Airbrush with your pressure-sensitive stylus to paint in glow effects at the left side of the object. Choose a medium-sized brush with a low opacity setting to get a wide, glowing line that partly falls behind the object. If you use the Outer Glow Layer effect instead, you will get the glow all over the object's edges and not exactly where you'll want it.

Figure 5.31
Use layer masks and
Gradient tools to add
shade and depth to a
picture.

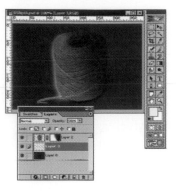

NOTE

There are plenty of filters that will let you create light effects and such in
your photographs, such as Photoshop's Lighting Effects. Some filters will
work only on the whole image, while others can be applied to selections. If
you don't get the options you need to create *exactly* the effect you want,
you're always able to manipulate your image manually. That's why you'll be
shown examples of how to create manual effects instead of just browsing
through all the numerous filters.

Distorting Objects

Another approach to creating interesting pictures of dull objects is to manipulate their size and
shape. As shown in Figure 5.32, you can easily distort objects by using the Transform > Distort
option. You can scale, rotate, skew, distort, or apply perspective to selected parts of an image,
entire layers, paths, and selection borders.

Figure 5.32
Use Transform > Distort
and drag the handles to
where you'll want the
distortion in the picture.

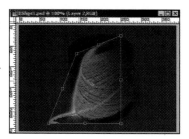

Photoshop 6 has a completely new set of distortion commands hidden under Image > Liquify.
Liquify lets you manipulate areas of an image as if they had been melted. The Liquify command
brings up a preview area you'll work with before applying the effects to the original image.
Using the Liquify tools, you can warp image pixels, as shown in Figure 5.33, or you can twirl,
expand, contract, shift, and reflect areas of the image. You can also "freeze" areas of the preview
image to protect them from further changes and "thaw" previously frozen areas, making them
editable. You can also fully or partially reverse the distortions by using several reconstruction
modes. When you're finished, you can apply the changes to the original image.

Figure 5.33
These images show the
effects of the Warp Tool
in the Liquify dialog
box.

The tools in the Liquify dialog box (see Figure 5.34) distort the brush area when you drag your Pen over it. The effects intensify if you drag over the same area several times. You can use Liquify on rasterized (bitmapped) layers only, so if you want to Liquify a Type layer, you have to rasterize it first using Layer > Rasterize > Type. Liquify has several tools available, among them the Twirl Clockwise and Counterclockwise tools, which rotate pixels as you hold down the mouse button or drag. The Pucker Tool moves pixels toward the center of the brush area, as opposed to the Bloat Tool, which moves pixels away from the center of the brush area. Wacom PenTools is an excellent set of tools for distorting an image as well, and we'll take a closer look at them in Appendix A.

Figure 5.34
The Liquify dialog box
and preview. You'll
work in preview mode
until you're satisfied,
and then apply the
effects to the original
image

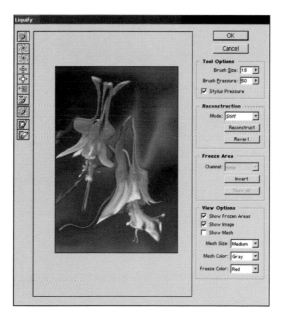

Creating A Photo Collage

In this section, we'll use some of the previous techniques to create a photo collage in Photoshop 6 and also look at a couple of new tricks. The five pictures you need to follow this tutorial, can be downloaded from **www.iril.no,** or you may use your own set of pictures.

As discussed in the layers and masks sections of Chapter 4, there are a lot of ways to merge pictures into a new image altogether. We'll take a look at how to make an image from several pictures.

We'll start with two pictures, a boy's portrait and a close-up picture of fur. Adjust the brightness and contrast in the two pictures before you begin, as previously described in this chapter.

1.   Start with the portrait, and have it as your background layer. Paste the fur image above the portrait layer. Adjust the opacity so you can move the fur to where it looks good over the face, as shown in Figure 5.35.

Figure 5.35
Adjust the layer opacity to move the fur to where it looks good over the portrait. To the right, you'll see all the images we'll use in this example.

2.   Select the Elliptical Marquee Tool and use a Feather setting of 12. Feathering "blurs" edges by building a transition between the selection and its surrounding pixels. This is yet another way of creating a mask without having to edit all of it: With the fur layer active, make a selection that covers the boy's face using the Elliptical Marquee Tool.

3. Click the Add a Mask icon. Select the mask, and with the Airbrush Tool, paint with black color over the eyes, nose, and mouth areas. Use a small brush with 30 percent pressure, and then swap to a medium-sized brush with a 10 percent pressure setting. This creates smooth transitions between the portrait areas you'll want to be visible and the fur.

    Adjust the opacity settings for the fur layer repeatedly as you work, so you can see the effects and see where you'll need further masking. Remove any fur that's outside the facial area by painting those areas black on the mask. Switch to the fur layer thumbnail, and use the Dodge and Burn tools to create highlights and shadows in the fur.

4. On the portrait layer, use the Sponge Tool with the Mode set to *Desaturate*. This will remove the bright pink color from his lips. Use a pressure setting of 20 or so and a small or medium-sized brush with the Airbrush Tool. Your image should now look similar to Figure 5.36.

5. Apply the mask and then merge the two layers. In the Layers palette, choose Merge Down from the menu.

Figure 5.36
When you're satisfied with the mask, use the Dodge and Burn tools to create highlights and shadows in the fur layer.

6. Paste the fur-and-portrait collage onto a landscape picture. Set the Layer opacity to about 80 percent so you'll see the background through the portrait/fur layer.

Part II Objects, Photos and Colors

7.   Create a mask for the portrait/fur layer. Use black as the foreground color and select the mask. Choose the circular gradient tool, with the *foreground to transparent* setting and opacity to 27 percent, and draw outward from his nose. Use the linear gradient with the same settings to create a smooth transition on the right side, and use the Airbrush for the last details. Set the portrait/fur layer opacity to 90 percent and make final adjustments to the mask by painting black on the left side. Use a brush size between 45 to 100 for this, with pressure at 38 percent. See Figure 5.37.

Figure 5.37
Set the portrait/fur layer opacity to 90 percent and make final adjustments to the mask by painting black on the left side.

8.   Apply the portrait/fur mask and merge the two layers: From the Layers palette, choose Merge Down. If you wanted his face to be only in the sky part of the image, you would retouch his jaw more. To create a more intense fur/portrait layer, try duplicating the layer and see what happens.

9.   Duplicate the fur/portrait layer by dragging the layer onto the New Layer icon. Scale it to about 150 percent and flip the layer horizontally with Edit > Transform > Flip Horizontal. Set the opacity of the new layer to 57 percent.

10.   When you're satisfied with the composition, merge all layers: In the Layers Palette, click the arrow > Flatten Image. See Figure 5.38.

Figure 5.38
Duplicate the fur/portrait layer by dragging it onto the New Layer icon.

Our collage looks absolutely fine, but you can continue to add more pictures or make more collages using the same methods as previously discussed.

11. If you have downloaded the picture of rippled water, you can paste the collage on a layer below it. Pick a blue color from the water and use Hue/Saturation > Colorize on the collage layer. Add a mask to the water layer, and set the layer opacity to 83 percent or so. Paint areas in the mask where you'll want the picture below to come through, and the finished collage can look like Figure 5.39.

Figure 5.39
Add yet another picture and adjust the Hue/Saturation. You'll get a different collage altogether.

12. Flatten the image again and copy the layer. Add an adjustment layer to the copy layer, and Choose Multiply in the dialog box. Select Blues and Cyan from the Hue/Saturation Edit menu, and set the Saturation to 0 in both. Click OK.

13. Merge the adjustment layer to your copied layer and create a mask. Use the Linear Tool set from black to transparency and drag the tool from left to right while holding Shift down, removing the left side of the dark (adjusted) layer. Apply the mask. You now have two layers, shown in Figure 5.40.

Figure 5.40
Dragging the Linear Tool from left to right will remove the left side of the dark (adjusted) layer, which is the top layer.

14. Select a picture of a beautiful flower and cut out the flower. Paste it into our picture using Ctrl+P (Command+P). Remove any remaining background pixels from the flower by using the Eraser Tool or creating a mask. When done retouching the flower, duplicate the flower layer and flip it vertically using Edit > Transform > Flip Vertical. Position it so it looks like it's a reflection in the water. Set this layer to 45 percent opacity.

15. Still on the flower copy layer, add a mask and erase the edges of the petals to make it look more natural. Use a 45 size brush with low opacity. A reflection will be more clear near the object it reflects. If you click one of the flower layers while on the other, just right of the Eye icons, you'll link the two layers together, as shown in the Layer palette in Figure 5.41. You may then move both layers around simultaneously while selecting the best spot for the flower/reflection.

Figure 5.41
By linking two layers together, you can move them around simultaneously until you're happy with the composition.

This chapter should have given you the creative input you need to start creating your own exciting photo collages and to adjust dull photographs. You should have picked up a few tricks regarding color adjustments as well, which leads us into the next chapter—an in-depth discussion of color.

6
Working with Color

This chapter will cover the basics of working efficiently with color in programs like Photoshop 6.0, Photoshop Elements, and Paint Shop Pro. The subject of color is so immense that it could be a book of its own, so we'll take a look at the most important topics and leave the details of this subject to others.

In this chapter, you'll get a deeper understanding of color and learn about:

▶ Colorizing photos and color replacement to create cool effects

▶ Creating and editing adjustment layers in Photoshop

▶ The different color modes and color calibration

▶ Fine-tuning photographs, by working with curves and levels

Adjusting Colors

This section will begin by discussing your color canvas. You can take what you learn from this discussion to adjust the color scheme of a photograph you'd like to tweak. Or you use your newfound knowledge to really manipulate the colors of an image to create "special effects" à la Andy Warhol.

Choose Your Working Space

"Working space" is a term you'll often see when reading about color. The working space is simply *the color space in which you edit* your photos or images; this will often be in RGB (red, green, blue) or CMYK (cyan, magenta, yellow, kohl) mode. RGB is a good choice when working with images to be used on the Web or viewed on other monitors; CMYK is used for print. (See the section in this chapter called "What Is Color: Technical Terms Defined" for more information.)

Because images created in RGB are considerably smaller in file size than those created in CMYK, you're usually better off working in RGB and later converting the file to CMYK. After the conversion, some colors will seem a little dull, so when you draw high-resolution (300 dpi or more) illustrations for print, exaggerate the color hue in RGB. Your monitor likely displays only 72 dpi, so set the resolution to 72 dpi when working with RGB files for the Web. Surprisingly, many people use higher resolution images on the Web, which lengthens downloading time unnecessarily. Calibrate your monitor with tools like Adobe Gamma and choose a color profile for the work you're doing. Files can have color profiles embedded, and some programs will let you convert them to another profile of your choice. (See the section called "Color Management in Photoshop 6" later in this chapter for further details about profiles.)

If you do a lot of work for both print and the Web, use the programmable menu strip on your Wacom Intuos tablet to easily access the different color profiles in your favorite program.

NOTE

The better photos you take at the outset, the fewer adjustments you'll need to make in process. To help you, there's plenty of information online about photography. Agfa's Online Photo Course at **www.agfaphoto.com/library/photocourse/** can help you get started.

At the time of this writing, more than thirty lessons were available. Subjects include "Shadows as a Motif" and "Panorama Photos." For example, you can learn a lot about light and reflection in the "Still Life" lesson. You can use this information both for taking photographs and for creating illustrations. Kodak's Web site has good information, too. It has a separate Web site for digital imaging, so if you're the happy owner of a digital camera, surf to **http://www.kodak.com/US/en/digital/dlc.**

Fine-tuning Your Photos

It's not easy to know where to begin when starting color adjustments. First, make sure you have the right workspace. Then you can do basic adjustments to a photo with regards to brightness and contrast, as shown in Chapter 5. After that, you can begin making color adjustments.

Hue, Saturation, and Luminosity

One way to describe color is to describe its dimensions, or attributes, if you like. Hue, saturation, and luminosity (HSL) are called *the three dimensions* of color. Hue—also called tint—is the basic color; green, blue, purple, and red are all hues. Saturation describes how dull or vivid a color is—that is, the purity of the color. Changing saturation means you change the amount of gray in an image. In Hue/Saturation dialog boxes, you'll see that dragging the Saturation slider to the lowest (negative) value will give you a dull, gray color. Luminosity—also called "lightness"—describes the brightness and darkness of the color. The Hue/Saturation dialog box will give you a lot of choices for correcting or manipulating photos, including creating "special effects" for a photo, as shown in the section "Changing Colors" later in this chapter. Now, let's examine how adjustments to hue, saturation, and lightness affect a photograph.

In Paint Shop Pro 7, you can use the Automatic Saturation Enhancement, as shown in Figure 6.1. On the menu, select Effects > Enhance Photo > Automatic Saturation Enhancement. Because the dialog box works with presets, the effects will not be "overdone." This is not a tool to use if you want to make special effects, but it's great for normal adjustments.

Figure 6.1
The Automatic
Saturation Enhancement
in Paint Shop Pro 7.

In Paint Shop Pro 7, you'll find the adjustments for Hue/Saturation and Lightness available as an adjustment layer. You can read more about adjustment layers later in this chapter. Select Layers > New Adjustment Layer > Hue/Saturation/Lightness. In Layer Properties, you can set the opacity and the blending mode in the General tab, and you also have a Colorize option on the Adjustment tab. In the Adjustment tab, drag the sliders or type in the desired values. Click the eye icon to preview the result. From the Edit drop-down menu, select Master to edit all the colors simultaneously or select the color you want to adjust separately, such as red. With Master selected, we'll make some sample adjustments to see how this works. See Figures 6.2, 6.3, 6.4, and 6.5.

Figure 6.2
The Saturation slider is
set to −98, and the
picture loses all color
and becomes gray.

Part II Objects, Photos and Colors

Figure 6.3
The Lightness
(Luminance) slider is set
to 50. The picture
becomes much brighter,
but just in lightness and
not in hue.

Figure 6.4
Dragging the horizontal
Hue slider adjusts the
hue in all colors when
Master is selected, and
this can be used to
create special effects.

Figure 6.5
Dragging both the
horizontal Hue slider
and the Saturation
slider can achieve neon-
like colors. (This is not
for the faint-hearted nor
for those without
sunglasses.)

Curves in Photoshop 6 and Painter

In Chapter 5, we saw how levels work. There's another way to adjust images in applications like Painter and Photoshop 6—curves. These are more precise, but also more complex. In Painter, you can find the Curves command button by accessing Effects > Tonal control > Color Correction. Take a look at the dialog box in Figure 6.6. In Painter's Curve dialog box, you can drag the curve to adjust the overall image, but not lock points to it (as in Photoshop) to preserve levels in highlight while adjusting midtones. Painter's Curve lets you adjust the gamma curves for red, green, or blue separately, or all three together. If you choose the Freehand mode, you can draw the curve just as you like it. This is very useful if you want special effects in your photo.

Figure 6.6
Painter's dialog box for
Curves.

In Photoshop 6, access the Curve dialog box by clicking Image > Adjust > Curves or use the shortcut Ctrl+M (Command+M). In the dialog box, you can choose to adjust all channels (colors)—or just a single channel—from the drop-down menu. See Figure 6.7.

Figure 6.7
Photoshop's Curves
dialog box.

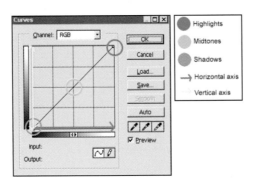

As with Levels, the Curves function lets you adjust the tonal range of an image. Instead of making the adjustments using the three variables—highlights, midtones, and shadows—in Levels, you can adjust any point along the 0–255 scale while keeping up to fifteen other values constant. The Curves function is, therefore, a more precise way of adjusting images. In the dialog box, you can click to add points to the curve, thereby "locking" values in the highlights, for example, while at the same time adjusting other values in midtones or shadows. The Curves Dialog box has a horizontal and vertical axis, as shown in Figure 6.7. Now, let's take a look at how Photoshop's Curves function behaves in Figures 6.8, 6.9, and 6.10.

Figure 6.8
This is the original
image, before adjusting
curves.

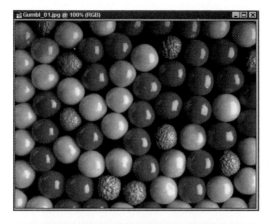

Figure 6.9
Note the adjustments in
highlights.

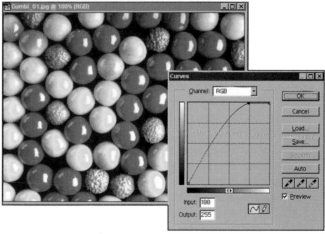

Figure 6.10
Look at how you can
add points to the curve
to create complex color
adjustments in a
picture.

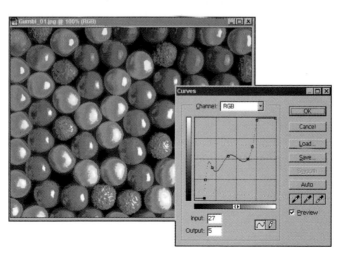

Part II Objects, Photos and Colors

Changing Colors

Want a red apple to become green? Blue eyes to be brown? This section will teach you how to colorize an image. You can start out by using the Color Range Command to make accurate color selections, or you can skip the next paragraph and learn how to colorize a photo.

Photoshop's Color Range Command

The Color Range command selects a specified color within an entire image or just in a selection. To refine an existing selection, use the Color Range command repeatedly to select a subset of colors. Choose Select > Color Range. Adjust the range of colors by using the Fuzziness slider or entering a value, as shown in Figure 6.11. The Fuzziness option partially selects pixels by controlling the amount of related colors that'll be included in the selection (similar to the Tolerance option for the Magic Wand). You can adjust your selection: Add colors to the selection by using the Eyedropper Tool marked with a plus sign. Now, click in the preview area or image. If you want to remove colors from the selection, select the minus eyedropper instead. You have various options for preview, where you can see your selection against different backgrounds. Note that if you want to replace a selection, be sure to deselect *everything* before applying the Color Range command.

Figure 6.11
You can use the
Fuzziness slider in the
Color Range dialog box.

Colorizing

There are endless possibilities to how you can manipulate color in an image. Let's take a look at how you can turn an ordinary vacation picture (see Figure 6.12) into a Warhol-like poster using Photoshop 6.

Open your image and crop it if necessary. Save a copy of your image before proceeding, because you'll use this copy later. Convert your image to grayscale: Image > Mode > Grayscale. Click OK in the dialog box. Duplicate this layer and hide it from view. Click Image > Adjust > Threshold. Adjust the Threshold slider, as shown in Figure 6.13, until you're happy with the result.

Figure 6.12
Our original, cropped holiday picture as it appears in RGB mode.

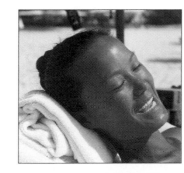

Figure 6.13
The threshold dialog box lets you posterize your image in pure black and white.

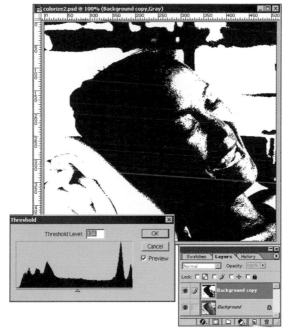

Now, convert your image to CMYK mode: Image > Mode > CMYK color. Click Don't Flatten in the dialog box, which always pops up when you convert between color modes. Open your saved copy. Use the shortcuts Ctrl+A (Command+A), and Ctrl+C (Command+C) to select and copy it. Switch to your black-and-white image and click Ctrl+V (Command+V) to paste the original image above. On the Layers tab, click Blending Options, as shown in Figure 6.14.

Figure 6.14
Blending Options in the
Layers tab.

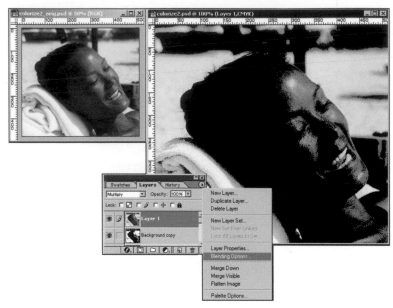

Choose Multiply in the Blending Options dialog box and set the opacity to 100 percent. Hide
this layer and select the black–and–white layer. Click on Image > Adjust, Hue/Saturation.
Experiment until you get a color you like, as shown in Figure 6.15. Make a rough selection of
the white areas in the face and Fill using the color you now have chosen. Deselect.

Figure 6.15
Use Hue/Saturation to
get a color you like on
your black-and-white
layer.

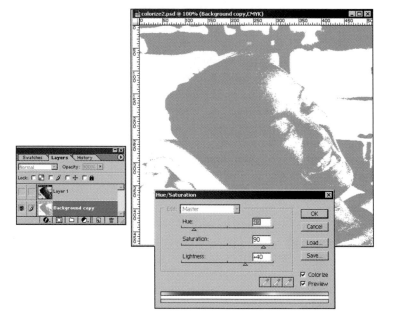

Now we'll take a look at the background. Using the Magic Wand Tool, select a white area. Go to the Select menu while the selection is active and choose Similar. Now all white areas are selected! Click the eye icon for the layer with the original image, so you'll see what you're doing—you'll still work on the colorized layer. Go to Image > Adjust Hue/Saturation again. Pick a foreground color that contrasts with your previous color choice. In Figure 6.16, I picked a purplish color. You have to set the Lightness value very low to colorize the white areas. When you're happy with the color, close the dialog box. With the selection still active, go to Select > Save. In the dialog box, name the selection Background. Click OK. With this technique, you can bring up this selection later if you want to make more adjustments.

Figure 6.16
Use Hue/Saturation to get a color that contrasts with your previous choice. Note the selection, which was created using the Similar command on the Select menu.

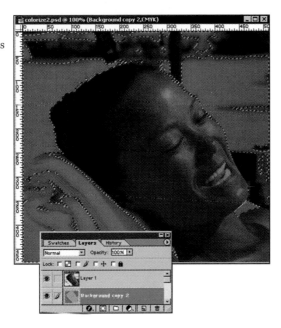

You may now select various objects in your picture, such as clothing items, furniture, sunglasses, or whatever your model has with her, and make adjustments to them. We'll select the towel under our model's head and turn its color to a bright blue, using the Hue/Saturation command as described above. The result may look like Figure 6.17.

Figure 6.17
Select various objects
and change their color
for additional effects.
Note that the color in
the Toolbox is lighter
than in the image,
because I've adjusted
the hue.

Move your duplicated and hidden grayscale layer to the top in the Layers tab. Click Image >
Adjust > Posterize and use a low setting of 4 or 5. Open Blending Options and select Multiply.
Adjust this layer's levels if the image is too dark: Open Image > Adjust > Levels and drag the
Brightness slider to the left while watching the Preview, as shown in Figure 6.18.

Figure 6.18
You can adjust levels on
your posterized layer.

Select your original layer again and adjust the Layer opacity to determine how strong your effects should be. In this example, the opacity is set to 39 percent. When you're happy, make the final adjustments to your model. This could be highlighting areas, such as colorizing the teeth (in Figure 6.19) or making further changes to the background by loading your saved selection. It is recommended that you duplicate your Layers and try out the effects before applying. You can also use the History option to bring back your previous versions. Remember that when you load a selection, you also have the possibility to invert it so you can work with other areas easily. The finished result is in Figure 6.20.

Figure 6.19
Use Hue/Saturation and colorize with white to give the model white teeth again.

Figure 6.20
The finished result. Noise is added to the saved background selection.

Replacing Color

The previous tutorial explained how to replace very large areas of color. In this mini-tutorial for Photoshop 6.0 and Elements, we'll replace very small areas of color.

You'll often retouch these areas by hand using a pressure-sensitive tool like a Pen or Stroke Pen with your favorite program. A combination of techniques is also a possibility. A quick way is, of course, to select an area with the Magic Wand, and in programs like Photoshop, you can use the Select Similar command to select pixels of the same color and then fill this selection with the color of your choice. You can also adjust the hue/saturation of the selection. Let's take a look at another easy trick for replacing a color in a photograph in Photoshop.

In this example, open your image, and select Image > Adjust > Replace Color. (In Photoshop Elements, choose Enhance > Color > Replace Color.) In the dialog box, you have three sliders to adjust: Hue, Saturation, and Lightness. You also have a Fuzziness setting, which determines how much of the *related* colors are included in the selection. Note the Fuzziness settings in the examples. See Figure 6.21.

Figure 6.21
This is our original image in 6.0, before replacing color. Note the Fuzziness setting at 54.

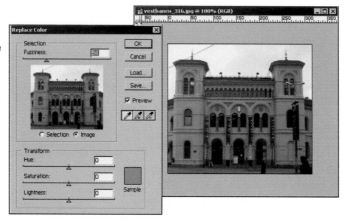

Use the Eyedropper and click in the preview area (or in the image) to select the color you want to replace. In our example, this is the main color of the building. See Figures 6.22 and 6.23.

Figure 6.22
A greenish hue is created by adjusting the slider. Note the Fuzziness setting at 130.

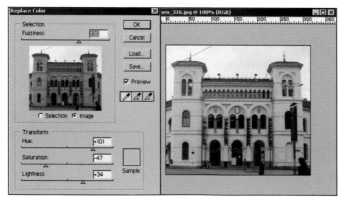

Figure 6.23
A red hue is created by adjusting the slider. Note the Fuzziness setting of 147. It allows for adjustments in some of the shadows on the building as well.

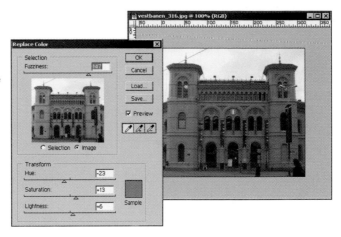

Replacing color is a neat effect you may use for an illustration or to make graphics for an interactive Web page. The example shown in Figure 6.24 was created for Brendmoe & Kirkestuen painters in Norway, where we used five differently colored images of the same building. The images were saved as JPEG files at 72 dpi measuring 202 × 181 pixels. Using Javascript, we created functionality so that when you move the mouse pointer over the small colored squares beneath the original image, the image "changes color."

Figure 6.24
The Web page with our finished result. Try the functionality of the script at **www.brendmoe-kirkestuen.no**

Part II Objects, Photos and Colors

Creating and Editing Adjustment Layers

We took a brief look at adjustment layers in Paint Shop Pro earlier in this chapter, and we will explore this option further in Photoshop 6.0 and Elements. Adjustment layers are great for making alterations without changing your original layer (image) directly and can be used both when working with photos and when creating illustrations. Adjustment layers in Photoshop have the same opacity and blending mode options as ordinary layers. Adjustment layers in Photoshop 6 have layer masks by default, as indicated by the mask thumbnail next to the layer thumbnail. You create an adjustment layer simply by opening your image, and then clicking the Layer Adjustment icon in your Layers Palette. Remember, an adjustment layer effect appears on *all* the layers below it. The advantage is that you can correct numerous layers by making a single adjustment, rather than having to make adjustments to each individual layer. The disadvantage is that you might want to leave some layers "unadjusted." You avoid this problem by rasterizing the adjustment layer and merging it with the layer(s) you want to adjust.

When you want to edit an adjustment layer, simply double-click the adjustment layer thumbnail in the Layers tab. You can merge an adjustment layer with the layer directly below it or with all other (visible) layers.

CAUTION

When you merge an adjustment layer, the adjustments are rasterized and become permanently applied. So make sure you've made all your adjustments before merging. You can also rasterize an adjustment layer without merging it, using the Layer > Rasterize command.

When creating the Web page for Harley-Davidson Christiania, a Harley-Davidson dealer in Oslo, Norway, we wanted a main image for the front page that stated what the Web site was all about. We picked an image of a biker, but the image was very dark and needed some adjustments to make it more exiting. Let's take a look at what we did using adjustment layers:

If your image is in CMYK mode (as ours was), convert it to RGB using Image > Mode > RGB Mode in 6.0. Elements does not have the option to work in CMYK mode. The image is high resolution, and because we'll use it on a Web page, we'll resize it to 72 dpi and make it 500 pixels in width (to correspond with our Web page layout). See Figure 6.25.

Figure 6.25
Click the Layer
Adjustment icon in your
Layers tab to view the
different adjustment
choices.

Part II Objects, Photos and Colors

Click the Layer Adjustment icon in your Layers tab as seen in Figure 6.25 and choose
Hue/Saturation from the menu. Drag the slider for Saturation to the far left; the picture should
become gray. You now have a new layer called Hue/Saturation 1. This Layer now also has a
layer mask in 6.0. If you're following this example in 6.0, you will work on the mask; if you use
Elements, you have to replace the following step with a Gradient Map instead. Select the mask
and choose the Linear Gradient Tool with the Foreground to Transparent setting.

In Photoshop 6.0, set the foreground color to black in your Toolbox. Drag the Linear Gradient
Tool from the left side of the image while holding down Shift and release somewhere over the
biker. When you look at Figure 6.26, you'll see there's an effect from a color picture fading
gradually into grayscale.

Figure 6.26
The adjustment layers
function enable the
gradual transformation
of an image from color
to grayscale.

Click next to the "eye" on the background layer to create a link between your adjustment layer
and the background layer. Click the arrow on the Layers tab and choose Merge Linked from the
menu, as shown in Figure 6.27.

Figure 6.27
Merge the two layers
after you've linked
them.

If you wanted to use the adjustment layer only in parts of the image, you could create selections on the layer mask with selection tools and invert and fill them with black color. You could also simply paint the areas you didn't want the adjustments on by using a pressure-sensitive Pen plus an Airbrush Tool or similar item.

Note that through the Layers tab, you can choose from several types of gradient fills. This is not the same as creating a gradient, as shown above. The Gradient selection on the Layers tab fills the layer with color, as shown in Figure 6.28, because it works on the layer and not the mask.

Figure 6.28
The Gradient selection on the Layers tab is not the same as creating a gradient on the layer mask.

See Figure 6.29 for the finished image for Harley-Davidson Christiania dealership. To get an even better look at the Web page in its entirety, visit **www.hd-christiania.com**.

Figure 6.29
This is the finished image, incorporated into the Web page for Harley-Davidson Christiania.

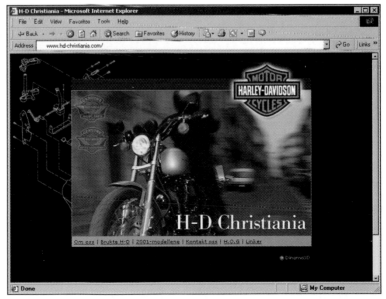

There are plenty of other choices on the Layer tab besides the Hue/Saturation settings. Take a look at Figure 6.30 to view some of them. Note that opacity settings and mask adjustments will be crucial to the results.

Figure 6.30
Various effects can be achieved with adjustment layers. Starting from the left is an image with a solid color of red at an opacity setting of 63 percent. Below is a Pattern fill with low opacity. The upper right image shows a Threshold adjustment setting at 27 percent opacity. At bottom right is the Selective Color option, which we've used to experiment on using various ink channels simultaneously.

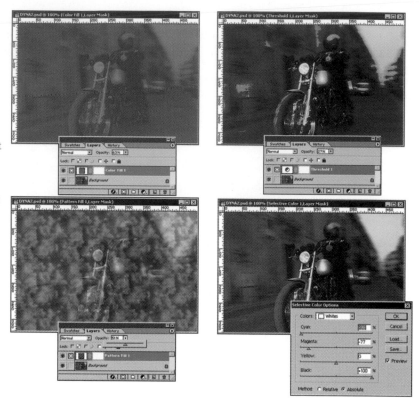

Color: Technical Terms Defined

Graphic production terms such as color models, color mode, CMYK, gamut, and others can be confusing if you've never worked with color before. This section explains the terms you should know if you want to delve into the subject of color and color management more deeply.

Color Modes and Models

We'll start our journey into color by looking at the different color models and color modes, explaining what they are and what they do. Choosing the right models will be crucial to your result, whether you work with Web graphics or print.

What Is a Color Model?

A color model is used to display and/or print images. Common models include RGB (red, green, blue), which is used on screen and for creating Web graphics; the CMYK model (cyan, magenta, yellow, black or kohl) which is used for print; and HSB (hue, saturation, brightness). The HSB color model is rarely used; it can be used to define color, but there's no HSB *mode* available for editing images. Programs like Photoshop 6 also include modes for specialized color output such as duotone or quadtone, as we'll see in a later example. The color modes determine the number of colors you can display in an image.

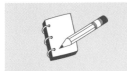

NOTE

Kohl, which means "black," is used instead of "B" in CMYK to avoid confusion with "B" for "blue" when printing.

Figure 6.31
Two of the most common color models are RGB (left) and CMYK (right).

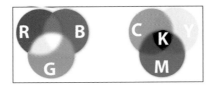

The RGB Model and RGB Mode

RGB images use three basic colors—red, green, and blue—to reproduce up to 16.7 million colors on screen. In fact, the RGB model is even used by computer monitors to display colors. This means that when you're working in image color modes other than RGB, such as CMYK or grayscale modes, applications temporarily use RGB mode for on-screen display. This is because your monitor is using the RGB model and can't use CMYK or other color models. With RGB mode, each pixel has an assigned value that ranges from a value of 0 (black) to a value of 255 (white). When the three components (R, G, B) are identical in value, the result is a gray color, as seen in the four examples in Figure 6.32. When the value of all components is set to 255, the result is pure white; when the value is set to 0, the image is pure black.

Figure 6.32
This image has four different grays. Note that the three RGB values are identical.

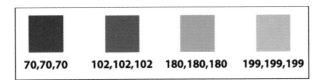

70,70,70   102,102,102   180,180,180   199,199,199

A large percentage of the visible color spectrum can be represented by mixing red, green, and blue colored light in various proportions and intensities. Where the colors overlap, they create cyan, magenta, yellow, and white. Because the RGB colors combine to create white, they are also called **additive colors.** Adding all colors together creates white. Additive colors are used for video, monitors, and lighting. Your monitor creates color by sending light through red, green, and blue phosphors.

Grayscale Mode

There are 256 shades of gray. Every pixel of a grayscale image has a value ranging from 0 (black) to 255 (white) in brightness. Grayscale values can also be measured as percentages of black ink coverage, which are commonly used in print. The higher the percentage, the darker the gray will be; 100 percent is pure black. As you can see in Figure 6.33, the levels in a grayscale image have only a black channel. When converting a picture to grayscale from RGB, remember to select "Don't Flatten" if you want to keep your layers.

Figure 6.33
The histogram (levels)
of a grayscale image.

CMYK Model and CMYK Mode

The CMYK model is based on the quality of translucent inks when they're printed on paper, and this is the method used in **four-color process printing.** When a white light hits the translucent process inks, some of the color spectrum is reflected back to your eyes.

As with the RGB model, cyan, magenta, and yellow should suffice to produce all colors, including black. In reality, C, M, and Y produce a very dark brown, so black (K) has to be added as a fourth print color. When you work in CMYK mode, you give each process ink a percentage value. To get a brownish color, you'd need a lot of magenta and yellow and a small amount of cyan; the percentage of black (kohl) will decide how dark your brown is. Just mixing magenta and yellow will create various nuances of orange and reds, depending on the percentages you use.

Your screen will never display CMYK with complete accuracy, because your screen works in RGB. Changes will happen to your ink colors when printing, such as an increased percentage of black (K), for example. You can make some compensation by calibrating your monitor and choosing color modes, but you won't be certain of the result before your work has been printed. Converting RGB to CMYK (or the other way around) won't do the trick—you have to make adjustments.

Duotones, Tritones, and Quadtones

Duotones, tritones, and quadtones are color modes that can be used as three easy techniques in Photoshop for transforming grayscale images into more exciting pictures. You have the option of working with presets in Photoshop, or you can create your own. We'll take a brief look at each.

Figure 6.34
This is our original grayscale image from the Photoshop 5.5 CD-ROM.

1. Open a grayscale image. (If you don't have one, simply convert an RGB or CMYK image to grayscale mode.)

2. Choose Image > Mode > Duotone. In the Duotone dialog box, you can choose between Monotone, Duotone, Tritone, or Quadtone from the Type drop-down menu, as shown in Figure 6.35.

3. Click the Load button to load one of Photoshop's presets or click the Ink color areas to manually select the colors you want. Note the small Curve buttons to the left (partly hidden under the drop-down menu), which you can use to adjust the curves for the inks you choose.

NOTE
The Duotone command in Photoshop 5.5 and 6.0 creates duotone (two-color), tritone (three-color), and quadtone (four-color) grayscale images using two, three, or four colored inks. Note that Photoshop Elements is made with the Web in mind and not print. It uses Greyscale, RGB, or Indexed Mode and does not offer duotones. To change the color using Elements, take a look at the options in Hue/Saturation using Adjustment Layers instead.

Part II Objects, Photos and Colors

Figure 6.35
This is the Duotone
Options dialog box.

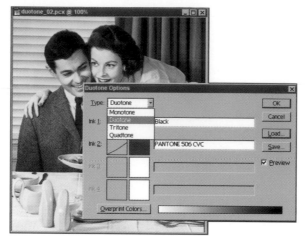

In Figures 6.36, 6.37, and 6.38, you'll see three examples of the same picture. In the first example, we've used duotones with dark brown and yellow inks. Next, we've created a tritone with three different shades of blue. When you select your colors, you can use the Eyedropper tool or select existing colors from the color swatches. Note the curves in the quadtone example.

Figures 6.36, 6.37, and 38
Here are your duotone mode variations: duotone (left), tritone (middle), and quadtone (right

Color Management

A color management system, or CMS, compares the color space a color was created in to the color space the same color will be output to. It makes the necessary adjustments to represent the color as accurately as possible. In this section, we'll take a brief look at color management and color management software. Luckily, the type of tablet you have will not affect your CMS. A CMS is software-based, so the tablet is of no consequence in regards to color management.

Color Management in Photoshop 6

Here's a quote from an article written by color management wizard Bruce Fraser at **www.CreativePro.com**: "No working space will, by itself, magically make your prints match your monitor, or your monitor match your original. To match up your colors, you need to use the appropriate ICC color profiles for your capture device, your output device, and your monitor, to convert the data going into or out of the working space. The working space is simply a safe place for your data to live as you take it from capture to output." It can't be said any more clearly than this.

NOTE

What is ICC? Color management workflows are based on conventions created by the International Color Consortium (ICC), hence the expression ICC color profiles. ICC was established in 1993 by industry vendors for the purpose of creating and encouraging the standardization and evolution of an open, vendor-neutral, cross-platform color management system.

Please don't confuse color *management* with color *adjustment* or color *correction*, which are what we've been talking about so far. A CMS (color management system) doesn't correct an image with color balance problems, it is just a tool to evaluate and standarize color in the images in the context of your final output. Many companies have developed tools to manage color, as you can see from our software selections later in this section.

Photoshop has collected most color management controls in a single Color Settings dialog box. You'll find this on the Edit menu > Color Settings, which is a huge and terrifying dialog box. Choose from a list of color management settings (predefined) or adjust the controls manually to create your own custom settings. Before you fiddle around with the settings, read Photoshop's manual to guide you through the color wilderness.

Color management gives you surprises when opening images as well: When you open an image with different CMS settings than the ones you've selected, you get a dialog box with options to leave as-is, convert, and so forth.

Using Adobe Gamma

To calibrate your monitor, create an ICC monitor profile for use in Photoshop, Illustrator, and other ICC-aware applications. Adobe Gamma is a control panel utility for Macs and PCs that is used for just such a purpose. Monitor calibration is best done with specialized software and hardware, but until you want to spend money on color management and calibration software, the Adobe Gamma panel can provide reasonably accurate calibration for your monitor, and it's better than nothing. Adobe Gamma has a good step-by-step wizard that I recommend you use the first time you try to calibrate your monitor.

It's very important that you calibrate your monitor, and here are a couple of things to remember before you begin: Your monitor should have been turned on for at least half an hour before you calibrate. Make sure the light in the room is as you would normally have it. Then set the background color on your monitor to a medium gray color. This way, desktop patterns or colors will not interfere when you calibrate your monitor. In Windows, start Adobe Gamma, which is located in the Control Panel folder or in Program Files > Common Files > Adobe > Calibration folder on your hard drive. In Mac OS, choose Control Panels > Adobe Gamma. (See Figure 6.39.)

Part II Objects, Photos and Colors

Figure 6.39
This figure shows the Adobe Gamma panel, using the wizard.

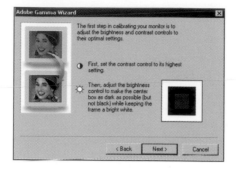

Color Calibration Tools and Software

There are a lot of color management tools available. Links to homepages, additional color calibration software, and further info can be found in Appendix B. Color calibration tools are designed to prevent changes in colors between devices so you can get an idea of how your work will look when printed. The price range is huge, so compare the different packages before buying. Let's take a look at some of them:

ViewOpen ICC and ScanOpen ICC

This software is for PC and Mac and generates ICC monitor profiles and characterization of color monitors. It lets you calibrate the brightness, contrast, color temperature, and so on of your monitor. The company states that ViewOpen offers the possibility to remove all color differences without expensive hardware investments. The individual color properties of each monitor are covered in an ICC profile, without distorting the gamma curve of the monitor. The adjustment made by the product can be completed within a few minutes. Heidelberg also offers ScanOpen ICC, which is a color rendering tool. Each input device, such as a digital camera or scanner, renders original colors in different shades. ScanOpen gives the user the possibility to characterize his or her devices to an optimum degree. The IT8 original is put in and analyzed, and the result is stored in the ICC profile. You can visit the company's Web site at **www.heidelberg-cps.com**.

Pantone ColorSuite for Businesses and the Pantone Personal Color Calibrator

This program is for the PC. ColorSuite for Business includes the Pantone OfficeColor Assistant, a plug-in for Microsoft Office. This is useful, for example, if you want to make sure your PowerPoint presentations will print correctly. The package also includes the Pantone Personal Color Calibrator, which provides accurate, predictable color matching between your screen and your printer by calibrating the colors on your monitor. You may also buy only the Personal Color Calibrator, which in my opinion would be a good choice if your cashflow is tight. This software takes into account the various viewing conditions you'll be working in, video card adjustments, and control settings. You'll also get the Pantone Digital Color System Guide, a reference of RGB and hexadecimal color values (see also ColorWeb Pro below) to reproduce the Pantone Matching System Colors. You can visit the company's Web site at **www.pantone.com**.

Pantone ColorWeb Pro

This software has little to do with calibration, but it deserves a mention nonetheless, because it involves the Pantone color system. ColorWeb Pro is software for the PC and the Mac that is designed to integrate Pantone Matching System colors into Web authoring software like Dreamweaver or FrontPage. It contains two color libraries, the Pantone Internet Color System with 216 Internet-safe colors plus the Pantone Matching System colors. This is a package some graphic designers will find useful, as it basically translates the familiar Pantone colors to Web colors. In my opinion, this is not the software you'll buy first if you already have Photoshop. If you have Photoshop 6, you can always look at the color palette and read off the Hex value to use in your Web page. Plus, very few users nowadays are using 256-color monitors, and new PCs often come with a "thousands-of-color" setting. You can read more about Web colors in Chapter 9.

Corel Premium Color Edition

This is a bundle for PC only. It contains the applications CorelDRAW and Corel PHOTO-PAINT, to name a couple. They come bundled with numerous calibration software programs, including products from Heidelberg (see ViewOpen and ScanOpen above) and ColorOpen ICC LE, an advanced color-profiling product. Included also is the AGFA IT-8 Scanner Target, to be used with ColorOpen ICC LE to create ICC profiles for your scanner. Corel has also thrown in a couple of handy publications, among them the X-Rite "Color Guide." And yes, you'll also get thousands of fonts and a lot of clip-art pieces as well. You can visit this company's Web site at **www.corel.com.**

NOTE

It is possible to simulate (or preview) printed colors on your monitor. This is called soft proofing. It requires color measurement devices and color management software for both your monitor and printer. If color is a subject that keeps you awake at night, try to get a copy of X-Rite's "Color Guide" from its Web site: **www.xrite.com.** This booklet has fifty-two pages of useful information that is absolutely free.

X-Rite ColorShop

ColorShop from X-Rite is a collection of tools for selecting and manipulating color available for both Mac and PC platforms. You may download a trial version of ColorShop from the company's Web site. ColorShop includes X-Rite color measurement technologies like Colortron, Digital Swatchbook, and Monitor Optimizer. ColorShop includes the Match Tool, which quickly references Pantone colors or your own custom palettes. If you're unsure about colors, you can use the Harmony Tool, which helps you select colors, or you can use the Compare Tool, which compares two colors visually and numerically. ColorShop has many helpful tools like the Lighting Tool, which lets you preview what your colors will look like under different lighting conditions. The Profile Viewer Tool lets you estimate CMYK process builds.

Part II Objects, Photos and Colors

When surfing on the X-Rite Web site, take a look at the Colortron Dual Color Measurement System as well. It includes features formerly sold separately, like the Profile Viewer Toolkit and the Density Toolkit. You can visit the company's Web site at **www.xrite.com**.

NOTE

Here's some suggested further reading about color.

There are lots of books about color and color management available. Take a look at Agfa's Web site and its book section at **www.agfabooks.com.** Most books have PDF samples so you know what you'll get. Worth looking at is *The Secrets of Color Management,* where you can read chapters on basic color theory, including "How Do We Perceive Color?," "Bit Depth," and "Monitor Limitations." Some books about color are bundled, so you'll get good value for your money. The Agfa Prepress and Production bundle includes *The Secrets of Color Management, An Introduction to Digital Color Prepress, A Guide to Color Separation*, and *PDF Printing and Publishing.*

Kodak ColorFlow Custom Color Software ICC

ColorFlow is a Photoshop plug-in for the Mac. It is a set of tools for adjusting the color performance of ICC profiles. With the Custom Color ICC plug-ins, you can use the familiar Photoshop Image Adjust features to fine-tune the color hardcopy output from a digital printer. You can also compare the printer's color match to another printing system. Experts believe that tuning color for high-end applications often requires fine control of CMYK or RGB output values. Kodak states that with Custom Color ICC, users can edit in CMYK for printers and proofing systems and in RGB for three-color printers or film recorders. Visit the company's Web site at **http://www.kodak.com/global/en/professional/products/software/colorFlow/ customColor/customColor.jhtml.** Or start at **www.kodak.com.**

Part III
Creating Graphics

7

Basic Drawing Techniques

In this chapter, you'll learn about creating your own bitmapped drawings on a tablet. Then, we'll explore some techniques using various applications that will get you ready for an adventure in cartoon land. At the end of this chapter, we'll explore the basics of vector graphics and bitmap images to get you set up for more advanced graphics creation concepts in Chapter 8.

In this chapter, you'll learn:

▶ How to draw and paint with a tablet, creating bitmapped drawings
▶ How to create a cartoon character
▶ The difference between bitmapped and vector graphics

Drawing with Brushes and Pens

There's some confusion regarding the expressions *painting* and *drawing* when using a tablet. You may have noticed that I use the expressions in regards to real-life painting and drawing. Applications like Photoshop have a tool called Paintbrush, and the name is quite accurate. But some manufacturers distinguish between painting and drawing—"painting" is often used when creating bitmapped images, and "drawing" is used when creating vector graphics. Drawing is then confined to *working with shapes*, which has nothing to do with real-life drawing. There's no reason to restrict the two expressions to vectors and bitmaps. Because some applications now support both formats simultaneously, this only confuses the user. You can read about vector graphics and bitmapped images later in this chapter.

The Wacom Intuos tablet provides up to 1024 levels of pressure-sensitivity. This means you can create both smooth and precise brush strokes and curves when drawing and painting. Some applications, like Painter, support tilt and bearing input as well. Read your applications manual to find out if you need to set any special preferences to take full advantage of the functions of your tablet or stylus. (For more information, also take a look at Chapter 3.)

Part III　Creating Graphics

Drawing in Photoshop 6

 Drawing and painting in Photoshop mean you have several tools available; these are described in the second half of Chapter 3. Adding several input devices, such as the Wacom Intuos range, means that you have unlimited options when drawing. Photoshop is not considered a drawing application because of its strength in image manipulation and retouching photos. Having the option to draw *and* do advanced adjustments to images simultaneously makes Photoshop an excellent application for artwork that involves photomontages. You can create your own brushes in Photoshop as well—we'll show you how in Chapter 11.

To demonstrate Photoshop 6's strength—combining drawing techniques with photos—I'll use an actual example. We'll create a Christmas card for Wacom, the tablet manufacturer. See Figure 7.1.

Figure 7.1
A simple sketch gets the artwork started.

1. Start by creating a sketch for your artwork. You can work with an RGB file of only 72 dpi resolution, because this is only a sketch. Use an input device such as a Pen or Stroke Pen and set the Photoshop Brush Dynamics: Opacity and Pressure to be controlled by the stylus. You don't have to do this at sketch point, but it's great for practicing your strokes anyway. Work with your sketch until you feel you have the composition right. Toggle between the Airbrush and Paintbrush tools in Photoshop. The Airbrush Tool is great for soft coverage of large areas like backgrounds. For outlines and rough details in the sketch, use brush settings of 3, 5, and 9 in size and also use Brush Dynamics settings for the stylus to control the size. This lets you create strokes of varying width.

2. Start your original image or resize the sketch. This example was created as an 8.25 2 4.15-inch (21 2 10.5 cm) image at 200 dpi. Now flip forward to Figure 7.10 so you can see what we're creating. This is the final artwork.

3. Create a white background layer. The sketch should reside on a layer above it. Set the opacity of the sketch layer so you'll barely make out the details; you don't want to get hung up in the sketch when drawing. The sketch is there to help you, not to annoy you. Note that when you resize a low-resolution sketch to 300 dpi, your strokes will seem wider on screen when working with it in 100 percent. Thus, I recommend working and viewing at 50 percent or smaller, or you won't see much of your artwork because of the high resolution. Create a new layer (Layer 1) above the sketch and start working on the sea, sky, or whatever you'd want the "background" of your artwork to be.

4. Start by creating a *rough* background. Fill in large areas using the various selection tools and the Airbrush Tool. Begin your work on the sky by painting clouds with the Airbrush Tool. (If you feel clouds are difficult to paint, take a look at the clouds tutorial in Chapter 11.) Use almost-white shades for the clouds and use only pure white for the finishing touches. You'll need to toggle between a medium-sized and a large brush when working on the clouds. Use *very* little pressure on the tablet to make the clouds smooth and soft. Use a medium-sized paintbrush and airbrush tools to create the darker areas of the sea, as shown in Figure 7.2. Use soft pressure and make sure you get the strokes blurred. Note that on the Intuos tablet, you have three pressure settings next to the menu strip, so if you have a firm pressure setting, click the Soft icon on your tablet to change it quickly without opening the tablet control panel.

5. Open your image files. In this case, it's a picture of an Intuos tablet and a picture of input devices. Images of tablets and input devices are available for free on Wacom's Web site (**www.wacom.com**).

6. We'll start with the tablet: Make an accurate selection of the tablet with the Lasso Tool. Make sure Anti-alias is selected before you create your selections.

7. Paste the image into your artwork, above the rough sea layer as also shown in Figure 7.2. Note that I've hidden the sketch when working with this.

8. To create perspective, transform and rotate the tablet image to align and match it with the waves.

Figure 7.2
Paste your image into your artwork, on a layer above your background(s).

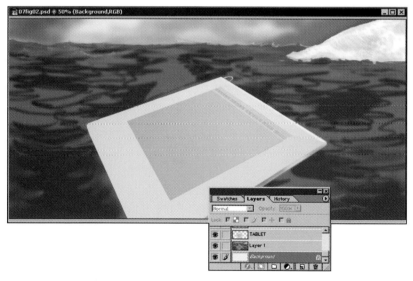

9. Create a new layer *above* the tablet layer for the waves and sea details and name it "Waves." Look at your sketch to see where the penguins are going (you don't have to create details where the penguins will cover them).

10. Hide your sketch, and use several blue colors (see Figure 7.3) plus shades of white to create the waves. Because you have the tablet image on a separate layer, you can select it, invert it, and switch to the waves layer to make sure you don't draw over the tablet. We want the tablet to appear as though it were sticking out of the water rather than just floating on top of it, so we'll want a couple of waves to go above it. Deselect when working on those. If you've remembered to save your selections, you can always load them again later—or Ctrl+click the layer to load the object residing on the layer as a selection.

11. To create the waves: Start with the darker areas of the waves, using various blue shades that are slightly brighter than the sea. The shades I've used can be seen in Figure 7.3. Use the Airbrush Tool for this, with very light pressure, and work with smooth, curved strokes. White was used to create the spray. Be very careful when working with white, because it is very dramatic and should be used only to enhance areas. Black and white are colors you should use at the final stage when creating artwork. When creating the spray, use the Airbrush to create "dots" with a single click, as this—when done correctly—gives the illusion of drops, as shown in Figure 7.4. I use a "Soft round 9 pixel" brush for most of the white water spray dots. Switch to a larger brush and create white effects in the areas that connect the spray dots with the wave. Remember, you can duplicate your work when working digitally, so you can always recycle some of your drawing!

Figure 7.3
Use several shades of blue to create waves. The numbers refer to RGB values.

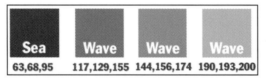

Figure 7.4
Remember the water spray when you're creating waves. Work from dark shades to bright shades to build the waves.

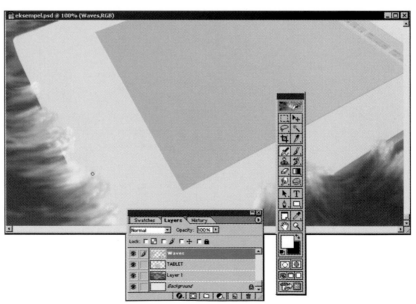

12. Create a new layer for your penguins and put it between the waves and tablet layer. You'll want the penguins to have some water on them as well. Now is a good time to view your sketch layer if it's been hidden.

13. Draw the outlines for your penguins first, then the beaks and eyes, and then hats and so on, using the Paintbrush with a gray or black color and a very low opacity setting. Use little pressure. The point is to create a rough sketch that you can draw accurate lines over afterwards. You can work on the same layer or create a new layer for the final drawing of the penguins, depending on how you prefer to work. Build your penguins the same way as the sea and waves; gradually working your way to brighter shades. Paint the main body color first, then add other colors and shades. Draw any crisp outlines when you're absolutely sure you have it right (that's why you drew with a low opacity setting to begin with). Add a white dot with a small Airbrush to create highlights in the black eyes. See Figure 7.5.

Figure 7.5
This is an enlarged view of one of the penguins. Note the variety in color shades in the body.

14. When you work with shadows, create a selection with the Lasso Tool to protect the areas you don't want the effect in. As seen in Figure 7.6, I've selected parts of the penguin's body to create a shadow next to it, inverted the selection, and then used a dark gray color, the Airbrush Tool, and a size 35 brush. This way, I can paint partly over the selection's edge, because the penguin itself is protected by the selection. Another way of creating shadows is to make another layer below the penguin and paint there instead. If you do this, you have to have a penguin that's completely opaque (filled with color), because any amount of transparency on the penguin's layer will make your strokes on the layers below visible.

Part III Creating Graphics

Figure 7.6
Protect the parts you
don't want color in by
using selections and
inverting them.

15. Add any other images to your artwork that you think would be right for the
    project. I used the mouse and pen sticking out of the water, because I thought
    those would be fun.

16. Adjust your waves correspondingly. Work with the light and shade on both the
    objects and the penguins. You have to decide where the light is coming from,
    and adjust it accordingly. Because you're working on separate layers, you can
    make a new layer just for light effects to have complete control. Otherwise, you
    can lock the transparency of your layers so that you draw light only on the areas
    of the object and not over the background. Your artwork should now look like
    Figure 7.7.

Figure 7.7
Light and shade are
added. The light in this
drawing is diffuse;
there's no bright sun or
any other light source
visible.

17. Now it's time for the Christmas card details. Add a new layer above all the others. Draw a pine twig, by starting with a small Airbrush. Draw soft strokes as a sketch for it, and then add pressure when you see you have it right. When drawing the green strokes, start at the middle of the twig and release pressure as you draw so you get a nice fade at the end. Draw the lighter, brown lines when you're finished with the green strokes. When you've finished drawing one twig, duplicate it and flip it, rotate it, and then you have another one without any effort! Be careful if you scale it, so you don't lose detail. Otherwise, it becomes too blurred.

18. Add yet another layer above the pine twigs for the two bells. You draw a single bell, starting with the medium-yellow color. Create a selection horizontally as an oval with the Elliptical Marquee Tool for the inside of the bell. Use several shades of brown to create the shadows inside the bell. Lock Layer transparency and add lighter areas to the bell. Unlock layer transparency. Make one bell and duplicate its layer and move the duplicated bell next to the first one. Merge these two layers when you're done.

19. Create a new layer below it for the red bands. Draw them with a Paintbrush Tool (choose a hard brush for crisp edges), and solid red color. Use an even, hard pressure on your stylus or turn off the pressure to be controlled by the stylus when you do this. Lock layer transparency and pick a darker red color such as RGB 126, 45, 30.Use a medium-sized Airbrush and soft pressure to create the shadows under the bells. When you're satisfied with the result, merge the bells and the layer with the red bands. You'll have one layer called Bells, which is above the Pine layer. See Figure 7.8.

You can now delete your sketch layer if you haven't already done so.

Figure 7.8
Duplicate layers to create copies of your object, and merge the layers when you've finished adding details like shade and light.

Part III Creating Graphics

20. How about some snow? Create yet another layer and place it above all the others. You can paint a few snowdrops by using your Airbrush Tool to make dots of various sizes in white. Work only in a small area of the image. When the dots look natural, select them all and resize (scale) them heavily so they become larger and blurred.

21. Copy your layer and move the snow copies around to fill the whole illustration with snow. (Remember to flip layers and rotate them so you don't get "patterns" of snow.) Merge all the snow layers when you have snow everywhere. Experiment with layer opacity settings for the merged layer if you painted the snow too white. Create a new layer above the bells to create snow areas on the bells and pine (or anywhere else you'd like amounts of snow) and use various shades of white and gray to create depth in the snow. See a detailed and enlarged example of snow and snow details in Figure 7.9. Erase any unwanted snowflakes over your penguins with the Eraser Tool.

Figure 7.9
Duplicate layers to create snow everywhere in your artwork. Finish off the image by adding snow details on a separate layer.

22. The final touch is to add some text for your Christmas card. I used a warm red color, copied the type layer, and filled the type (below the copy) with white. Moving it up a pixel or two created an instant highlight for the red type on the above layer. In Figure 7.10, you can see the result. This was a Christmas card created for Wacom GmbH Europe.

Figure 7.10
This is the finished
result.

Some examples of Brush strokes in Photoshop 6

The first square at left shows the Airbrush tool with the Brush Dynamics settings. The size and opacity are to be controlled by the stylus. The Brush used is *Hard, round 9 pixels*, and the Intuos Pen is used. The next is the same Brush Dynamics setting, but with the *Soft, round 9 pixel* brush. The third square is the same brush, but using the Intuos Airbrush, with color controlled by the stylus as well. The fourth is made with the Intuos Stroke Pen at the same settings. The fifth is created with the Intuos Pen and the Paintbrush Tool, a *Soft, round 9 pixel* brush. Size and opacity are controlled by the stylus. The sixth has the same settings and tool, but with a *Hard, round 5 pixel* brush. The seventh is the same, but with Wet Edges turned on. The final one, No. 8, is the Pencil Tool with a *Hard, round 5 pixel* brush, where the stylus controls opacity and pressure.

Part III Creating Graphics

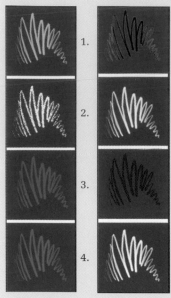

Layer Blending Modes
in Painter and Photoshop

1.

5.

All brush strokes are white; they are on layers above the blue background. Here are the layer settings: 1: Difference, 2: Dissolve, 3: Overlay, 4: Soft Light, 5: Exclusion, 6: Lighten, 7: Hue, 8: Normal.

2.

6.

In Painter, the blending modes are called Composite Method; in Photoshop, they are called Blending Options. Nevertheless, most of them have the same names. When working in Photoshop, I recommend opening the dialog box, rather than using the Blending Options drop-down menu in the Layers Palette. In the dialog box, you can display the Advanced Blending Options, where you can select Fill Opacity, Knockout, and so on. These Advanced options are not visible in the Layers Palette.

3.

7.

4.

8.

Drawing in Painter 6

Painter has an edge over Photoshop because of the incredible variety of preset brushes you can use; you can also create your own. You will no doubt spend hours learning them all (some are briefly described in Chapter 3). Painter has Brush Tracking Preferences that lets you adjust the program to match your stroke strength. Unfortunately, this information is not saved, so you have to set Brush Tracking each time you start Painter. (How to do this is also described in Chapter 3.) You'll use the same techniques when working in Painter as described in the Photoshop section. You'll see how to build your artwork, from sketch to backgrounds, and on to more detailed work. See Figure 7.11.

Figure 7.11
Painter has a layers capability as well, which comes in handy when creating artwork like this.

Painter's brushes create effects very much like those you'd get if you were working with real oil paints or acrylics. These brush tools cover existing brush strokes; some are even capable of multi-colored strokes. Some brushes react with underlying pixels, like the Smoary Flat brush. When you select a brush, Painter loads its default setting. Then, it's up to you to change it to suit your project. You can change the size, pressure, and other settings, such as Expressions.

TIP

When using Painter's Brush Control palette, you can customize and create brushes. You can adjust size, flow, and how the dabs (or dots) are repeated in the strokes. The Expression Settings in the Brush Controls give you numerous choices for Pressure, Direction, and so on, to control everything from Size and Opacity to Angle, Jitter, Grain, and Color. See Figure 7.12. This means that you can tie a Brush feature like *Size* to the stylus, and if you set Min Size smaller than the brush size, you can paint strokes with great variety in width, depending on the pressure you use. Painter supports Tilt, so be aware of how you hold the Stylus to get the desired results when drawing.

Figure 7.12
This image shows Painter's Brush Controls.

When you start working with Painter, go through the Art Materials palette. You can fill your canvas, or a selection, with the art material of your choice. This can be color, pattern, gradients, weave, and so on. Go to the Effects menu > Fill or use the Paintbucket tool. In Figure 7.13, there's a pattern added to the background, an image on top with Layer Opacity set low, and a new layer for drawing. Parts of the pattern in the background are painted over.

Figure 7.13
Use patterns and other fills to create quick backgrounds.

When drawing, set Size and Opacity to Pressure in Brush settings. This way, your tablet and stylus have control over your brush strokes. I've used the Digital Airbrush in this example. (Some of Painter's Water Color brushes have limitations.) If you try to paint with a brush on the layer you're drawing on, you get a message telling you this brush can be used only on the canvas. Unlike Photoshop, where you can use the brushes on any layer, Painter is very serious about its canvas. You can work around this issue by using the Liquid Brushes instead, even though they create a smeared effect. Some brushes can seem outright silly for the experienced artist, like Auto van Gogh, one of the Artists Brushes. This could easily have been a filter instead of a brush. Some brushes will surprise you, as they don't care about your pressure settings at all—their "nature" is to be completely opaque, like the Captured Bristle. You'll need to spend some time learning the tricks and limitations of the different brushes.

Painter also gives you the clever option of using pre-made paper textures, and some are really good. You'll find this in Effects > Surface Control > Apply Surface Texture, as shown in Figure 7.14. You can create your own textures as well (I'll show you how in Chapter 12). If you draw with a brush that interacts with paper grain, and you like the result, you can save this combination for later use.

Figure 7.14
Painter's Papers feature
has a lot of options for
surface texture. You can
apply this at any time in
the creation of your
artwork.

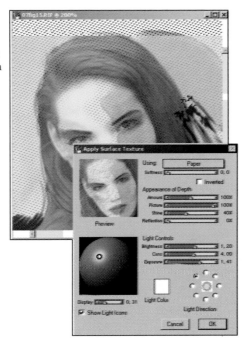

Drawing Cartoon Characters

Cartoons are fun, and when you have a tablet, they're easy to create with pressure-sensitive pens
and a few basic tricks. This section will go through the basics of creating your own cartoon
character. Plot and story will be totally up to you.

Cartoon Character Elements

When you read cartoons, you probably don't think about how they're created. You read the story
and laugh at situations and their funny expressions, completely unaware of the techniques and
tricks behind the cartoon. But a cartoon follows several rules, which we'll explore in this
section. The basics of any cartoon character are shape, proportion, identity, and expression.
Expressions, or emotions, are what makes a cartoon character great. There's really a *puzzle* of
different shapes that form a character. The shapes are the reason you recognize your favorite
cartoon character instantly.

When you start drawing cartoons, you'll want your characters to look the same when viewed at
different angles, so it's important that you know how your characters are put together. Even if
you create a character just by doodling on a napkin one night, create a "handbook" of how it
should look using shapes (see the next section). When working with a tablet, creating these
shapes is a breeze. You can draw a few shapes with the pen, and then you can use functions in
your software to manipulate it, flip it horizontally, vertically, stretch its lines, and so on. This is
also handy when working on expressions when very small adjustments are necessary.

Shapes

The character shapes in Figure 7.15 were created with a Wacom Intuos pen and tablet while working with a file in RGB mode in Photoshop. You can easily use programs like Painter or Photoshop Elements instead. In the "tool department," I used black color and the Paintbrush Tool with a 3 pixel brush and 100 percent opacity. By creating shapes like these, you'll always know what parts your characters are made of. In this example, the nose shape, hair style, and eyes will make you recognize it later on, even when its expression changes. You create the body of a cartoon character the same way, and the same method applies whether your character is an animal, human, or something entirely different. Building cartoon characters from elements is not just a method for amateurs, but very common in cartoon creation. The famous cartoonist Carl Barks created detailed instructions for how the various Disney characters should look and also wrote notes on what made them different from each other. This way, other cartoonists had a "manual" of Donald, Mickey, and all the other characters.

Figure 7.15
You construct your character by creating shapes and "filling them in" later.

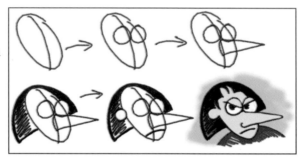

When you work on the shapes, consider what your character will be like when it's finished. I'm not talking about lines and details, but about personality and attitude. Are you creating a cute dog? Vicious cat? Friendly mouse? A general characteristic can help you on your way to get the character right regarding shape and proportions. Think also of how it should relate to its surroundings: Will it be the oldest one in the family? The smallest dog? The largest mouse? What makes it look young, old, tired, or vivacious?

Proportion

When you've created a rough draft of a cartoon character that you're satisfied with, you can use a simple trick to help you maintain the proportions of your character. Besides character identity and expressions, proportions are vital for recognizing the character and getting it right in various situations. I'm not asking you to create mathematical equations to get it right; just a simple set of "help lines," as seen on a child's writing paper, will get you going. Until you can draw your cartoon half asleep, this is a very useful trick: Divide your character into natural pieces, such as head, torso, legs, and feet. Make an example of your character with a couple of sketches, as shown in Figure 7.16, just to help you see the divisions. A quick glance at this "tool" can help you discover what's wrong with a new drawing—for example, if the head's too big for the body. You can often detect whether a cartoonist has just started out by the proportion mistakes he or she makes. As you work on a tablet, use an application with layers so you can keep a set of help lines on a layer *beneath* the one you're drawing on.

Figure 7.16
To maintain proportions, use help lines to divide a body into several pieces.

TIP

The best cartooning advice is basically to "keep it simple." If you want to create a character that is fast to work with, as in short comic strips, you need to consider a few things. The more details you create in your character, the harder it will be to get them right every time *and* it will take a lot of time each time you draw a new one—even if you know how to duplicate layers. There is a reason why many famous cartoon characters consist of few lines and not so many details. Look at Bart Simpson, Mickey Mouse, Dilbert, or other famous characters and try to imagine what it would be like to draw them repeatedly if they had big, curly hair with lots of details, a jacket with fringe, glasses, and beards.

Unless you have unlimited time and/or want to create artwork such as that seen in the Sandman comic books, keep your character simple. The fewer lines the better. Moreover, that is where the challenge lies—to create a distinctive character with just a few lines drawn on your tablet. Pay extra attention to details as well, if you use them: Three strands of hair are not the same as two or four, and five fingers are not the same as four. The number of holes in the lacing of a shoe and so on are also important.

Character Identity

When working with cartoons, it's vital that your character can be easily identified. Think of Mickey Mouse's silhouette, with his face and ears. You instantly recognize Mickey, right? To see if your character has a great identity, you can simply fill an outlined drawing with color using your Brush or Pen in Painter or Photoshop. If what you have created doesn't look like anything else, then you have created an easily recognizable figure. Make several drawings of different views so you'll know you have it right. You don't want your character to be seen just from behind or in profile. See Figures 7.17 and 7.18.

Part III Creating Graphics

Figures 7.17 and 7.18
Draw several silhouettes of your cartoon character to see if it's easy to recognize.

Attitudes and Expressions

After you have established an identity for your character, you'll need to look at attitudes and expressions. This includes how the character walks, moves, makes gestures, and shows expressions. Because most characters are made up of very few lines, it's very important for you to have decided upon your character's persona when starting with expressions. Minor adjustments and changes to the eyes, for example, are enough to show various expressions. In Figure 7.19, you'll see how very small changes make a huge difference.

Figure 7.19
Variations to the eyes and mouth are generally enough to create different expressions. Observe that in these ten examples, no eyebrows are needed for variations—the eyes and eyelids are enough.

Attitude is often expressed by the cartoon character's body. When you see cartoon drawings or watch cartoons on TV, note that various cartoon types resemble each other. The villains and thieves are often drawn similarly. They can be thin with a sneaky look and curved back, and they lift their knees high when walking. These are often the "clever" bad guys. They are also drawn as big, bulky figures when they're supposed to be the dumber villains. Many head honchos of criminal gangs are depicted as small guys, with huge "torpedoes" at their sides—at least in cartoons and movies. You don't have to stick to this kind of simplistic view of how criminals should look, but this kind of knowledge is helpful when you want to create simple characters that your audience will recognize instantly. When drawing short cartoon strips, this is vital. If you're making a comic book, you can use several pages to build a character, but you won't have that opportunity in a comic strip. Try to be brave as well, and stay away from stereotypical details, because not all "truths" apply to all audiences. I bet there's a couple of nerds out there who don't wear glasses and who don't survive exclusively on pizza and Coke. This may not be the best example in the world, but you get my meaning. There's no cartoon bible that you can consult that states that all characters have four fingers. Just use your imagination.

Below, you'll find several examples of clip-art cartoons that have various expression and attitudes.

Figure 7.20
There's no doubt as to what these expressions are!

Part III Creating Graphics

From Sketch to Drawing

Never start to draw aiming for a finished version of your cartoon right away. Even the most professional cartoonists, whether they're working digitally or on paper, start with sketches and storyboards. If you prefer to create your sketch on paper, slide the sketch under the protective layer on your tablet and trace your cartoon with your Pen. Use a small, hard brush for this. This is a great way to work, but you can also scan your sketch and work with it in programs like Painter or Photoshop. Both methods require a tablet and a pressure-sensitive Pen or Brush Pen.

Sketches, Sketches, Sketches

The great advantage of making sketches is that when you create one, you draw more freely than you would when you're working on "the real thing" right away. When creating a sketch, you'll see if your idea is good enough and whether the cartoon or character "works." Don't get hung up on details, because you can always add details later. Using a program like Painter or Photoshop, create a grayscale image of approximately 600 × 500 pixels with a resolution of 72 dpi for the sketch. And pick a good tool, such as a Pen or a Brush Pen. Use the Airbrush or a Paintbrush Tool in the application, with the brush size set at only 3 to 5 pixels wide. The typical creative process for an illustration or cartoon would be like what is shown in Figures 7.21a, 7.21b, and 7.21c.

Figures 7.21a, 7.21b and 7.21c
This is "Ziggy the Cigarette" in three stages. The first (a.) is a rough sketch nobody usually sees but me, the second (b.) is a more detailed sketch sent to the client, and the last (c.) is the final result. This is an illustration for a brochure targeted towards doctors to inspire them to help their patients to stop smoking.

a.

b.

c.

1. Pick your brushes (and tools) before you start, so you don't get unnecessary pauses in the creative process trying to find the "right brush".

2. Draw a very rough sketch in black and white. Concentrate on what you have to say, and work with fast, swift movements. If you see that a line is wrong when drawing, don't pause to correct it. Instead, draw it where it should be. When you're happy with the sketch, start working on details and color (if you're working with color at all). If you want to work in color, change the image mode to RGB.

   At this point, you're still nowhere near a finished cartoon. I often send sketches to clients for approval before submitting the original artwork, so they get a sketch that is a bit more detailed and precise than I normally would make. That's because, while I can visualize the finished result, they sometimes can't see what I mean by looking at a rough sketch, so I have to show a detailed sketch to them so they see exactly what I'm thinking. This way, I can be sure that the result is what the client wants. An example of this type of sketch is in Figure 7.21b. When the client is happy, it's time to create the artwork on the tablet.

3. Keep the 72-dpi setting if your cartoons are going to be shown on a monitor (such as on a Web page). If your work is going to be printed, resize the file to a 300-dpi setting or more for good results. Now finish the artwork.

Sometimes you can work directly on your sketch, but you will benefit most from working in a program that has layers—Painter, Illustrator, or Photoshop. This way, you can adjust the opacity on the sketch layer and start drawing on a new layer above it. The sketch is still visible, but it won't "interfere" with changes you might want to make as you go along. Some artists stick to the sketch they've created when drawing, but others create a lot of new stuff. This depends on the quality of the sketch, combined with how satisfied you are with it.

Action Lines

An action line is a help tool, just like the lines you create for controlling proportions. An action line is used to mark the *direction* of a pose, like falling, sitting, bending over, running, and so on. You start by drawing the action line itself and then draw in the character. This is again where layers are very helpful, because you can keep the action line(s) on a separate layer. And why not use the same action lines repeatedly? You can make a whole library of them if you like. See Figure 7.22.

Figure 7.22
Action lines (shown here in orange) are great tools to control movement and direction, as shown in this rough sketch. When you've done the character, erase the action line or the layer that it's on.

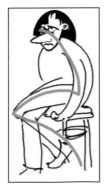

Part III Creating Graphics

Color

Not all color "survives" print. Working for the screen is easier because you can stick to a color palette of 216 "Web safe" colors to be viewed on most monitors and browsers. Just as you created a "handbook" of shapes and expressions, take note of what colors you use in your cartoon. This is vital when it comes to skin tones, which can be tricky. If you use Photoshop, you have the option of creating a palette for your cartoon. If you use other programs, create a new file with squares of the colors you use, and always have it open when drawing so you can access the colors with the Eyedropper Tool. If you have several characters, don't let them share too many colors—you want them to be as different as possible. Use a palette of 216 Web-safe colors if you plan to publish your cartoon on a Web page, and you also want to be sure the cartoon can be viewed properly on monitors with 256 color settings. This will get you in trouble when selecting skin tones, so take care to select your colors from the Web-safe swatch palette when drawing. You can read more about the pitfalls of Web graphics in Chapter 9.

Storyboard

Storyboards aren't something used just in movies and commercials. With a storyboard, you can see how your story will look before drawing it properly, and you can divide up your work as well, if necessary. In a comic book, this means you can start drawing anywhere in the story, as long as you stick to the storyboard. You can also use a storyboard for comic strips. A storyboard can be as small as you'd like, just as long as it's legible. You can create it on paper or on screen. The latter is strongly recommended, because it's easier to edit and it gives you a lot more options. You can use it to make notes and comments regarding shadows and light, coloring, and more. As seen in Figure 7.23, you can create the storyboard in full color, and with the Airbrush Tool you can easily brush in light, shadows, and so on. It may not be so beautiful to look at, but the whole point is to see if your composition works as you intended. You should create a storyboard in a size comparable to your finished work. It doesn't have to be exactly 1:1 in size, but the *proportions* should be right, such as for landscape or portrait, A4 format, and so on.

Figure 7.23
A storyboard is a great tool that gives you full control over your artwork.

Vector Graphics and Bitmaps

The overarching term "computer graphics" has two main categories, namely *bitmap images* and *vector graphics*. You have to know the differences between these two main categories of graphics to work efficiently with them and to get good results when printing. You may have heard or seen these terms several times, but in this section, we'll take an in-depth look at what they are, their differences, and, most importantly, when each is appropriate to use. You can work with both types of graphics simultaneously in many applications today, including Illustrator 9, Photoshop 6, CorelDRAW 10, and so on. Photoshop 6 will now enable you to create and work with files that contain both bitmap and vector data.

Vector Graphics

Vector graphics are made up of lines and curves defined by mathematical objects. These objects are called *vectors*. They describe an image according to its geometric characteristics. You can scale, rotate, or resize vector graphics without losing quality. See Figure 7.24 for an example.

Figure 7.24
This is an enlarged vector graphics example from a Photoshop 5.5 tutorial CD. The lines of a vector graphic stay crisp regardless of how those lines are manipulated.

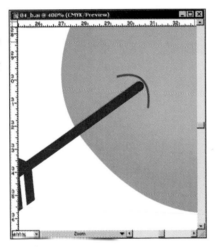

Vector graphics don't care about resolution. Vector graphics can be scaled to any size without losing detail and still be printed perfectly. This means that vector graphics are an excellent choice for representing graphics that must remain crystal clear when scaled. Typical examples of vector graphics are logos or detailed line art, often saved as EPS (Encapsulated PostScript) files. Animation software uses vector graphics, and so do many printers, such as Postscript printers, for example. Fonts represented as vectors are called vector fonts. We'll take a look at creating vector graphics (working with shapes), in the next chapter.

Bitmap Images and Anti-aliasing

Bitmap images use pixels to represent images, as shown in the enlarged illustration in Figure 7.25. Each pixel is assigned a precise color and location. When you create and work with bitmap images, you edit pixels instead of objects or lines as in vector graphics. A scanned photo is a bitmapped image.

Part III   Creating Graphics

Figure 7.25
Here is an enlarged
bitmap image. The
squares (pixels) are used
to represent the image.

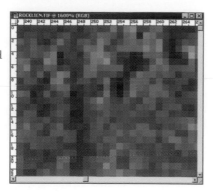

Bitmap images can represent subtle gradations of color, nuance, and shade; thus, the bitmap is the perfect choice for photos. Bitmap images are *resolution-dependent*. This means that the number of pixels used to represent the image is fixed. For Web graphics, this is 72 dpi, because that's what the screen is designed for.

Bitmapped images have their drawbacks, though. They lose detail and can become "jagged" or blurred if they are resized (scaled) or if they are printed at a different resolution than they were created for. For example, if you take a 72-dpi Web graphic and print it on paper at 300 dpi or higher, the higher print resolution will reveal jagged edges. You can also see a pixelated effect in heavily compressed Web graphics. An example of a resized bitmapped image is shown in Figure 7.26.

Figure 7.26
The small image on the
left is the original 72-
dpi image. The top right
close-up is just an
enlarged copy of the
same image at the same
resolution. Note the
clear pixels at the jagged
edges. The bottom
image is a resized image
at 600 dpi, shown at
100 percent; note the
blurred edges.

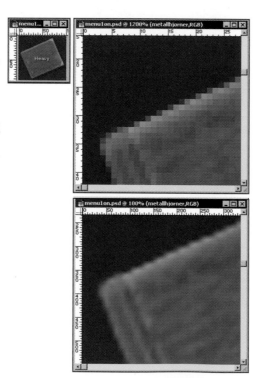

TIP

Here's a tip to improve how you work with bitmapped images. First, know your output. When working with bitmaps, it is essential that you know beforehand whether your work is to be printed or used on the Web, or both. You can resize to a lower resolution more successfully than the other way around, so if you are working with something that is supposed to be both printed *and* displayed on the Web, focus on the print resolution. This should be at least 300 dpi for good results.

So how do you fix the jagged edges when bitmaps are scaled? The answer is anti-aliasing. Anti-aliasing creates transitional pixels along the edges of an object, type, or line to smooth the transition between the edge and the surrounding image or background. A typical example is a black object on a white background: With anti-aliasing, you'll see pixels of gray between the black edge and white background, as shown in Figure 7.27. Anti-aliasing, therefore, reduces jagged edges. When you draw with brushes and pens in applications on your tablet, you work with anti-aliasing turned on or you'll draw jagged edges every time. The only occasion where you'll want the anti-aliasing turned off is when you need straight lines with crisp and clear edges, like when you create icons.

Figure 7.27

Anti-aliasing reduces jagged edges in bitmapped images. The left image, (at 300 percent), has no anti-aliasing. The right image (enlarged to 1600 percent) has anti-aliasing and has gray pixels of various shades at the edge of the black object.

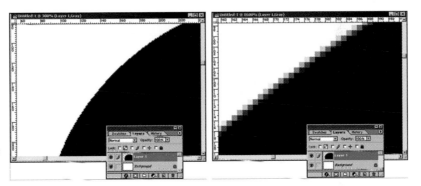

Combining Vector Graphics and Bitmapped Images

Even though programs like Illustrator, Painter, and CorelDRAW have recently added a lot of filters and effects, you'll turn to programs like Photoshop to add cool or natural effects to a vector graphic. Importing vector graphics is an uncomplicated procedure. You can use File > Place or the paste commands to paste your vector graphic into an existing Photoshop 6 file. This psd (Photoshop) file must be in the resolution you'll want later—such as 300 dpi or more—for print. With your Photoshop file open, choose File > Place and browse to your vector image on your hard disk. When it appears in your Photoshop file, you'll see that it appears jagged, even though anti-aliasing is turned on. This is only a temporary preview, because you'll use the handles surrounding the vector graphic to scale and move it exactly where you want it, as shown in Figure 7.28. Double-click or click your Move Tool to bring up the Place dialog box, where you have the option to Place or Not Place the vector graphic. You'll see it rasterize (convert to a bitmapped image), as in the lower image in Figure 7.28. Note that if you don't use anti-aliasing, you'll get jagged edges.

Figure 7.28
The first image (upper left) shows the vector graphic as imported. The second (below) shows the graphics after the Place command has been used, and it's rasterized. The final image, (top right), shows the result after Layer effects have been added. I've used drop shadow and outer glow; I've even played around with Blending modes. I used Multiply on the top layer and Overlay on the other rasterized layer. I've also airbrushed in some black color to darken the background.

This chapter should have given you the knowledge you need to start some '"serious" drawing with a tablet and for creating your own cartoon characters. You should know the main differences between vector and bitmapped graphics, and that leads us into the next chapter, which gives you an in-depth knowledge of working with vector shapes and objects.

8

Creating Graphics

Past chapters have covered photographs and drawings as bitmap images. In this chapter, we'll look at vector graphics and how they're created. After you finish this chapter, you will have the necessary knowledge and confidence to work with vector graphics and bitmaps using your tablet. You will also have learned a few tricks when working with icons and how to get professional-looking results out of clip art.

This chapter will show you how to:

▶ Work with vector shapes in Adobe Illustrator

▶ Work with paths and strokes and add effects to them

▶ Create a composition using both vector graphics and bitmaps

Creating Vector Graphics

Vector graphics can be used for creating logos and other illustrations that need to be independent of resolution. This section will discuss vector basics, starting with shapes. Then we'll work our way through paths and strokes. Finally, we'll convert a vector graphic to a bitmap so we can add filters and effects.

Shapes

You can create shapes in programs like Adobe Illustrator 9 by using the Rectangle Tool, Rounded Rectangle Tool, Ellipse Tool, Polygon Tool, and so on. For those unfamiliar with Illustrator, these tools may seem similar to tools you've seen in other programs that work with bitmapped images. We'll play around with various shapes and see how they behave, using the same example throughout the following sections.

Creating Shapes in Adobe Illustrator

1. Start with an RGB mode file in Illustrator, sized to about 500 × 500 pixels. Choose the Rectangle Tool and create a rectangle, filled with one of Illustrators default colors from the Swatches palette. I've chosen Periwinkle. (It's RGB values are: 153, 102, 204 in case you have another version of Illustrator.) Outline is set to transparent.

Part III Creating Graphics

2. From the Object > Transform menu, choose *Shear* and set the angle to 30 degrees horizontal, which creates a parallelogram.

3. Make a new layer using the Layers Palette—this palette works just like Photoshop's—and create a new parallelogram of lavender fill color with Shear settings of -45 degrees horizontal.

    In the Transparency dialog box, set the opacity on the Lavender shape to 50 percent. Use selection tools to move or resize your shapes. When you draw a shape, holding down the Ctrl key (Command) will get you the Move tool. This way, you can move the shape around as well, before continuing to adjust it.

TIP

Use the Lock option to be sure you're not selecting the wrong layer or shapes when working with multiple layers and shapes. Ctrl+right clicking over an object (shape) doesn't select it on the correct layer as in Photoshop. You may select multiple shapes on several unlocked layers by dragging a rectangle around them with the Selection Tool.

4. Now, make a new layer called Ellipse. Choose the Ellipse Tool and create an ellipse of Lavender color, but with opacity set to 20 percent.

5. Make a new layer called Star, select the Star Tool (hidden under the Ellipse Tool in the Toolbox), and create a star filled with a Pale Yellow color with object opacity set to 30 percent in the Transparency palette. Your artwork should now look similar to Figure 8.1.

Figure 8.1
Create shapes with various tools in Illustrator. You can adjust the opacity settings in the Transparency palette to make the objects transparent.

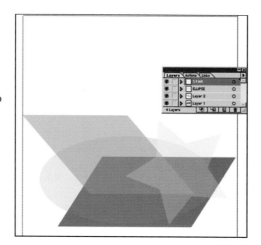

NOTE

Shapes are defined as geometric objects (also called *vector* objects). For example, if you draw a circle using the Ellipse Tool, the circle is defined by a specific radius, location, and color. Working with shapes has some advantages. Shapes are object-oriented, which means they can be resized, selected, or moved just like objects. Shapes are also resolution-independent, so they don't get blurred or "pixeled" when they are resized or distorted.

You can quickly select the entire circle and move it, or you can edit the stroke of the circle to distort its shape. You can also adjust the fill of the circle, which you'll see how to do in this section.

Using Filters with Shapes

You can modify shapes by scaling them, rotating them, using the Transform command, or modifying them with other neat effects. Filters give you a lot of versatility when you work with shapes. You'll often want to use the Free Distort command under the Filters menu.

1. Beginning where our previous example left off, choose the layer with the lavender parallelogram and select Filter Distort > Free Distort. You'll get a dialog box, shown in Figure 8.2, where you can manipulate your shape to whichever new shape you wish. Simply drag the handles in the preview to distort your shape. Click OK.

2. Now rotate the shape. When your mouse pointer is next to a corner, you get a rotate symbol when your shape is selected. Drag the shape in the direction you want and click a bit away from the shape to apply.

Figure 8.2
Distort your shapes using the Free Distort command.

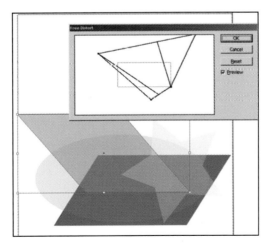

3. Select the layer with your Periwinkle parallelogram (Layer 1). Choose Filter > Distort > Punk and Bloat. In the dialog box, use a –12 setting. Click the Preview button to see what you're doing. Click OK to apply. Experiment with the other filters as well (see the ZigZag filter for example). Look at Figure 8.3 to view the effect of Punk and Bloat.

Part III Creating Graphics

Using Effects with Shapes

You can rasterize any shape using the Rasterize command. This converts the vector shape (or text) to a bitmapped shape, which means it can no longer be resized or adjusted as a vector shape. This means a loss of details when resizing, so make sure you're finished editing the shape before rasterizing. You can also add effects found in programs like Photoshop.

1. First, choose the Lavender Ellipse layer, then select the shape and choose Effect > Texture > Stained Glass. Use the default settings of the filter. Illustrator first rasterizes the shape, and then it applies the filter effect. At this point, if you set the object opacity to 45 percent after rasterizing, Illustrator re-rasterizes your object. This can be a tiresome procedure if you're working with large files, so try to plan ahead. Your artwork should now look like Figure 8.3.

Figure 8.3
Apply effects to your shapes by rasterizing and using the options on the Effects menu.

2. Lock the Ellipse layer for now.

3. Create a new layer called Type above the ellipse layer. Write "Hello" in Arial Black, size 72 points, and use the Purple color as fill. The handles around the type let you stretch and resize the letters. From the Effect menu, choose Distort & Transform > Free Distort.

4. Drag this layer onto the New Layer icon in the Layers Palette to create a duplicate of your type layer. Lock and hide the upper layer and select the lower layer to create a shadow for your type.

5. Fill the type with Faded Blue color and set opacity to 38 percent. Resize the type so it's bigger than your original type. See Figure 8.4.

Figure 8.4
Resize the second type layer to create a "shadow."

Blending Modes

Just as in Photoshop, you have blending modes in the Transparency palette: Multiply, Darken, Lighten, and so on. Use them to create special effects in your artwork when working with objects on separate layers. Blending modes let you differ the ways in which the colors of shapes on a layer blend with the colors of shapes on underlying layers. You can also create Knockouts using Blending modes.

1. To see how Blending modes work, create a new layer and call it Spiral. Use the Spiral Tool and a fill with Pale Light Green color and create a Spiral on your new layer. Test the various Blending modes in the palette, and you'll get results similar to the four examples in Figure 8.5. Also, try to move the layer so you can see what changes are created in your artwork.

Part III Creating Graphics

Figure 8.5
Use Blending modes for effects. The first example (upper left) is with the Normal setting. Below it is Multiply, the upper right shows Screen, and in the bottom right is Overlay.

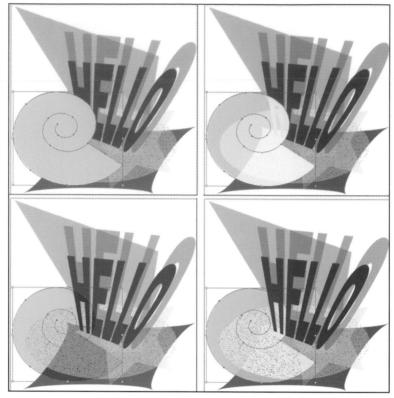

2.   Add a stroke to the spiral by clicking the Stroke icon and the Forest Green color. You can adjust Blending modes for the Shape (Object) as a whole, or you can adjust the Stroke and Fill separately. Either way, be careful what you have selected in your Appearance palette when you make your adjustments.

3.   Select the Star layer. Now, make sure the object is selected in Appearance and choose Multiply from the Transparency palette. Set Opacity up to 100 percent. While you're at it, set the stroke of the Star to orange. Add a Pale Blue stroke to the purple type "Hello" as well. Move the Spiral layer below the two type layers and move both Hello layers a little to the left. Holding down the Ctrl key while clicking the objects will help you select both so you can move them simultaneously.

Paths and Strokes

A path is made up of one or several straight or curved sections that are also called *segments*. A path can be open or closed; an oval is an example of a closed path. At the start and end of each section, you'll see *anchor points*, which you can adjust. You change the shape of a path completely by editing these points. At the anchor points, you have direction points as well, which are used to control the curves of a path. If your path is open, the first and last anchor points are called *endpoints*. These are common terms used in most vector programs.

Constructing a Path

Here is how a path is constructed. In Figure 8.6, No. 1 shows a curved line drawn with the paintbrush. The whole line has every section (segment) selected and moveable. No. 2 shows one section selected (with the Direct Selection Tool), with the direction points and their direction lines visible. No. 3 shows how you can adjust the curve of that segment (section) by moving one of the direction points. No. 4 shows what happens if you click the endpoint (start point) and drag it downwards.

Figure 8.6
This illustration shows how a path is constructed.

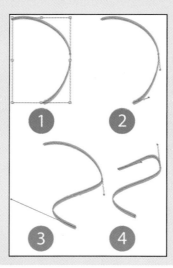

Drawing Freehand Paths

We'll create a few paths for our artwork, which by now looks like Figure 8.7. When you draw freehand paths in Illustrator, you use the Stylus with the Paintbrush Tool or the Pencil Tool.

Figure 8.7
Before we begin adding paths and strokes to our artwork, it should look something like this.

Part III   Creating Graphics

1. Create a new layer and call it Paths. Select the Paintbrush tool. We'll create a question mark for our "Hello" letters.

2. Set the Stroke to a Purple color (6-pt. Flat) and the fill to Pale Orange. Draw the question mark in two parts.

3. Draw a circle to the right of the last letter in "Hello" to create the dot in the question mark. Release and move your tool upward until you're at the top of the letters.

4. Now, draw a shape similar to the first stroke you would make if you were writing the number "2." Stop drawing just above your circle. *Do not release your tool*, but continue to draw a short horizontal line to the left about as wide as the circle, and trace to the left of your first line upward until you're about a half-inch (or a cm) below your starting point.

5. Continue to draw a vertical line up to your starting point to connect.

The idea here is to draw this continuously to get a whole shape, so that when you select the shape you've drawn, it doesn't split up into different shapes. Use the Direct Selection Tool to select anchor points and adjust curves if you're not happy with what you've drawn. The question mark can look like Figure 8.8 when you're finished.

Figure 8.8
Drawing a question
mark with the
Paintbrush Tool.

Creating Brushed Paths

Notice the variation in the width of the stroke in the question mark in Figure 8.8. If you double-click Strokes in the Appearance palette, you'll see the settings for the Calligraphic Brush with Angle, Diameter, and so on. Note that if you have a setting of 6 pt., with 2 pt. in variation, and use the Pressure setting, you'll get variations in your stroke by applying different pressures on your tablet. You can make adjustments to your stroke by adjusting the settings of the brush with your path selected as well.

NOTE

There are several types of vector brushes you can use to create your artwork. Here are some of the major ones:

Illustrator Brushes—Illustrator has four brush types, called the Calligraphic, Scatter, Art, and Pattern brushes.

You can modify them, create new brushes, or import a brush from Brush Libraries.

Note that when you create a brush, that brush is associated only with the file you're currently working on! Each Illustrator file can have a different set of brushes. If you create a set of brushes you use often, you might want to create a customized Illustrator startup file that includes these brushes.

CorelDRAW Brushes—Corel lets you select the Brush button in the Artistic Media Tool palette to create effects for your brush strokes. Choose from twenty presets. You can also save a graphic (or text) object as a brush stroke. Or choose the Calligraphic button to draw calligraphic strokes. The most interesting preset is the option to draw in Pressure-sensitive mode. Open the Curve flyout menu and click the Artistic Media Tool. Select the Pressure button on the Property Bar.

Click the Freehand Smoothing box and move the pop-up slider to select a smoothness setting. On the Property Bar, type a width in the Width box; this represents the curve's maximum width. Just as Illustrator lets you brush with patterns instead of a regular filled stroke, CorelDRAW has the Object Sprayer. Using this, you can draw a series of objects along a curve. The Object Sprayer can be adjusted in regard to rotation, offset, dab settings, and more. As shown in Figure 8.9, you can then select anchor points or directions points and adjust the path sections.

Figure 8.9
This illustration shows the use of the Object Sprayer in CorelDRAW 9, with adjusted path segments.

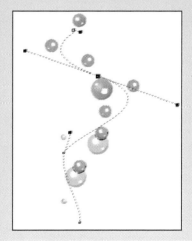

Applying Effects to Strokes

Stroke settings (or attributes) in Illustrator are available only when you *stroke a path.* These settings control whether a line is solid or dashed, thick or thin, and so on. View Stroke settings by choosing Window > Show Stroke. You can apply various effects to strokes.

1. Select our previously drawn question mark, which is two stroked paths. Use the Direct Selection Tool, click the circle and hold Shift down, and click the other shape to select both.

2. Go to Window > Show Styles. In the Styles palette, you can choose between different presets: Some are for strokes, some are fills, and some are both. Select the one called Bizzaro, as shown in Figure 8.10.

Figure 8.10
Use Styles to apply effect to strokes. The Bizzaro effect is shown here on the question mark.

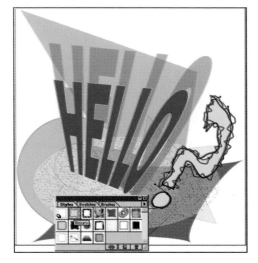

You can edit Styles as well, if you're not happy with how the Style looks by default. You can apply effects to strokes after they're drawn, or you can establish your settings and then draw. You can adjust them by changing the Fill or Stroke settings, or use other techniques. For example, try this:

1. In the Appearances palette, leave the strokes alone but select Fill. Turn to the Swatches palette and click the Swatch called Clown Attack. Then, adjust the blending options in the Transparency palette and choose Multiply. As shown in Figure 8.11, your question mark really looks different!

Figure 8.11
Edit the styles you
apply by changing
blending modes.

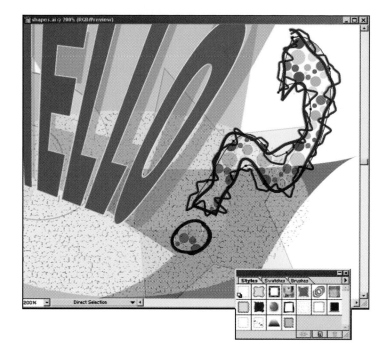

2. Open your Brushes palette and select the Charcoal Brush. This is a brush with
    an effect to the stroke. Because we already have a funny fill selected, we'll
    continue to use that and not make the fill transparent. Now, create a new layer
    called Curve. Select your Pencil Tool and draw, with the Charcoal Brush
    selected, a curve that follows the outline of the green spiral. Start at the "H" in
    "Hello," and draw a downward curve from left to right tracing the green spiral.
    Release it approximately at the question mark. Your artwork should look like
    Figure 8.12, with a half-moon shape filled with Clown Attack.

Figure 8.12
Have fun with your
brushes. You should
adjust effects and
settings to strokes before
you draw anything.

3. Drag the Curve layer above the Spiral layer but below the Type layers. Choose Luminosity as the blending mode. Move the Star layer above the Curve layer. Change blending mode to Overlay, and with the star still selected, click the Fudge Brush in the Brushes palette to add effects to the stroke.

4. For some final touches, we'll look at our purple type. Select the type with the Selection Tool. Go to Effects > Stylize > Outer Glow. Use the default settings in the dialog box and click OK. We're finished, and the colorful result—hey, this is an *example*—can be viewed with sunglasses on in Figure 8.13.

Figure 8.13
Our finished artwork. Note that changing the background color can create huge effects. Try this with a black background and see what happens to the transparency!

Composition with Vector and Bitmap Graphics

Sometimes you'll want to create artwork using several programs, because they will have different options and advantages. Here's an example of how a composition is created with Illustrator 9 and Photoshop 6, using the best of both programs.

Starting in Illustrator 9

 Let's say you have a rough sketch of your artwork, created digitally or on paper and then traced into your favorite program using your tablet. Open this sketch in Illustrator. We want to view the sketch while creating our artwork, so set the Layer opacity of this sketch to 50 percent by opening Layer Options > Dim images to: 50 percent. You can also double-click on the layer to open the Layer Options dialog box. Take a look at Figure 8.14. This is our sketch, dimmed to 50 percent, with a new layer for our drawing plus a few drawn lines. You can download the sketch for free from my Web site, **www.iril.no**, and follow this tutorial.

Figure 8.14
This is our sketch, with a couple of layers and some test strokes to try out the new brushes. The finished image (see Figure 8.25) was created for *LMS Magazine* in Norway to illustrate an article about a severe condition that figuratively "chains" you to the toilet all day.

Part III Creating Graphics

Before we begin drawing, we need a couple of items. First, create two new Calligraphic Brushes to draw with. (If you don't know how, turn to Chapter 11 and read the section entitled, "Creating Brushes.") The new brushes should have diameters of only 2 and 3 points. Then we need a set of six swatch colors. In the Swatches palette, click the arrow and select New Swatch. In the dialog box, enter the following names and RGB values with *Color Type: Process color* selected:

Table 8.1
Colors for example
Swatch

Color Name	R	G	B	
Dark Blue	16	61	125	
Medium Blue	95	136	195	
Dark Moss Green	40	111	20	
Green Bright	65	158	23	
Skintone	250	246	225	
Skintone Pink	251	228	229	

Now we're ready to start!

1. Open the sketch and dim it as described above. Select the Paintbrush Tool and use your two new brushes to create strokes. Double-click the Paintbrush Tool to bring up Paintbrush Tool Preferences, as shown in Figure 8.15. Now, choose the following settings: 4 in Fidelity, 0 in Tolerance, and all three options checked. Fidelity values are the number of pixels (up to 20) the stroke can deviate from the path you draw to produce smooth curves. The higher the value, the smoother the stroke or curve. Experiment with these settings to see what suits your strokes. Smoothness values are the *percentage* stroke (and curve) smoothness.

Figure 8.15
This illustration shows
Paintbrush Tool
Preferences in
Illustrator.

2. Add a new layer called Background for the floor and walls, which is what we'll begin to work on. Lock the sketch layer and any other layers. Create the shape for the floor using the Pen Tool by clicking the "corner points" of the floor, following the sketch. Fill it with our Dark Blue color. Adjust the anchor points of your shape by using the Direct Selection Tool. Create the walls the same way, but these will be separated. On the floor layer, create the right wall and fill it with Medium Blue color.

3. Create a new layer for the left wall.

    Draw the left wall the same way, using Medium Blue color, as shown in Figure 8.16. Select the left wall, go to Filters > Color > Saturate and click the Preview box. Drag the intensity slider to -27 percent to lighten the color. To make sure you don't select the wrong shapes when working, lock the layers that you are not working on. Simply click next to the eye icon to lock layers in the Layers Palette. You can draw and select colors afterwards or select colors first—both fill and stroke—so you're drawing with the correct colors right away.

4. Create a separate layer for tracing the outlines of your sketch. Work with your Paintbrush Tool and draw black strokes (transparent fill) to trace your sketch. This is where our new brushes come in handy.

Figure 8.16
Use Filters > Color >
Saturate to adjust colors
of shapes.

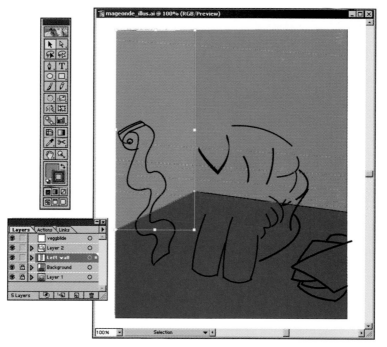

Part III Creating Graphics

5.   Create a layer below the one with the black strokes and name it White. Create shapes with a white fill and a transparent stroke where all the white areas are, such as the straitjacket, toilet roll, and so on. Make sure they fill the areas completely, so you don't get glitches between the shapes and your thin black strokes.

6.   Create a separate layer for the trousers, and use the Dark Green color as fill for the trouser shape, which is also created using the Pen Tool. As shown in Figure 8.17, drawing paths and shapes lets you adjust the path segments at any time. It doesn't matter if you've deselected; just use the selection tools to select the sections of any path. You can also group the paths when you're happy with your work.

Figure 8.17
Working with shapes and strokes lets you adjust the path segments at any time.

7.   With the trousers selected, choose Effects > Stylize > Drop shadows to create a shadow for the trousers. The black "outline" for the trousers is drawn with our 3-pt. brush on the black strokes layer.

8.   Create a new layer for the skin, make shapes, and fill with the pink skin tone. Make a separate layer for the toilet and create shapes filled with the Pale Blue color from the original swatch palette. Use the eye icon frequently to view your sketch when necessary.

9. On your black strokes layer, draw the shoes and fill them with the Dark Moss Green color. Then draw the newspapers on the floor and the toilet roll, plus the lightbulb. The lightbulb is drawn with the Paintbrush using black stroke, white fill, and the 2-pt. brush. The newspapers are drawn the same way, with the 3-pt. brush and object opacity set to 62 percent. We don't want the whole layer set transparent, so make sure the object is selected when adjusting opacity. Go over your artwork and make final adjustments before exporting the file to Photoshop.

Exporting Illustrator Files to Photoshop

As shown in Figure 8.18, this is how the artwork looks before exporting it. Select File > Export. In the dialog box, Choose *Photoshop 5 psd* for file type. Choose RGB for your color model. Resolution should be High (300 dpi) because we'll soon send this off to a printer. Make sure both Anti-alias and Write layers are selected. Check "Include hidden layers" just in case. Click OK.

Figure 8.18
This is how our file looks before leaving "vector world."

Part III Creating Graphics

Finishing Touches in Photoshop

 In Photoshop, you can add loads of effects not available in Illustrator. Note that we're now leaving vector graphics and will be working in bitmapped mode, so make sure you've done any adjustments in Illustrator before exporting the file.

Figure 8.19
This is how our file looks when opened as a bitmapped file in Photoshop.

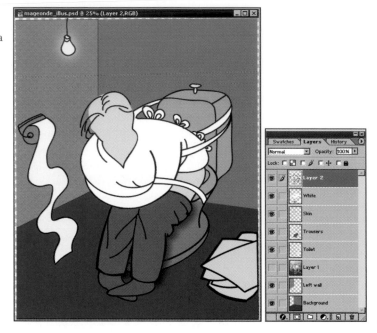

1. Open the saved psd file in Photoshop 6. Note that in Figure 8.19, the white background (canvas from Illustrator) is "missing" and the layers reveal their transparency. Take a look at how the layers themselves are intact.

2. Create a layer to become the background and fill it with white. Merge this layer with the right wall and the floor layer to keep the amount of layers to a minimum.

3. Create light for the lightbulb by making a feathered selection using the Ellipse Tool, while holding down Shift to constrain. Use a feather setting of 12 pixels, and do your work on a separate layer below the lightbulb layer. Fill the feathered selection with white.

4. Create a new layer above it, and with a pale yellow color, use the gradient (radial) from yellow to transparent; drag from the middle of the bulb outward. Release, and it should look like Figure 8.20. If the light becomes too bright, use the layer opacity slider to adjust it until you're satisfied that it looks natural and not like a "drawn shape."

Figure 8.20
Create light with feathered selections and fill them with white and pale yellow.

5. Select the left wall layer and lock its transparency. Use the linear gradient upwards from the bottom, with a Dark Blue color (RGB 9, 38, 79). Drag from the right bottom corner of the wall to the left at a 45-degree angle. Release approximately at the toilet roll.

NOTE

Because we're working in 300 dpi, many of the large brushes in Photoshop seem to have shrunk! Create a new, 600-pixel brush with a spacing of 25 percent, hardness 0, angle 0, and a roundness of 100 percent.

6. Create a Shadow layer beneath the Toilet layer for the wall-and-toilet shadow. Use very little pressure and the Airbrush Tool with black color—and you've set the pressure to Stylus in Brush Options, right?

Part III Creating Graphics

7.   Select the Trousers layer. Choose Filter > Texture > Grain. Set the Intensity to 16, the Contrast to 24, and then choose Contrasty from the Grain Type menu, as shown in Figure 8.21. Add new layers for light and then add shade for the trousers. Use sizes 100 and 200 brushes with both brighter and darker shades of green for adding depth to the trousers. Paint with the Airbrush Tool and have Opacity set to Stylus. More work will be done with the trousers later (as shown in Figure 8.24).

Figure 8.21
Use Filters to add texture to those boring, flat, colored shapes.

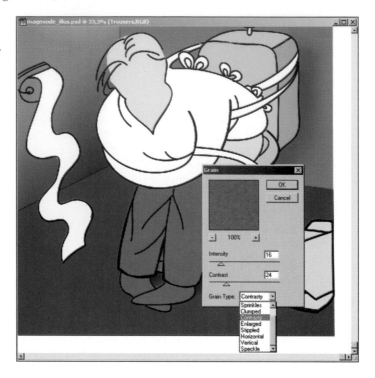

I recommend that you work in 25 percent or 50 percent view (zoom out) most of the time when creating this artwork. Because the file is in 300 dpi, you won't see much of your artwork in 100 percent view.

8.   Create yet another layer called Details. Draw the newspaper details there and, if necessary, zoom in to 100 percent to see the details clearly. Take a look at both trouser and newspaper details in Figure 8.22.

There are big advantages when working with separate layers—and you simply can't have too many layers. Besides, you can always merge them. When working with this type of illustration, create separate layers for light and shade so they're easy to delete or adjust.

Figure 8.22
Zoom in when you
draw your details.

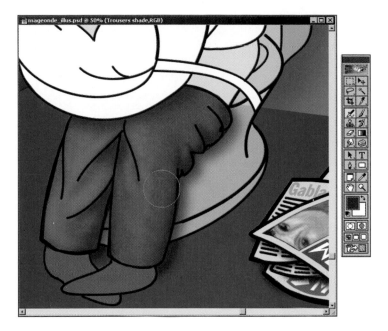

9. On a shade layer, use a large brush and load the *selection* of the White layer to
    create shade for the white areas—but make sure the Shade layer itself is the layer
    you're working on. Draw shades with a dark gray or black color, with the
    pressure controlled by the Stylus and a very light touch. Always use a soft
    medium-sized or large brush for shadows.

10. Switch to the face layer and airbrush in other skin tones that are lighter and
    darker than your main skin tone. This will add depth and shape. Create hair
    with the Paintbrush Tool and some black color, and then make a new layer
    below it and brush in various shades of brown color. Choose a large brush and
    brush in some light (there's light coming from the lightbulb) on the hair. Make
    sure you use darker shades of brown where you want shade to appear in the
    hair, and remember to use darker shades of the skin tones where the light won't
    fall, such as on the sides of the face, under the cheek, on the neck, and so on.
    Remember the light in the eyes—I use white color, a soft Airbrush, and very low
    pressure settings, to be on the safe side. Ordinarily, I'd paint the iris in several
    shades of blue, but because I use large areas of "flat" color in this illustration, I
    must be careful not to overdo details, because this will look weird. As you see in
    Figure 8.23, the eyes are painted with just black and blue (the blue color is RGB:
    68, 102, 205).

Part III Creating Graphics

Figure 8.23
Airbrushing other skin
tones that are lighter
and darker than your
main skin tone will add
depth and shape.

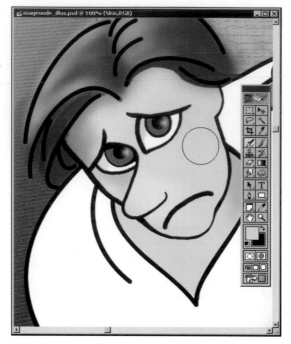

11. Using various filters can enrich the background of this illustration. To get started,
    create rough selections that you can duplicate and to which you can add various
    effects. Use tools like the Smudge Tool to create soft transitions between areas or
    simply blur the transitions using your Pen. Duplicate the Trousers layer yet again
    and use a mask to remove some of the green color. Use the Airbrush Tool and a
    large brush with low pressure when working on masks if you want soft and
    almost invincible transitions between very different areas. If you have the Intuos
    Airbrush, use this device instead of the pen when working with large areas of
    soft colorings. Red and green seldom work well together as colors, but because
    white is added, this combination looks like some of the floor is reflected on the
    trouser leg. The effect is enhanced compared to "real life," because even though
    colors on surfaces will reflect off each other, this is too much—nevertheless, the
    result is rather nice. See Figure 8.24.

Figure 8.24
Make duplicates of your layers to create almost abstract "color reflections" on surfaces (like these trousers) by removing some of the color so that the colors on the layers beneath become visible.

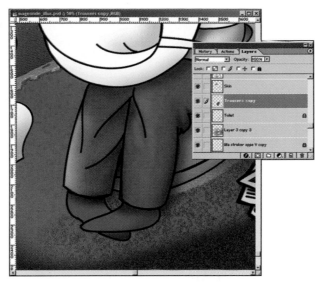

12. Finally, you'll work some more on the background. You'll use filters and effects such as Ink outlines, Noise, Spatter, and Texture, which enable you to make fast and easy effects. Remember to use the History palette to go back to previous versions of your artwork if you feel you're going down the wrong path. Or, as I've said before, you can't have too many layers. Duplicate layers and add effects, then simply delete the layer if you're not happy with the result. Use Opacity settings to control transparency, and take advantage of Blending modes if you want an effect to either highlight or darken large areas. Use your Pen plus Photoshop's Dodge and Burn tools to work with smaller areas. Because this illustration is going to a printer, the last thing on our agenda is to convert the file to CMYK mode. See Figure 8.25 for the finished artwork.

Figure 8.25
The final result with all its layers. Merge layers only when you're absolutely sure you're satisfied.

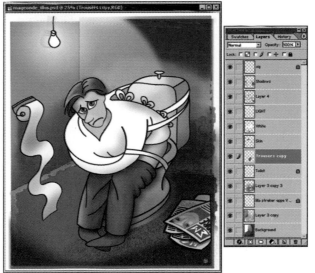

Part III   Creating Graphics

Clip Art and Icons

When working on a computer, you can't escape icons and clip art images. Icons are all over your desktop, and clip art comes bundled with many programs to help you get started with presentations. There will be times when you're fed up with both and want to create or manipulate them yourself. This is exactly what we'll do in this section.

Working with Icons

An icon is defined as a small picture that represents either a program or even a function within a program. Some examples are the icons in your browser. On your desktop, you click on icons to start programs. Some icons are single files, while others are enclosed within program files such as DLLs on a PC. Icon editors can open BMP files and also read (and save) many common image formats apart from ICO (see Note below) formats, including JPEG, GIF, and TIFF, just to mention a few. You can use special Icon Editors to create icons, but you can also create icons in other applications. Note that you have to use a program that lets you save to the ICO format or at least as a BMP file.

NOTE
When working with icons in Windows, you'll come across two file extensions that probably are unfamiliar to you—.ICL and .ICO.

.ICL—This is an Icon Library. Icon Libraries are used to store several icons as a group. ICL files have the same format as many of the DLL files in Windows.

.ICO—This file contains a Windows icon image. Windows icons are usually 16 × 16, 32 × 32, or 48 × 48 pixels in size. They are created with the Windows color palette. See Figure 8.26.

Figure 8.26
Some editors come with icon libraries, like IconForge.

Creating Icons for Windows

Icons often come in one of the standard (Windows) sizes, such as formats of 32 × 32 pixels. This is the size of your desktop icons. We'll start by manipulating a familiar Windows icon for practice. Open the Explorer icon in your icon editor program. Browse to your Windows folder (called Winnt in Windows 2000) and click *explorer.exe*. This program file has the icon built in. Save the file under a different name, such as "myicon.ico," because you don't want to destroy the original icon. See Figure 8.27.

Figure 8.27
This is a typical icon editor—Icon Collector Graphics Editor, a shareware program. If you use an existing icon file, remember to rename the file before you start working on it.

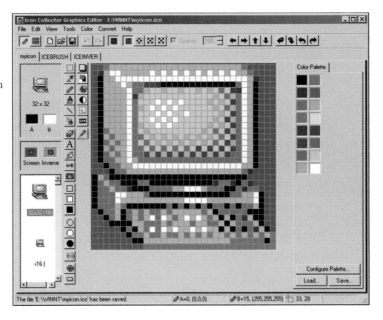

As you can see from Figure 8.27, you have many of the same tools as in other paint programs. You have the Bucket for filling, Eraser, Pencils, and so on. Drag Pencils to cover several pixels (seen as squares) at once or click single pixels to fill them in one at a time. Now, convert your icon to 256 colors (it is currently only 16 colors), because we want a more colorful Explorer icon! Working with a tablet when creating icons doesn't let you take advantage of pressure-sensitive tools—because the programs don't support pressure sensitivity—but the tablet is great for precision when you want to work on single pixels. Clicking and painting with a Pen beats using a mouse on any given day.

Start with the easy parts, such as changing large areas. Zoom in if you have problems seeing (or clicking) single pixels. Work with the Line Tool to create straight lines or click-and-drag with a Pencil or Brush Tool to color more pixels simultaneously.

Part III Creating Graphics

Icon editors don't grasp the concept of anti-aliasing, so if you want shades or gradients, you have to use slightly darker or brighter colors and make a pattern by filling every other pixel. Look at Figure 8.28 and note the upper right corner. It is filled in this fashion, with two different shades of blue. When you're happy with your "creation," save the file as a BMP file. That's not really a *proper* icon file, but it' sufficient for display on your desktop. On your PC desktop, create a new shortcut, and in the dialog box, click Change Icon and browse to your BMP file. Use it for your favorite program or file. Now see Figure 8.29.

Figure 8.28
This illustration shows how to create your own personal Explorer icon. You guessed it—it's a penguin!

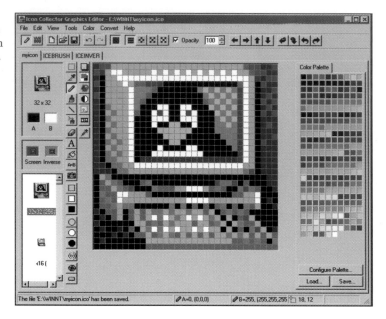

Figure 8.29
This figure shows both icons side by side on the desktop.

NOTE

There are numerous icon editors out there, almost too many from which to select just one. Your best bet is to go to a shareware site like Tucows (**www.tucows.com**) or to DaveCentral (**www.davecentral.com**). Look in the Icon Editors folder, download evaluation versions, and try them yourself. What you're looking for is a program with a friendly interface that is intuitive to use. The two editors used in this section are randomly chosen, because, I have to admit, I have not tried every single one of the 135 or so editors out there. Try to pick an editor that has a library of icons. It's far easier to start manipulating existing icons than learning from scratch. You can also download icon archives from all over the Internet until your ISP sends you flowers for being such a great customer.

Icons in Photoshop

 If the thought of downloading icon editors seems like a bad idea at first, try creating an icon in Adobe Photoshop 6. Adobe would probably faint if they knew we were using their expensive software for such a task, but then again, it's fun to do something different.

Create a file of 72 dpi in RGB mode that measures 32 × 32 pixels. Open Preferences > Guides and Grid. Set grid to 1 pixel and afterwards, on the View menu, select Show Grid. You now have a file divided into 32 × 32 squares, each representing a pixel. Zoom in to 1200 percent or so. That's right, 1200 percent. Note that you can use programs other than Photoshop, as long as you can divide a grid to suit your preferences.

Open the Swatch with 256 Web colors and use them when drawing your icon. Also set Snap to Grid in View preferences when working with large areas. Use the Pencil Tool, because it's perfect for the job. Set Brush Dynamics to Off. Use the Selection tools, such as the Rectangle, to select and fill numerous pixels. Turn off Snap to Grid when working on single pixels; the pen is precise enough and you won't draw wide of the mark if your hand is steady. Save your file as a BMP when you are finished. You can open it later with an icon editor and save it as an ICO file if necessary. See Figure 8.30.

Figure 8.30
You can also create icons in Photoshop with a couple of adjustments to the preferences.

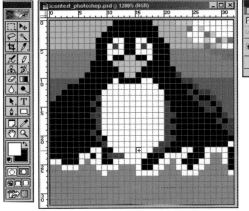

Using Clip Art

 Most computer artists look for a barf bag when they hear the words "clip art." Many vendors hand out hundreds of clip art images with their programs so that the end user can easily create simple presentations in a jiffy without being able to draw at all. What are those loathed things? "Clip art" is a term for illustrations that can be inserted into many types of documents, such as Microsoft Word or PowerPoint files. They can be of various file formats. Many clip art packages are available; Corel is famous for supplying thousands of clip art images with its applications. These packages are often sorted into themes, such as office-related illustrations, everyday objects, or just fun images. The packages often come with a clip

Part III Creating Graphics

art viewer of some sort, so you can browse through, and search, the collections. You can open and edit clip art in various programs when they are available as single files, or you can use Copy and Paste techniques to get to them.

PowerPoint, one of the programs in Microsoft Office 2000, comes with a lot of clip art sorted into different categories. These are built into PowerPoint, so you have to open PowerPoint to view them. We'll look at a very simple way to edit a piece of clip art to suit your presentation.

1.   To begin editing, open an existing PowerPoint file or create a presentation. Click Insert > Picture and choose Clip art to get the dialog box shown in Figure 8.31. Select a category and browse through until you find a cool clip art image. You can convert it while in PowerPoint or paste it into a drawing program like CorelDRAW. Simply select your image and use Ctrl+C (Command+C) to copy it to the clipboard.

Figure 8.31
This is a typical clip art dialog box, shown here from PowerPoint.

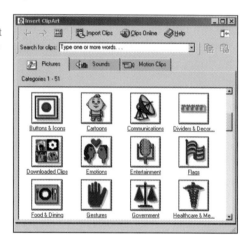

2.   Now, open CorelDRAW. Create a new file and use Ctrl+P (Command+P) to paste your clip art. When pasted into CorelDRAW, as shown in Figure 8.32, you can resize or do other adjustments to your image. You can even ungroup it so you can select its various components and change the separate shapes and strokes. You can also change colors, the behavior of its strokes, and so on.

3.   Use the Strokes palette in CorelDRAW to apply various effects and colors to the image. You can change the color of an applied stroke simply by selecting it and then selecting the color you want. Fill it with different colors, add effects to it, save it, and place a whole new clip art image in your presentation when you're done! The point of this procedure is that you can customize existing images to suit your presentations colors. Who says a frog has to be green?

Figures 8.32
By pasting your clip art images into programs like CorelDRAW, you can manipulate them.

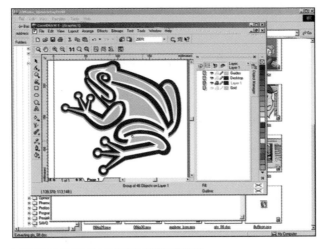

TIP

Clip art images are universally disdained because, if you use them as they are, chances are many people have seen them already. The same applies to other "helpful" stuff like FrontPage themes and PowerPoint presentations. That is a disadvantage if you're trying to create a unique presentation at work. You've probably seen a lot of clip art pieces at the office, and they're widely used for in-house papers like invitations, reports, and other documents. Use clip art for parties, letterhead, and informal papers. Even though many packages have great borders and detailed illustrations that would take you hours to draw yourself, try to give the images your personal touch anyway.

Part III Creating Graphics

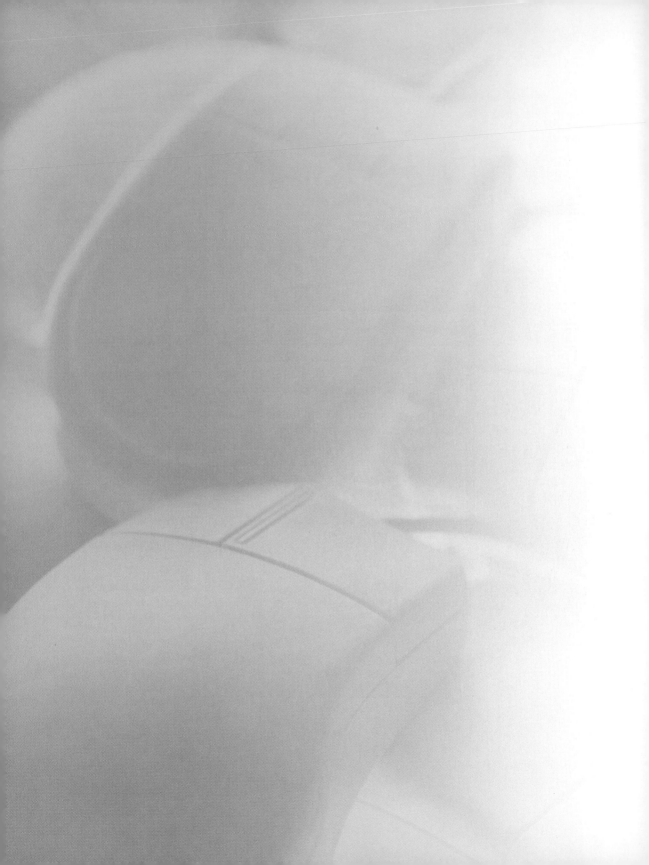

9
Creating Web Graphics

Everybody complains the Internet is slow. True, some people have slow dial-up connections, but the biggest problem is the inconsiderate use of heavy graphics by Web designers. In this chapter, we'll create professional-looking Web graphics that both look nice and download fast. In this chapter, you'll discover:

▶ The difference between GIFs and JPEGs and how to use them correctly

▶ How to create transparent GIFs

▶ Why type is a challenge, and how to use type on Web pages

▶ How to create type effects

▶ Techniques to optimize Web graphics for fast downloads

After finishing this chapter, you'll be confident working with type. We'll cover the basics, making simple type effects and utilizing type on Web pages. Web-optimized graphics—including buttons, animation, and effects—will finish out this chapter.

File Formats and Image Compression

To create good Web graphics, there are some basic techniques and rules that apply: You need to balance image resolution with download speed (GIFs and JPEGs), you need to understand how your browser works, and you need to be concerned about transparency. You also need to understand screen and print considerations for your images, and, lastly, you need to understand how colors behave on the Web.

GIFs or JPEGs?

Which is the best file format for images on the Web—GIF or JPEG? You, as the Web designer, need to balance resolution and speed considerations. First, understand the type of image you're working with. Photos and other continuous-tone graphics with colors that blend into one another, or that have shadows and/or gradients, are better saved as JPEGs. If your image has areas of flat color, it will compress better as a GIF, both from the aspect of file size and appearance. You can *interlace* a GIF, which is an advantage on the Web for those occasions where you can't avoid using a large illustration. Interlaced GIFs appear first with poor resolution and then gradually improve until the entire image has been loaded into the browser. You get a good idea of what the picture looks like while waiting, which is great when you're downloading large images from the Web. Note that you don't always see this effect on the Web, though, because for you to notice this, the GIFs must be extremely large in file size or the Internet speed very slow.

Another plus for the GIF is that it can be saved as transparent, which means that you can place a graphic without clear (rectangular) edges against the background of your Web page. Note that this method doesn't do much to the file size, but it helps you create better design solutions. Finally, GIFs can be animated, which we'll take a brief look at later in this chapter. In the examples below, you can study some of the differences between GIFs and JPEGs, to see what works in both formats when the images are compressed.

The Original Test File

Figure 9.1 is our original test file of six squares. The first set has clean, flat-colored squares that will get best results saved as GIF files. The second set has been embellished with an Airbrush, a Pen and the Smudge Tool, various brushes, and Photoshop's Dodge and Burn tools. Using these tools creates transitions between the colors that will give us trouble when saving them as GIFs. There's also a layer shadow added.

Figure 9.1
The first set of squares is clean, but the second set has numerous enhancements.

Figure 9.2 shows the test file saved as three various GIFs. The first two examples are with Diffusion dither at 100 percent, saved as 256 colors, and as 32 colors. Note the amount of dithering—visible as the coarse dots—in the lower set of squares. The example to the right is saved at 256 colors but without dithering, which makes the transitions between the colors even more uneven. Notice how the example in the middle has a nice set of squares at the top; this will also have the smallest file size because we used only 32 of the 256 colors available in the palette. When you save graphics for the Web, you can choose the amount of color from a drop-down menu—see "Exporting Web Graphics" later in this chapter.

Figure 9.2
Notice the imperfections
in the enhanced
squares.

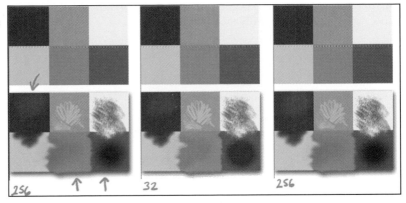

Now, in Figure 9.3, our squares are saved as JPEGs, at compression rates of Medium, High and Maximum. (Forget about saving at the Low setting, because it will rarely be acceptable.) Notice how the Medium setting is not good enough in either set of squares. The High setting is good for the lower set of squares, but we have to use Maximum to get the clean, flat-colored squares to appear correctly—and then we're at file sizes considerably higher than the GIF. See Figure 9.3.

Figure 9.3
These squares were
saved as JPEGs at
settings of Medium,
High, and Maximum.

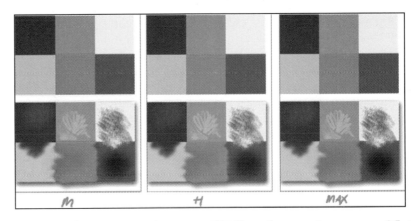

As we've learned from the examples, save your images as GIF files when you have areas of flat color, and save your images as JPEGs if you have areas that are smudged, that contain gradients and areas of continuous tone, or other types of color detail. When you export as GIF or JPEG, try out the various settings to get a result that is acceptable both in file size and quality. When you are exporting from Photoshop 6, Elements, or ImageReady, the preview tells you both file size and how it looks, so you can switch between the various modes until you're happy with the result.

When creating Web pages, remember you can fill tables and cells with color. So, crop your images as much as possible and paste them into the cells instead of creating graphics with vast one-colored areas. This often results in your having to work harder at the Web page design, but it saves considerable download time.

Table 9.1 compares characteristics of GIF and JEPG files.

Part III Creating Graphics

Table 9.1
Compares some characteristics of GIF and JPEG files

| GIF | | JPEG | |
Pros	*Cons*	*Pros*	*Cons*
Can be animated	Shadows and gradients look horrible	Great for photographs	Can't be animated
Can be transparent	Often poor results with pictures of people or other photographs	Best choice to display gradients and shadows	Can't be transparent
Downloads gradually if interlaced	Dithers easily when exporting		Does not download gradually, but linearly
Can be matted in transparent areas		Can be matted in transparent areas	

Application and Browser Dithering

Those "dots" of color you sometimes see in a GIF, as in Figure 9.2, are the results of a problem called *dithering*. *Application dithering* creates two pixels of different colors to simulate a third color. For example, a dark green color and a yellow color can dither to produce a brighter green color. Dithering makes your file size a bit bigger, so try out dithering settings when exporting your graphics. *Browser dithering* happens because the browser attempts to simulate colors in the graphics that it doesn't actually have in its own color palette, so the browser fails to display the colors properly. This is clearly seen in Figure 9.4, which is a Web page that contains many difficult graphics. This page might not look difficult at first glance, but there are many images and photo collages created with a tablet that naturally include several transitions and gradient masks. These masks were created freehand, using the Airbrush tools and the Intuos tablet and Pen. Figure 9.5 shows the improved image.

Figure 9.4
A Web page displayed at a setting of 256 colors, with dithering occurring in both JPEG and GIF images.

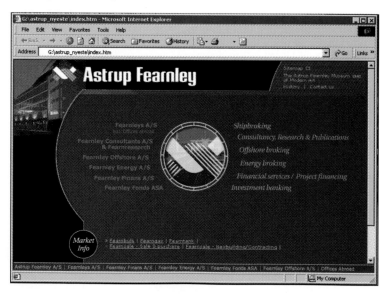

Figure 9.5
The same Web page at a color depth of 32—a remarkable improvement!

Transparency

How do I create a transparent graphic? This is one of the most frequently asked questions in newsgroups and other forums from people new to Web graphic creation. Transparency makes it possible for the designer to place a graphic without clear (rectangular) edges against the Web page background. Background transparency preserves the transparent pixels in the original image. These pixels "blend" with the Web page background in the browser. You can create transparent GIFs, but not transparent JPEGs.

With JPEGs, you need to fill your background with the same color as on your Web page. You create your transparent GIF in applications like Photoshop or ImageReady and *hide the background layer*, as shown in Figure 9.6, before exporting—it's that easy. Select the background color before you export, type in the values in the Export dialog box, and check off for transparency. Beware that if you have used hand-drawn masks on your graphics, you can get into trouble when exporting as transparent if you haven't been careful enough to remove every pixel in the transparent areas. Hide the background layer (or change its color) when working with masks so you can view any mistakes.

Background matting is another technique used to achieve "transparency," or, rather, to blend the image into a colored background. Background matting works by *filling* the transparent pixels in an image with a color you choose to match the Web page background where the image will be placed. Of course, you must have decided the color of the Web page background first. Background matting works properly only if the Web page is a solid color, otherwise, this technique would have a weird effect on a multi-colored background. Take a look at Figure 9.6 to see the transparent graphic on a Web page with a dark blue table background. You can't see where the graphic ends and the background begins, because the color used is exactly the same.

Part III Creating Graphics

Figure 9.6
This is our GIF inserted
into a Web page table
with the same
background color as in
the GIF.

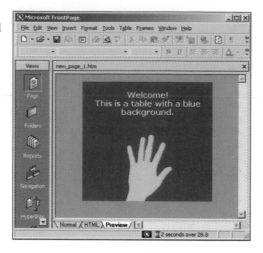

TIP

A quick way to select the background color for matting in Photoshop is to
use the Eyedropper Tool (Color Picker) and copy the Hex value in the color
palette dialog box, as shown in Figure 9.7. Paste the six-digit Hex value into
the dialog box for matting during Web export.

Figure 9.7
Copy the hex value
circles with blue (left),
hide the dark blue
background, then Save
for Web (Photoshop),
and, finally, paste into
the matting dialog box
(right) later when
exporting. Notice that
transparency is selected.

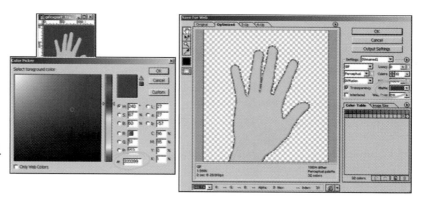

Anti-aliasing visually smoothes out the edges of images by mixing the color of the edge with the
color of the background, and this demands several shades of the same color. If you create a GIF
with anti-aliased edges against a transparent background, you often get unwanted results. You'll
see anti-aliased edges in your work, because this is a natural occurrence when drawing graphics
or creating photomontages. Not only is there a risk of dithering, but often fringes will be visible.

Remember that only **one** individual color will be transparent when you export, so if you have
several shades of blue in the background, the other shades will still be visible. This causes that
ugly fringe around your image. Pick your Web page background color first and then use that

same color for the background in your GIF. The anti-aliasing will be created with the correct color, and the fringe will blend in with the background color. This does not work if you have an image in your background containing several colors; you can still see the fringe in Figure 9.8. Type in graphics can be a challenge as well because of anti-aliasing, which we'll take a closer look at in the next section.

Figure 9.8
This is our GIF inserted into a Web page table with an image in the background. Notice the thin blue fringe.

Screen and Print Considerations

When you create Web graphics, you need to use a setting of only 72 dpi when you create your files. PC monitors in general have a limit of 72 dpi, so there's no reason to make 300-dpi graphics. Monitor resolution determines the display size of an image. When importing a vector file, open it in 72 dpi at the size you want, so you don't need to resize it as a bitmapped image. Resizing bitmaps will always create some loss of detail that we want to avoid, especially because we're going to compress the graphics for the Web as well. But if you're creating graphics for both the Web and for print, you need to consider the resolution more carefully. You can convert a 300-dpi graphic to 72 dpi with better results than you would get by converting a 72-dpi graphic to 300 dpi. When delivering 300 dpi (or better) graphics for print, the layout people can always scale your graphics to 120 percent without visible loss of detail. Try this with a 72-dpi graphic and they will object and call you funny names—not to mention insist you deliver a higher resolution graphic.

NOTE

LPI (lines per inch) is used for printing, where dots are arranged in lines. The LPI value refers to the number of lines, so the higher number, the smoother and better printed graphic. **DPI** (dots per inch) refers to the actual number of dots per inch that can be viewed on a monitor. DPI is also used in print. PPI (pixels per inch) describes screen resolution. A 800 × 600 setting is capable of displaying 800 distinct dots on each of 600 lines. Most modern monitors can display at least 1024 by 768 pixels.

A graphic on a Web page with dimensions of 100 × 100 pixels will be the same viewable size on a Web page when saved with various resolutions. The graphic will download more slowly if you save it at 150 dpi, but it will be the same size and not look any better since your monitor is at 72 dpi. But when you print these graphics, you will notice the difference in quality and resolutions.

You will also need to consider your use of color modes. The screen uses RGB (red-green-blue), and print uses CMYK (cyan-magenta-yellow-kohl). You can read more about color modes in Chapter 6.

Part III   Creating Graphics

Some colors will not convert very well between the two color formats. You need to save two versions of your original, which is adjusted individually for each use. I often work in RGB, and I save a copy in CMYK mode, which I compare to the RGB file. I almost always have to adjust the CMYK color saturation, because the colors often get too bland. I have to remember to calibrate my monitor as well. The correct color workspace is an absolute necessity when adjusting RGB and CMYK. The settings should be saved so you can easily move between the two at a later time.

The Web Color Palette

The more colors your graphic has, the more file space the color information will take up. The color information is represented as bit depth or the actual number of colors. GIFs have a limit of 256 colors, which is also known as 8-bit color. You want the color depth as low as possible, but without losing any detail in your graphics or getting ugly dithering. By working only with Web-safe colors, you can be sure that the graphics you create for the Web will not dither on a computer with the display set to 256 colors. Use as few colors as possible when creating graphics so you get the smallest file sizes when exporting. Remember that adding shades to an object or type creates more colors—not just the black shade—because of color blending. See Figure 9.9.

Figure 9.9
The Web color swatch
in Photoshop 6.0 is
available from the
Swatches palette drop-
down menu. Just click
the arrow in the
Swatches palette.

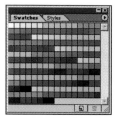

Working with Type

Type is a nightmare for Web pages and has thrown many people with backgrounds in desktop publishing into hair-ripping frustration. Let's have a brief walkthrough of the fonts and their uses, and see which ones you should use. We'll start with some type basics and finish this section with some examples.

Type Basics

The term *font* is widely misused instead of *typeface*. A typeface consists of the letters, symbols, and numbers that make up a *design* of type. A typeface design is basically a style of print. An original typeface design might be compared to an original song that uses a set series of notes to form a unique tune. Examples of typefaces are Helvetica, Gill Sans, and Times Roman. Times New Roman Bold set in 10 pt is a *font*.

A *font family* is a group of fonts related to each other, originating from the same typeface, such as Arial Narrow and Arial Black. In traditional typography, typefaces are classified based on design characteristics, such as serif or sans serif, and their history. Examples are Gothic, Roman, Sans-serif (or Grotesque), English, and Decorated

Popular typefaces for Web use include Arial, Times New Roman, and Verdana.

Type: A Mini-Dictionary

Alignment—The positioning of text, as in left, right or centered.

Face—One of the styles in a family of faces. Example: The black style of the Arial family is a face.

Family—Also called font family. A collection of faces designed to be used together, such as Arial regular, Arial Italic, Arial Black and so on.

Font—One weight, width, and style of a *typeface*. Arial Black 24 pt is a font. So is Arial Narrow 12 pt.

Point—Unit of measure in typography. There are 72 points to an inch.

Style—Variations of a face are also called style, such as bold or narrow.

Typeface—The letters, symbols, and numbers that make up a *design* of type. A typeface design might be compared to an original song that uses a set series of notes to form a unique tune. Examples: Helvetica, Gill Sans, Times Roman.

TrueType and PostScript

TrueType (bitmapped fonts) and PostScript (vector fonts) have technical differences (see note) and your computer manages them differently. Bitmapped fonts represent each character as a grid of pixels. It is difficult to change the size, shape, or resolution of a bitmapped character without significant loss of quality, just as with bitmapped images. Outline (vector) fonts have each character drawn mathematically as a series of lines and curves. When a character from an outline font is printed, it must be rasterized into a bitmap. This is the same rasterization as for any vector turned into a bitmap.

If you work with type in programs like Adobe Illustrator and save it as vectors, you can scale it later and still keep it sharp. If you save it as bitmapped files, you have *rasterized* it. All output of a display screen or printer is in raster (bitmap) format. You have to rasterize vector graphics (and fonts) before printing them. You should stay with the size you rasterize in, or you will get jagged lines if you enlarge (or scale) your bitmapped (rasterized) type elements later on. Keep this in mind if you create graphics with type that might be used for print and not just for the Web.

Part III Creating Graphics

NOTE

The difference between TrueType and PostScript fonts is in the "mathematics" used to describe curves. TrueType rasterizing is built into both Mac and Windows operating systems nowadays. Scaling PostScript fonts requires Adobe Type Manager software to handle rasterizing on-screen, and this software also rasterizes the fonts for non-PostScript printers. TrueType fonts have all the data in a single file, while PostScript fonts require two separate files: one for metrics data like character width and one for the character outlines.

Many software packages include thousands of TrueType fonts, and most are converted Type1 (vector) fonts. The cheapest font collections often include poor quality fonts, with converted Type1 fonts that weren't any good to begin with. Many TrueType fonts are "standalone" fonts, meaning they don't belong to a font family but exist just in one version. An example of this are the many dingbat and symbol fonts. Some PostScript devices, such as imagesetters, have problems with TrueType fonts in general. As a general rule, use Type1 fonts when working with print, unless you want the printers to call you funny names.

Serif and Sans-serif Fonts

A *serif* font has various decorative elements, or wedges, added to the basic character forms. A serif is the term for the tiny line or wedge added as decoration to the basic form of a character. You'll see examples of serifs in Figure 9.10. Serif fonts are easy to read on paper, because serifs help the reader follow the lines of text—that is why they're used in newspapers, books, and magazines. Examples of serif typefaces are Times, Garamond, Caslon, and Bodoni. This book is printed in Melior, a serif typeface.

A *sans-serif* font is made up of simple lines; it's plain to look at and has no decoration on the characters. It's used for headlines, road signs, posters, and other jobs that demand easy-to-read fonts. Some examples of sans-serif typefaces are Verdana, Arial, Helvetica, Gill Sans, and Futura. *Sans* is a French word that means "without," so a translation of "sans serif" means a font "without serifs." Sans-serif fonts are *the best choices* for readability on screens and displays such as your monitor because they are less tiring on your eyes than serif fonts. Far too many Web pages use serif fonts like Times New Roman Regular or Bold. They should instead use a sans-serif typeface like Verdana. See Figure 9.10.

Figure 9.10
Serifs are the small decorative lines added to a character; here some are marked with red circles. The typeface is ITC New Baskerville.

TIP

Not only is the font you use vital for good readability, but the column widths
are equally as important. Columns more than 300 pixels wide should be
avoided. There's a reason why newspaper columns are narrow—they're easier
to read that way. The wider the columns, the more problems you'll have
following a line of text.

Anti-aliasing

Many applications now have anti-aliasing of type by default for screen display. If you are using
programs like Adobe Photoshop to create text, some fonts will look better with anti-aliasing
turned off at sizes below 10 points. In Photoshop 6, choose "none" from the drop-down instead
of "Crisp" for sans-serif fonts below 10 points and see how they look. The typefaces Pixel and
Sevenet in Figure 9.11 were created for small sizes. These faces look horrible when used in
larger sizes but are better for very small Web page graphics.

Figure 9.11
Pixel classic and
Sevenet, custom-made
faces for the Web, must
be used small and with
anti-aliasing turned off
for good results. Shown
here are sizes 10, 8, and
6 points.

Drawing Letters

Instead of using a font that looks like handwriting, you can write the letters yourself when
creating titles or small amounts of text. Use the Paintbrush Tool in Photoshop or similar
programs and the Pen, and then select a hard and round brush of 2 or 3 pixels. Set Brush
Dynamics to stylus in size, but set the opacity to Off unless you want color variations in your
characters. This depends on what kind of ink you're trying to simulate. In the example in Figure
9.12, I used solid black, writing on what seems to be a Polaroid photo. (Of course, it's not.) I've
made a white frame, pasted the image into the selection of the frame, and added shade. If you
use a font instead, the viewer will see the mechanical uniformity of the characters and not the
small uneven differences that real handwriting has.

Part III Creating Graphics

Figure 9.12
Draw letters yourself to create real-life effects. If your handwriting is a little ugly or uneven, it just adds character to the natural look.

TIP
If your hand-drawn lettering is not solid enough with ink, I have a trick that will work for any program with layers. It's really simple: Duplicate your layer with the writing and merge the two layers! You'll see that the lettering instantly gets twice as dense.

Simple Type Effects

There are hundreds of simple ways to make your type stand out. For instance, outlines provide one of the fastest ways to add life and style to text. Even a simple 1-pixel line around your characters will make them stand out from other graphics and add a crisp look, especially with noisy backgrounds. Read on for more of these tips and tricks.

Type in Illustrator and Photoshop

With vector programs like Illustrator, you can also add a twist to your type. Draw a freehand path with your Pen and the Pencil Tool and type text at the path, as shown in Figure 9.13. Use a bold sans-serif face; I've used Frutiger. You can scale it, fill it, add effects to it, draw textures, and so on. You can also paste images into your type using masks, as shown in Figures 4.20 to 4.27 in Chapter 4.

Figure 9.13
This figure shows type on a path in Illustrator with a drop shadow added.

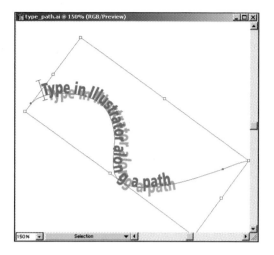

Photoshop 6 has some exciting features regarding type if you want to use fonts and not draw the letters yourself. I haven't found a text-to-path trick yet, but there's plenty of other stuff to be excited about—like converting type to shapes. When you convert type to shapes, a layer with a vector-based clipping path replaces the type. You can edit the layer clipping path and apply styles to the layer, but as soon as you have converted it, you can't edit the characters as text any more. In Figure 9.14, I've used the Nueva face in brown on an apricot background (RGB 255, 204, 153). On the Layer menu, choose Type > Convert to Shape.

Figure 9.14
This illustration shows type converted to shapes in Photoshop 6.

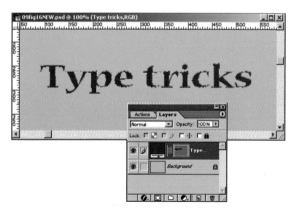

For example, you can now paint the border of the path with a stroke, as shown in Figure 9.15. In the Paths palette, click the Selection icon to load it as a selection. In this palette, you can create several paths to work with, based on your layer path. Make a new layer, choose Edit > Stroke, and enter the values. I used white color at 2 points, set outside the selection.

Figure 9.15
You can easily stroke the path to create a perfect outline. Note the clipping path.

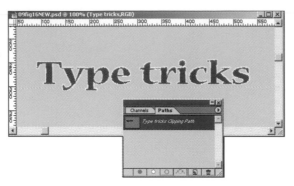

You can also fill the paths you create in the Paths palette with color or patterns, or you can disable the path for other quick results, as in Figure 9.16. Right-click over the layer path and choose disable. You can enable it again at any time.

Figure 9.16
Disabling the path makes just the outline visible and does surprising stuff to your colors.

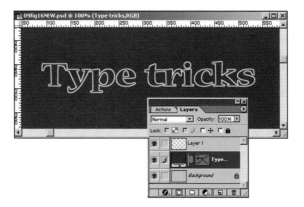

Because the shape (our previous type) and the outline are on different layers, you can paint effects on layers in between or even adjust them separately. Working on countless layers gives you more options than doing everything on one. You can rasterize your shape to create additional effects. It's a good idea to save a path in your paths palette before doing this. You can use Blending modes to adjust the layer and warp effects to distort type in the shape of, for example, an arc or a wave. Remember you need to work with it as a type element to warp, because warping shapes isn't possible. While it's a type element, you can still edit it. Look at Figure 9.17 to see a warped effect for type. I've applied the Outer Glow effect with the following settings: Opacity, 75 percent; Noise, 78 percent; Spread, 16 percent; and Size, 13 pixels. Blending mode is set to Multiply. I have a layer below my warped type where I've airbrushed in a pattern to create a better background for the type.

Figure 9.17
You have almost unlimited possibilities using combinations of type, shapes, warp effects, and so on.

Icy Type

You can easily create cool effects in a flash, like icy type. This kind of effect should be used with a sans-serif typeface, and preferably with a bold font. In this example, I've used the TrueType font Tahoma Bold 30 pt.

Start with a dark blue or black background in Photoshop. (I used RGB 5, 58, 77.) Type your letters in white, at your preferred size (in this case, 30 points). On the Image menu, choose Rotate Canvas > 90 degrees Clockwise. On the Filter menu, choose Stylize > Wind. You'll be asked to rasterize the type, which is all right as long as you have chosen the right size and don't need to resize later. Select "from the right" in the Wind dialog box. Rotate the canvas back (90 degrees counter-clockwise) and you have the text in Figure 9.18. Lock transparency on your rasterized text layer, and fill it with a pale blue color like RGB 187, 196, 240. Then choose Edit > Stroke and select white as the Stroke color. Use settings of 1 or 2 pixels, with the location set to Center. You now have a white outline on your letters.

Figure 9.18
You now have icy type, but we're not finished yet.

Part III Creating Graphics

Copy this layer by dragging it onto the New Layer icon. Select the top layer of the two layers you now have. Use the Wind filter again, and select wind from the right. This will look weird and pixelated, because the transparency is locked. Choose Filter > Blur > Motion Blur and a 90-degree angle, 10 pixels' distance. This smoothes out the blue and white colors, which makes the text more naturally icy than in many other "ice text" tutorials I've seen. The finished result is shown in Figure 9.19. If you want to use this on a Web page, you have to save it as a JPEG because of the blended colors of blue and white.

Figure 9.19
Just looking at this type gives me the shivers!

Type on Web Pages

With the introduction of the <font face> tag in HTML, we could specify what font the browser should display. Unfortunately, fonts on the Web aren't that simple. The font you specify has to be installed on the viewer's system for it to be displayed. If you use a non-standard font, chances are there will be plenty of viewers who don't have that font. Say you use a TrueType font like Comic. Another viewer doesn't have this font, and what happens is that the browser replaces the font with a standard Web font based on the browser settings. In other words, you don't have control over how the Web page looks on other computers when you use non-standard fonts. The latest browser versions come with a set of fonts, which is why we have the term "Web safe fonts." This means that everyone who has downloaded Microsoft's Internet Explorer 5.5 browser has the same fonts.

Recommended Fonts

Sans-serif fonts are the best choice for text on Web pages. Italic fonts fight against the constraints of the square pixel grid of a computer screen and should be avoided if possible. And, if you insist on using serif typefaces, try fonts from the Georgia font family instead of using Times, because Georgia was designed for the screen.

Recommended Typefaces

> ▶ **For text**: Verdana (best) and Arial
>
> ▶ **For headings:** Verdana, Trebuchet, and Arial

You can download these fonts (Mac and Windows versions) from Microsoft's Web page at **www.microsoft.com/typography/fontpack/.**

If you work with Web pages already, you may know that you'll have additional options for fonts if you use CSS (cascading style sheets) like line height in percent, and so on. This improves readability when used correctly.

TIP

When creating Web pages and using standard Web faces like Verdana or Arial, you have an advantage when converting pages to Adobe PDF files. You get smaller PDF file sizes, because you can choose **not** to embed fonts in your PDF document—Verdana is a font "everybody" has nowadays. Always consider cross-platform and cross-file type differences when you work. In this digital age, you never know what file format the client will ask for later!

Type as Graphics

As you saw from the list of recommended typefaces, there aren't many to choose from. So what do you do when you want to use other fonts? You have to create graphics and use those instead. Note that this means that you can't edit or update the Web pages as easily, because you have to replace the graphics. Typical uses for text saved as graphics are headlines on pages, navigation elements, menu items, company logos, and so on. See Figure 9.20. Of course, soft drop shadows and other effects added to type demands you save that as graphics as well, because this is not a function in HTML. We'll take a look at some really cool type effects in Chapter 10, where we'll create type in Gold.

Figure 9.20
The menu items on the left side of this Web page for Ecological Chemicals (**www.ecolchem.no**) are a combination of icons and text, saved as single files that were stacked vertically.

Creating Web-optimized Graphics

Graphics dominate Web pages today, and the secret to fast-loading Web pages is reducing the file sizes of your graphics. You may want to know exactly what "optimizing" an image means. It means reducing the file size of a picture while preserving image quality so that the image loads in a browser as quickly as possible.

How to Create the Best Web Graphics

ImageReady and Photoshop have color palette reduction settings for exporting Web graphics. Let's take a look at some compression settings and color palette tweaking.

Color and Compression

There are two ways to save color raster images: Indexed (like GIFs) and RGB (JPEG). Indexed formats are mapped to a palette of 256 or fewer colors. RGB, or true color, has a 24-bit palette that can hold up to 16.7 million colors. For index-based formats such as GIF and PNG, fewer colors mean smaller files. Unlike the GIF format, JPEG retains all color information but compresses file size by selectively discarding data.

When exporting your Web graphics from Photoshop 6, Elements, or ImageReady, you have four options for changing the color palette reduction settings. This is called the *Color Reduction Algorithm* and is a pop-up menu in the Optimize palette. In Photoshop and ImageReady, use the Optimize palette and try out the different settings while previewing the result. See Figure 9.21.

Choose "Perceptual" to create a color table that prioritizes the colors that your eyes are sensitive to or choose "Selective" (the default), which favors large areas of color and at the same time preserves Web colors. You can choose "Adaptive," which will sample colors from the range *most common* in the graphic. Lastly, you can choose "Web," which uses the 216-color palette. This is what Netscape and Explorer browsers share, so a 256-color palette isn't 100-percent Web-safe. If your image has *fewer* colors than the total number specified in the color palette, unused colors are removed and the file size becomes smaller. The Web palette setting can create larger files and is recommended only when you want to avoid browser dithering. You can save color tables from optimized images to use later on with other images. When opening your file in ImageReady, you instantly get the Optimize palette. In Photoshop, this is "hidden" under File > Save For Web, but the settings are the same.

Figure 9.21
This is a snapshot from ImageReady. In the red circle, you can see the size of the file, which in this case, displays the original file size because the preview is of the original.

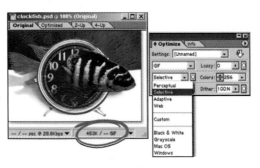

Compression Tools

Compression techniques are divided into two categories: "lossless" and "lossy." Lossless techniques compress image data without removing detail; lossy techniques compress images by removing detail. When exporting from ImageReady or Photoshop, you can choose "lossy" settings as well. (Refer to Figure 9.21.) Some designers prefer to use custom-made applications for compressing images. See the following Tip for some of them.

TIP

Here are some compression packages you may want to look at:
Spinwave—Spinwave, at **www.digfrontiers.com**, offers several graphics-reduction tools: JPEG Cruncher Pro and GIF Cruncher. The company offers both online and desktop versions that are designed to crunch your images into great-looking JPEGs and GIFs that speed up download times considerably. From the company's HVS Series comes ColorGIF 2.0. This Photoshop plug-in (filter and export) is said to optimize any image for the best color and the smallest file size. HVS JPEG 2.0 is a program for handling JPEGs.

DeBabelizer—This program, from Equilibrium (**www.debabelizer.com**), was one of the first compression tools on the market. Some folks still swear this is one of the best image crunchers.

ImageVice—This Mac and PC Photoshop plug-in is a great tool, and Boxtop Software (**www.boxtopsoft.com**) has a couple of other great tools as well: ProJPEG, GIFmation, and Colorsafe.

Exporting Web Graphics

Here's how to export Web graphics using ImageReady. We have a photo collage of a fish and a clock as seen previously in Figure 9.21. Let's look at how we can optimize this. We can try the setting "Web" for our color palette. This makes a nice 14 K image if we don't use Diffusion dither. However, look at how the colors dither anyway when we turn dithering up to 100 percent in Figure 9.22. This happens because we turned the amount of colors to Auto, and from the color table below the Optimize palette, we can see that only 71 colors are used.

Figure 9.22
Our image with GIF settings using the Web-optimized color palette.

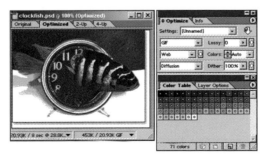

Now let's try the Selective palette instead. Just changing the menu selection automatically gives a 256-color setting in the Colors field. We tried fewer colors, but that only made dithering worse. In Figure 9.23, you'll see these choices in action. Note that the file size jumped up to 30 K, which is on the high side.

Figure 9.23
This illustration shows
GIF settings using the
Selective color palette.

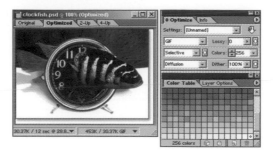

This complex image is better saved as a JPEG, so the reason we're experimenting with the GIF settings is just to show you how quickly dithering can occur. Let's try some JPEG moves instead. On the drop-down menu, choose JPEG. Use "High" in compression and a quality setting of 60. The file size is down to 19 K (which is better), and finally we have a graphic with the shadows and details but without application dithering. Of course, we had dithering in all of our GIF examples of 256 colors. If you look at this JPEG on a 256-color setting browser, it will dither anyway. Luckily, most people run their computers with "thousands of colors" in their display settings nowadays. See Figure 9.24.

Figure 9.24
Finally, we get to see
the JPEG version.

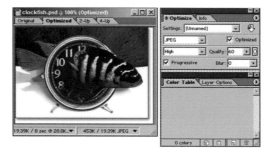

Creating and Exporting Buttons

"Buttons" in this setting means an object that's obviously clickable on a Web page. This could be a menu item or a home button, an icon of an envelope for sending e-mail, and so on. We'll look at some easy, quick-to-make menu buttons.

Create Easy Buttons

In Photoshop, start with a file big enough for menu buttons; 200 × 200 pixels or so will suffice. Make a new layer and create a rectangle some 20 pixels high of almost full width. (You don't know exactly how big this is going to be until you've created the type.) In this example, I created a rectangle in RGB 153, 51, 102. This color is very dark, but this is just an example. Use 12 pt. Verdana Bold with "Crisp" or "Smooth" settings, in black or white color, and type your text. I use black in this example. Drag the type layer onto the New Layer button in the Layers Palette to create a duplicate. Change the type color to white afterwards; this layer is below the black type layer. Now switch to the Move Tool. Move the white type 1 pixel to the left and up by clicking the arrow keys once in each direction. On the Layers Palette, change Blending mode from Normal to Soft Light. Take a look at Figure 9.25 for the result. Crop to the buttons edges and save for Web.

Figure 9.25
A quick button like this has a little effect on the text using layer duplication and blending modes.

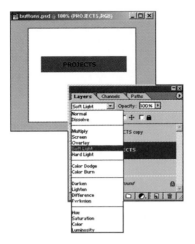

You can create rounded corners on buttons very easy, and avoid rectangular buttons. Select the rectangle layer and load the selection by holding Ctrl down while clicking the layer. Go to the Select menu and choose Modify > Smooth > 10 pixels. You now see that the selection has rounded corners. Go to the Select Menu again, choose Inverse, and click Delete. Choose Inverse again to bring the selection back to the button. Create a new layer, choose Select > Modify > Contract > 12 pixels. Fill this selection with 25 percent White. Choose Select > Feather, set 5 pixels, choose Inverse selection, and press Delete. Move this selection to the top of the button, just a pixel from the top edge. Hit Blur twice on the Filter menu.

There are hundreds of cool Photoshop tutorials for buttons out there, which you probably have seen already if you're interested in this kind of thing. This is one of the most popular, where we create a capsule look-alike button. See Figure 9.26.

Figure 9.26
Create highlights on your button by using selections and filling them with white.

Part III Creating Graphics

Create a new layer above the white highlight and choose the Linear Gradient Tool. Load the
button selection again on this layer. Fill with white to transparency from top to bottom. Set
Layer Opacity to approximately 15 percent. Add a shadow on the button layer by using the
Layer Effects option and, finally, hide our black type layer so only the white is left. You may
wonder why it's necessary to have the white type. For the sake of this example, that's why. See
Figure 9.27.

Figure 9.27
Our finished button.
The beauty of this is
that you can create all
kinds of nice colors
simply by changing the
color on the button
layer.

Before I export this button, I'll make another easy effect. Make the black type visible again and
change the color to be a somewhat darker shade than the button background. Presto: instant
bevelled type. Now, take a look at this button as we save it as a GIF file in ImageReady. You
might think it should be saved as a JPEG because of the color transitions and shadow. Nope.
Look at the color palette in Figure 9.28. Notice that the palette now consists of 256 colors, which
covers all the nuances in our graphic. We would have dithering if we had used more colors in
our original, but because we have only white, black, and magenta, the palette creates all the
nuances in between—which is sufficient for a good result.

Figure 9.28
Notice how the color
palette consists of 256
colors, which covers all
the nuances in our
graphic.

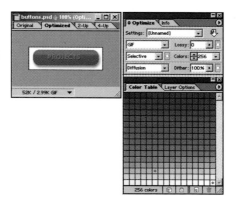

Droplet—A Time Saver

When exporting a number of GIFs to be used on the same Web site, you often use the same settings because your original file has many of the same colors as when you split it into smaller graphic elements. Use batch processing to ease your workload, and look at the "Droplet" feature in ImageReady. Droplets are the same as batch processing with Actions in Photoshop, but with one cool extra feature: Droplet creates a file that you can place, for example, on your desktop. Drag and drop a single file, a folder, or several files, onto this Droplet. Every file dropped will be processed using the settings you defined in the Droplet. Create a Droplet called "WEBGIF" and let it create an optimized GIF file to your preferred export settings. When the files are processed, they can reside in the same folder as your original file, but as a GIF. It doesn't get any simpler than this.

And it's easy to create a Droplet. With an image open in ImageReady, choose your settings in the Optimize palette. Choose Create Droplet, as shown in Figure 9.29, from the Optimize palette menu. Name the droplet, choose where you want the droplet to be saved, and click Save.

Figure 9.29
Create a Droplet by clicking the Droplet icon, marked with red.

GIF Animation and Effects

Animations are overused on the Web and should be reserved for special cases where they are absolutely necessary. They will quickly devour your bandwidth, and nothing is more irritating to the eye than numerous animated banner ads and other animations on Web pages. Surveys have shown that animations are annoying to Web surfers and will make them go someplace else if they have a choice. Create your animations carefully and use them with caution.

Because JPEGs can't be animated (unless you implement them into a Java applet or something like that), we're talking about GIF animations—Shockwave or Flash for Web pages these days. In Photoshop or another program with layers, it's easy to create animations. You can number the layers, copy them, do some tweaking, export one layer visible at a time as GIFs, and then merge them all into an animation using a GIF animator application. Because animations consist of several GIF files rolled into one, you'll get huge file sizes. Consider this and use as few colors as possible. In ImageReady, use the Animation palette to create animation frames from an image with several layers. You can assign a delay time to each frame, specify looping, and more.

Open a multi-layered graphic in ImageReady. On the Animation palette, select "Make Frames from Layers" from the drop-down menu on the arrow. ImageReady then automatically creates frames based on the order of your layers. See Figure 9.30 for how this looks in ImageReady. Use the Animation palette to adjust delays; note that you should select all frames before adjusting delays, unless you want some frames with different delays than others. Preview the animation by clicking the Play button on the palette. After you have made your adjustments, export the animation: Choose File > Save Optimized and then save as a GIF. Note that GIF animation applications have several options that ImageReady doesn't have. These options can add effects to your frames, including transitions of various kinds between frames. Download evaluation versions and try them out before buying.

Figure 9.30
ImageReady creates
Frames for your
animation based on
your layers.

There you have it. We've just finished creating buttons and Web-optimized graphics. Using what you just learned about type, you have all the skills you need to create sharp-looking and fast-downloading Web site content.

10 TIPS TO GOOD WEB SITE CONTENT

1. Your motto should be: Content is King.
2. Use few colors when working with graphics, and know when to use GIFs and JPEGs.
3. Use standard Web fonts.
4. Be careful when using animations—don't overdo it.
5. Think download time—use small thumbnails viewers can click on instead on loading a huge image on a page.
6. Make the Web site easy to update.
7. Text should be easy to read.
8. All optimized graphics combined should never exceed 100 K.
9. Web site navigation should be clear and available on all pages. Viewers should not need to use the browser's Back button to navigate.
10. Give your viewers the opportunity to choose what they want to see— don't force them to view long Flash intros they can't skip or overwhelm them with full-screen pop-up windows.

Part IV
Special Effects and Filters

10

Shadows, Depth, and Special Effects

What elements make for a great illustration? Apart from composition and color, they are perspective, shadows, and light. The correct shading and light draw the eye to the focal point of the image, enhance the best areas, and give a more professional look overall. This chapter will focus on how you can use your tablet to draw shadows and light, add depth, and inject some special effects into your artwork.

This chapter will guide you through:

▶ Creating natural-looking shadows, drop shadows, and cast shadows

▶ How to create depth and perspective

▶ The process of creating industrial objects and effects, such as gold and brushed metal

Shadows and Light: Occurring Naturally

There are numerous filters available to help you create shadows and light, but they are seldom true to reality. If you study real-life shadows, you'll see what I mean. A true shadow is not as flat as the filters make it; it will always be darker and denser when it's close to the object. Other objects will affect it, as will ambient light sources. The filters simply add a *shade* to an object and don't really create a proper *shadow*. Let's see if we can create some natural looking shadows using various techniques.

True shadows can look like the shadows shown in Figure 10.1. Notice how the boat casts two shadows instead of one. Notice how one is dark and close to the boat, and the other is more subtle. If you had made a selection of this boat and used a shadow filter on it, you'd get *one* shadow.

Figure 10.1
The water in this image creates an uneven shadow, which would be impossible to achieve with just a shadow filter. You'd have to ripple the shadow afterwards to simulate this. (Photo: Gunnar Homdrum)

There are plenty of different shadows, such as cast shadows (which create perspective), drop shadows (which lift the object from the background), and natural shadows that objects will create when you add a light source. Let's take a look at cast shadows first.

Creating Cast Shadows

Some filter packages create good cast shadows, but you can make these yourself, especially when you want to add a cast shadow to type. To show you how, I'll make an autumn picture with plenty of shadow.

For this tutorial, you can use any application that has layers, such as Painter or Photoshop Elements (I use Adobe Photoshop 6 in the following examples). Fill your background layer with a medium green color like RGB 77, 118, 37, add an image of leaves as a backdrop if you like, and then type your letters in black. Use a sans-serif font such as Arial Black or Verdana Bold (I use Gill Sans Bold). Find a nice autumn picture to use for the letters and press Ctrl+click (Command+click) on your text layer—this action will load the selection and paste your picture into it (or cut out the selection and paste it on the layer). (The paste-into technique for Photoshop 6 is described in detail in Chapter 4.) Your image should resemble that in Figure 10.2. We're going to work on the background as well, so create a thin outline on your text by stroking it with light green color at 1 point outside the selection: Select Edit > Stroke and choose color and width. This will make the text stand out better from the background later on, when we're adding elements to the background.

Figure 10.2
Paste-into techniques always come in handy and can instantly create letters that are more exciting than those that are simply filled in with color.

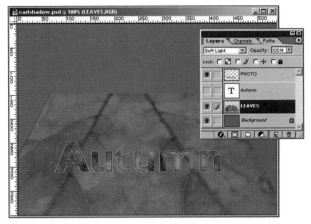

TIP

When creating artwork or photomontages, it's very helpful to add a photo to the background while working. This is a good aid to help you remember the colors you use, even though you might remove it altogether later. Adjust the layer opacity so it doesn't disturb you.

Create a new layer called Shadow below your text layer, and then load your text selection (Ctrl+click or Command+click the text layer) to this layer. Hide your original text layer for now to view clearly what you're doing. Set Foreground 100 percent to transparent and fill your active selection with a Linear Gradient. Use a dark green color, as in Figure 10.3, and draw the gradient from the bottom and upwards. The dark green I used is RGB 46, 80, 10.

Figure 10.3
Fill the Shadow layer selection with a dark green linear gradient.

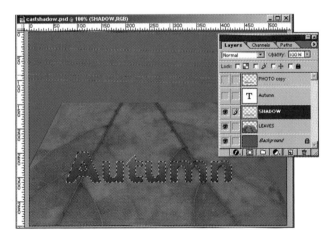

On the Edit menu, select Transform > Distort. Drag the two upper corner handles sideways and upwards to skew the selection to the right, as shown in Figure 10.4. Try out various distortions and keep in mind what the light source would be to create this kind of shading. Because this is an autumn illustration, we imagine the sun is low and therefore casts a long shadow.

Figure 10.4
Distort the shadow layer with the Transform option to create a cast shadow.

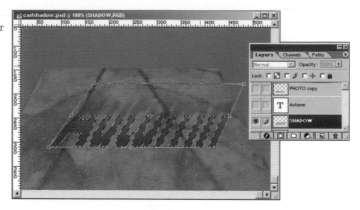

Create a new layer above your shadow layer and load the shadow selection on it. Name it "Dark Shadow." Use the Airbrush Tool at brush sizes 45 or 65. Set Pressure and opacity to be controlled by the stylus in Brush Dynamics. In one sweeping stroke, draw horizontally from the very bottom of the text selection so you'll get a darker shade next to the original text. Use a light hand, because you don't want the shadow to be completely black. Hit Delete to clear the selection if you're not happy with your first drawn stroke and try again. We're doing this on a separate layer because you'll have the option to make the darker shadow lighter by adjusting layer opacity if you're not happy with it. See Figure 10.5.

Figure 10.5
Use the Airbrush Tool to draw a dark shadow at the bottom of the cast shadow.

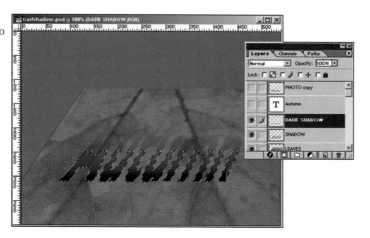

Now, view your original text layer now to see how it looks. On the Dark Shadow layer, choose Filters > Blur > Gaussian Blur and use a setting with a radius of 1 or 2 pixels. We want just a small amount of blurred effect here, because this darker shadow should be more solid and crisp. Your artwork should now be similar to Figure 10.6.

Figure 10.6
This is the text with our two shadows applied.

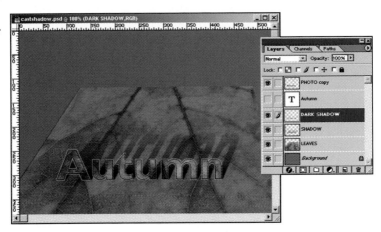

In the next step, we'll draw a shadow completely from scratch. This brings us to the next step in our shadow walk-through: We'll use a picture of an object, such as a nut, a single leaf, or a butterfly, for our autumn collage.

Using Layers

You can draw the most beautiful shadows yourself just by using layers and Airbrush tools. I've pasted a gorgeous butterfly on a layer above all the other layers. Naturally, I masked it first to remove the background. I used several medium-sized soft, round brushes and the Airbrush Tool, with a setting of 30 percent pressure in Brush options. I applied the mask when I was finished. I hid all the background layers and used the Eraser Tool to remove any unwanted pixels, which can be hard to see with multi-colored backgrounds under an object. (A dire example of how easy it is to miss pixels when creating masks can be viewed in Chapter 4, Figure 4.32.) Remember to set Color to Off in Brush Dynamics when you draw masks, unless you want parts of the background visible.

At this point, you should work on the Butterfly layer. I recommend brushes in sizes 35 and 21 with the dark green color. Use a very light hand, or set Brush pressure to 20 percent or so to be on the safe side. We could have created this shadow on a separate layer, but this is a new trick that comes in handy when your objects are semi-transparent and you don't want to see the shadow through it. On the Brushes options menu, choose Behind as the mode. See Figure 10.7. Notice that you can now paint all you want without affecting your butterfly! If your mask isn't precise enough, you'll see a fringe on the edge of the butterfly.

Figure 10.7
Draw shadows directly
on the same layer as
your object by choosing
Mode > Behind, circled
with red.

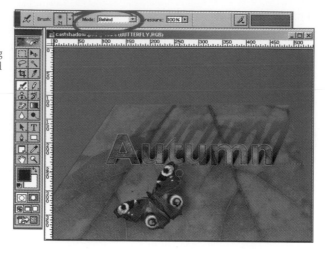

Because we want the butterfly to look natural against the letters, we have to repeat the cast shadow technique we used for the text. We want the butterfly to "hover" a bit above the background, so we don't want to distort the butterfly shadow quite so much as before. We'll also set the opacity of the butterfly shadow layer to 60 or 70 percent.

Move the butterfly and its shadow around until you're happy with its position. I moved it close to the letters, because this adds shadows cast from the butterfly onto the letters as well. (Look closely at the lower parts of the letters "m" and "n" in Figure 10.8.) In this image, I've added several leaves from four other photos, making sure they are in the same color range. If you're using several photos, adjust their colors before merging the layers that you've pasted them onto.

Figure 10.8
We're almost finished.
Later, we'll add some
light to this artwork.

Shadows and Drop Shadows

Duplicating layers is one of the fastest ways to create the ubiquitous drop shadow. You simply duplicate the objects layer, place the copy layer below, fill the copied object with black, and then use the Blur or Gaussian blur filters to smoothen the edges. Adjust the layer opacity to values between 30 and 70 percent, move the shadow to where you want it, and then you're done. This creates a flat shadow, which has nothing to do with reality, but it nevertheless makes a nice effect in some illustrations.

Drop shadows are great for flat objects, such as paper clippings, icons, photos, and other items where you want them to stand out from a background. Drop shadows are also good for text, for the same reasons. But simply adding a drop shadow to a 3D object will not do. Take a look at the dice in Figure 10.9. This is the original photo. Notice the shadows: They are a little darker close to the dice, and very soft. Let's say we'll want those dice on another background. That means we'll have to create a selection, paste them on a new layer, and then add new shadows.

Figure 10.9
This is the original picture.

Create a new file of 400 × 300 pixels and fill the background with two areas of brown color (RGB 204, 153, 102 for the light brown and RGB 51, 0, 0 for the dark brown). Paste the dice and remove the background completely by using your Stylus and the Lasso Tool. Go over the edges with the Eraser, using modest amounts of pressure to get the edges smooth. When you're finished, go to Layer Style > Drop Shadow and try to simulate the shadow in the original picture. You just won't be able to, as seen in Figure 10.10. The shades won't look right no matter what angle you try, because the drop shadow style perceives the dice as flat objects.

Figure 10.10
Layer Style doesn't do much at all for 3D items.

Figure 10.11
Adjust layer opacity if
the shade is too dark;
the lower image has
opacity set to 40
percent.

To simulate the original shadow, you'll have to paint it by hand. Use the techniques as
previously mentioned or paint it from scratch. First, we'll paint the softest shadow. Create a new
layer below the dice. Use black color and select a brush size of 65 or 45. Set Brush Dynamics to
let pressure be controlled by the stylus. Don't worry if the shading gets too dark. As in the top
picture in Figure 10.11, getting the shade even is more important. Simply adjust layer opacity to
40 percent or so when you're finished, as in the lower picture in Figure 10.11.

Create another layer for the darker shade and select a smaller brush to paint with. A soft, round
13-pixel brush will do nicely. Draw very carefully, because you will not adjust the opacity on
this layer. Keep the brush partly behind the dice to get smooth edges. When you're done, create
a selection for the soft cast shadow on the right die. Use a 1-pixel feather and draw a selection
with the Lasso Tool, as shown in Figure 10.12. Switch to a 65 brush with 5 percent pressure
setting. Barely touch the tablet, and draw a short stroke from the corner of the die and to the
right. Adjust the edge of the shadow with the Blur Tool. Take a look at the finished result in
Figure 10.13.

Figure 10.12
Use selections when creating straight shadows and adjust the edges with the Blur Tool afterwards.

Figure 10.13
This is the finished result.

TIP

Using selections is a great help when working with cast shadows. Selections enable you to be certain that you get color just where you want it, but the drawback is that the edges will often become too sharp. Adjust the edge of the cast shadow afterwards by using the Blur Tool.

We'll leave our hand-made shadows for the time being. At this point, we'll now look at how shadow filters can help you. We'll still use the dice image for an example and look at some of the most popular shadow filters available.

Creating Shadows Using Filters

The following are some of the most popular shadow filters. Alien Skin's Eye Candy and Xenofex, plus Andromeda's Shadow filter, are among them.

NOTE

Before you start having fun with filters, make a copy of the layer with your objects, because the filter applies itself on your object layer. If you want to change anything later, you're lost if your history palette is all used up.

Alien Skin's Eye Candy 3.1 and 4000

The popular Eye Candy filter package for Photoshop and Painter has a perspective shadow that's really good. This filter is especially useful when you want objects to seem like they're almost touching the surface, as when using the Classic setting (see Figure 10.14).

Figure 10.14
This figure shows the Eye Candy 3.1 dialog box with the Classic setting.

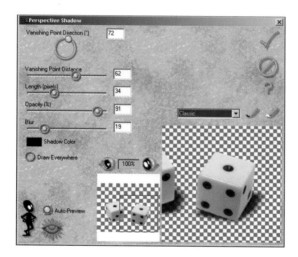

Alien Skin has released two more filter packages, Xenofex and Eye Candy 4000. Eye Candy 4000 has the Shadowlab filter, in which you can use numerous preset shadows such as the Short Perspective shadow, shown in Figure 10.15. (You can also create your own from scratch.) Just as in previous packages, you have options for setting Opacity, Blur, Offset Distance, and so on. If you're looking to buy a good overall filter package, I can recommend Eye Candy 4000, because you get several other filters as well. After applying the filter, you can go to the Edit menu and fade the effect. I also like the intuitive interface.

Figure 10.15
This is Eye Candy 4000's Shadowlab dialog box. It is not the discreet Settings menu choice that hides a lot of presets.

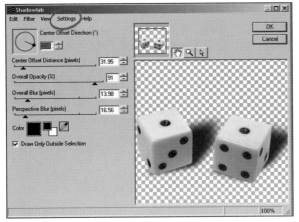

Andromeda Shadow

Another cool shadow filter comes from Andromeda, shown in Figure 10.16. I have tried only the demo version of this filter, but the settings and options are quite impressive. Like Eye Candy 4000, the interface is intuitive. Andromeda has some more advanced features, including adding a camera and rotating the objects. The ability to move shadows around simply by dragging them—instead of entering values—has me completely hooked on this product. If you're looking only for a Shadow filter package, Andromeda is it. This is as realistic as you'll get without drawing the shadows yourself.

Figure 10.16
Andromeda Shadow has unlimited options and 3D shadows.

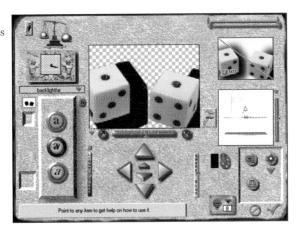

Part IV Special Effects and Filters

Light

Let's pick up our autumn collage again. This time, we'll see if we can add some light as well. We know that the light source is coming from the left and the front because of the shadows, so we can't just add light anywhere. We'll create a soft, afternoon light. First, create a new layer. With the Lasso Tool, create a cone-shaped selection with a 10 Feather setting, as shown in Figure 10.17. Pick a light yellow color; RGB 250, 215, 146 should do nicely. Use a large Airbrush and paint carefully from the edge of the canvas towards the letters. You can also use the Linear Gradient Tool for this. Set the gradient from 100 percent to transparent. Adjust layer opacity afterwards to approximately 55 percent. You can scale and distort this light to fit the object you want lit.

Figure 10.17
The Lasso Tool is at work at this stage of our collage.

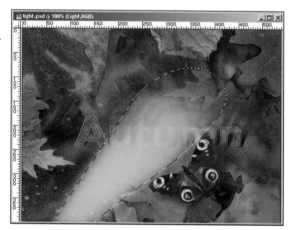

You can achieve an effect of light "hitting," or reflecting on, your letters simply by loading the letters as a selection. On a new layer, paint them with the same color that was used as the light source. Beware that this brushed light will always create a very soft light effect unless you paint really hard and with full pressure. See Figure 10.18. But it's a handy effect that can also be used to create underwater light and other more diffuse light sources, which we'll look at in the next section.

Figure 10.18
Create a soft light by using a Brush and a Selection.

Creating Depth

Light and shadow are the best architects of depth in your artwork. Let's take a look at how adding just a little of each of them will achieve good results.

Shadows and Light

In this section, we'll return once more to Photoshop 6 (or Elements) and our autumn artwork. This time, we want to achieve better depth. We also want our image to look as if we are viewing it just before the sun goes down, as the scene is getting darker. To do this, we have to adjust the lighting and add a lot of shading.

Begin by enhancing the visible shading in the artwork on the leaves and in the background. Use black color and brushes of sizes 45 and larger. Use very little pressure; it's better to draw twice than get dizzy using the Eraser tools. Use the Burn Tool as well, with Range set to midtones and exposure to 25 percent. Paint over the leaves. Hide the light effects we created while doing this, because you can more easily determine just how dark you want your artwork to be. When painting with black color, use a pressure setting as low as 7 or 8 percent. Paint repeatedly, because this will create a better effect than just going at it with full pressure. Darken all of the areas somewhat, except where you want the light source. Move the light a bit to the right, make it thinner by distorting it, and lighten some of the leaves in the background. Duplicate the text shadow layer to create even harder shadows.

Finally, the result simulates looking through a shrub with thin light shining through the branches. Finally, desaturate the butterfly (it's outside the light source). Use the Sponge Tool with Mode > Desaturate. Be careful to adjust the letters that fall outside the light as well, plus their shading. The final result should look similar to that in Figure 10.19.

Figure 10.19
And now it's darker. Compare this image to the previous versions to spot the adjustments made with the Burn and Sponge tools plus the black ink brushes.

Adding Depth with Light

Rays of light can add depth to an illustration, just like shadows can, as we'll see in the next example. Let's look at an underwater illustration of a mermaid, created with a combination of photos and drawings. Start with a nicely colored fish that was applied in this image using masks. Then, draw the outlines of your mermaid, as shown in Figure 10.20. Create a background that resembles a sea using the same techniques as the penguin postcard background in Chapter 7.

Figure 10.20
To begin creating a mermaid, add a fish, draw outlines, and then create a sea-like background.

Now it's time to finish the mermaid. Pick the colors from the fish to apply these same colors to the rest of her. Use the two smallest brushes for tiny details like strands of hair, the details on the arms, and so on. Use the Smudge Tool at the ends of the strands of hair if you can't get them to fade correctly at first. In the background, add areas that are both darker and lighter than your basic colors. We want the light to come from above, so add a very soft and very large whitish area here with a large Airbrush. See Figure 10.21.

Figure 10.21
Start creating depth by adding large areas of light and dark shades with the bigger brushes.

Create Depth with Objects

Create depth by drawing objects (seaweed and similar items in this case), both in front of and behind our mermaid. Paint those in the back darker than the ones in front; notice that one in the front is also dark. This makes the front object seem to be very close to you and far away from the light. Notice that the rays of light are in the back of our drawing. See Figure 10.22.

Figure 10.22
Place objects behind (and in front) of the mermaid to add to depth and paint them accordingly.

Now, use the same light techniques as before. Duplicate the image three times and then move the resulting objects close together. Merge layers or link them when you move them around. Add a fish for company. Place some rays of light on the layers below the mermaid and a few in front of her (this makes the image seem more natural). Notice that I haven't placed light rays everywhere, but that I'm sticking to the left side of the artwork. See Figure 10.23.

Figure 10.23
Notice the rays of light coming from above.

For final touches, copy the fish and place it in the foreground. Re-paint it just enough so that it isn't exactly the same as the other one. Then, make another copy and scale it down to less than half that size. Fill the copy with black color and adjust layer opacity. Duplicate this a dozen times or so to create a school of fish in the background, seen as silhouettes towards the light. Notice how they seem to be farther away. Both the size (they're smaller) and the lack of detail add to this effect. Merge all of the layers with the small fish to reduce the number of layers; we're down to eleven layers in the finished artwork. See Figure 10.24.

Figure 10.24
This is the finished result.

Perspective

By now you've seen that light and shadow can easily create good perspective effects. Let's look at two other quick methods: copying your object and resizing and duplicating your object.

Copy Your Object

Copying your object several times can get you the effects you want. Take a look at the examples in Figures 10.25a and 10.25b. I have copied the ball, filled the copy with black, and then skewed it to create a shadow. I adjusted it by loading its selection after I was happy with its position; I then painted in darker areas of black with a brush. I copied the shadow, filled it with white, and moved this layer above the ball. I then adjusted the opacity of the layer and resized the white area.

**Figures 10.25a
and 10.25b**
Notice how different the ball looks when we adjust the light. In a., the light is set to 36 percent layer opacity; in b., it's up to 100 percent.

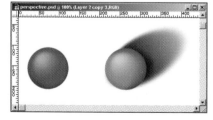
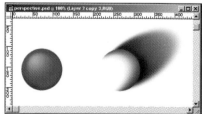

a.   b.

Resizing And Duplicating

Resizing (scaling) your object after duplication creates perfect copies of your object that you can place to create perspective. In the next example, look at how the balls seem to be glued together. They are copied, resized, and moved. Then all three layers are merged, copied again, and filled with black. This layer is placed above the balls with Blending mode set to Overlay. This is the dark shadow on the balls themselves. Then this layer is duplicated and placed beneath the Balls layer. This shadow is then distorted to create the cast shadow. Quick and easy—the result is shown in Figure 10.26.

Figure 10.26
Resize and duplicate your objects on various layers to create a shadow, which also creates perspective.

Industrial Effects

A couple of the hot topics on the Web are how to create metal objects and industrial effects. It's tough to find a graphics-heavy Web site that hasn't got a wire or two in the interface and/or brushed metal buttons. Let's take a look at how these effects are created in Photoshop 6.

Creating Metal Effects

It really helps to look at pictures of metal objects when you're creating metal effects. This will give you a good idea of what colors to use until you perfect your eye for these things and can select colors in your sleep.

Brushed Metal Plates

Start with a grayscale image of 500 × 300 pixels. Make a new layer and fill with a light gray color (RGB 170, 170, 170), as shown in the small square in Figure 10.27. On the Filter menu, choose Noise > Add Noise. Use Gaussian at 35 amount, and select Monochromatic. Click OK. Go to the Filter menu again, choose Blur > Motion Blur. At an angle of 0 degrees, use a distance of 90 pixels. Adjust the brightness and contrast (I used a Brightness of −11 and a contrast of −39).

Figure 10.27
Fill your layer with
Gaussian Noise.

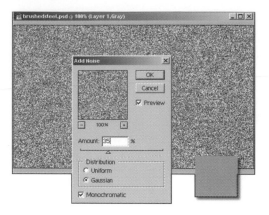

Brushed Metal Letters

To create instant steel lettering, you could use Photoshop's Layer styles or a combination of highlights and the shadow techniques you've learned thus far.

For the Steel letters, follow these easy steps:

1. Create letters that measure 130 points and use a sans-serif font such as Gill Sans Bold or similar. Warp the text if you like (I used the Fish warp). Copy an area of your background that's a bit larger than your letters. Create a new layer above the text layer, load the text layer as a selection on it, and paste your metal pattern into it.

2. Apply the layer mask and use Filter > Blur > Blur. On the Layer menu, choose Layer Style. Use Drop Shadow at a 120-degree angle. Set Opacity to 52 percent and use a distance of 8 pixels.

3. Under Quality in the Drop Shadow dialog box, choose the first contour in the second row of available contours. Select Inner Glow from the Styles main menu and use opacity of 75 percent, a Blend mode of Screen, and the default settings.

4. Select Bevel and Emboss. Use the Inner bevel as Style and Smooth as the technique. Set the depth to 100 percent and the size to 5 pixels. The rest are default settings. Voilà! You have steel letters. See Figure 10.28.

Figure 10.28
You can create quick
and easy steel letters
with Photoshop's Layer
styles.

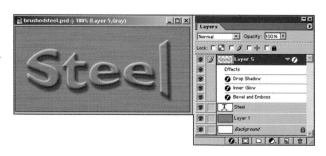

Silver Effects

To achieve a more silvery effect, adjust your steel letters. Convert your grayscale image to RGB mode. Adjust the colors in Color Balance: Image > Adjust > Color Balance. Use Midtones to set Cyan to −26 and Green to +11. And then adjust the brightness to +60 percent or so. The adjusted example is shown in Figure 10.29. Add more light to adjust the shine if necessary.

Figure 10.29
You can have quick and easy silver letters by adjusting color balance.

Create Gold Letters

Creating gold effects is easy if you stick to filters and channels when you're working with letters. Create a file measuring 500 × 400 pixels and fill the background with black. Type your letters at approximately 150 points, use white for your color, and then select a serif font. (I used a font called Amaze.) Set anti-aliasing to Smooth. Press Ctrl+click (Command+click) on your text layer to create a selection. Open your Channels palette and click the Save selection as Channel icon. See Figure 10.30.

Figure 10.30
Save your selection as Channel icon.

Select this new channel, called Alpha 1, and fill your selection with white color. Duplicate this channel by dragging it onto the New Channel icon. On your Alpha 1 copy channel, use Gaussian Blur with a setting of a 3-pixel radius. Still working on the copied channel, press Ctrl+click (Command+click) and select Alpha 1 to load its selection on the Alpha 1 copy channel. On the Select menu, choose Inverse and press the Delete key. Deselect. Your image should look like Figure 10.31.

Figure 10.31
On the copied channel, load the selection from Alpha 1. Now choose Inverse and press Delete.

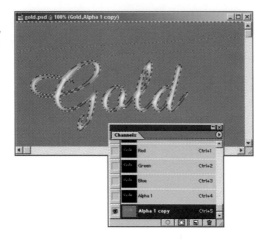

On your Layers Palette, select your text layer. Go to the Filter menu and choose Render > Lighting Effects. Click OK to rasterize the layer in the dialog box that comes up automatically. Use the settings as in Figure 10.32. The most important point is that your Texture Channel is set to Alpha 1 copy and that the colors are right. Use yellow RGB 246, 213, 32 and orange RGB 251, 180, 67. Save the settings for later by clicking the Save button and naming it "Gold letters" or something else that is descriptive.

Figure 10.32
This is the Lighting Effects dialog box. Make sure your Texture Channel is set to Alpha 1 copy.

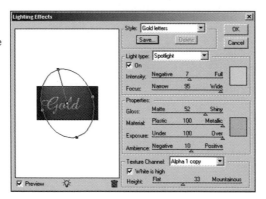

Create a new layer called Beige above your text layer. Select the Alpha 1 channel and click the Selection icon. You have loaded the selection on your layer when swapping to it. (You can Ctrl+click (Command+click) your text layer instead, of course.) Fill the selection with a beige color, (RGB 243, 204, 158) at 60 percent. Set Blending mode to Color on the Layers Palette. See Figure 10.33.

Figure 10.33
Set the Blending mode to Color on the Beige layer.

Now these letters could pass as brass letters perhaps, but they don't yet look quite like gold. Drag your Beige layer onto the New Layer icon and rename it White. Lock transparency and fill with 100 percent white. Unlock transparency. Load the text selection and contract it by 2 pixels, Choose inverse and hit Delete.

Set Blending mode to Color Dodge and then set Opacity to 35 percent. Create yet another layer and call it Lights. Load your text selection, contract it by 2 pixels, and then fill with RGB 253, 242, 199, which is a very pale yellow. With the Lasso Tool selected, move your selection two pixels down and to the right using the Arrow keys, and press Delete. Deselect and adjust the light if necessary; I moved mine up and to the left. (This varies depending on the font you'll use.) See Figure 10.34.

Figure 10.34
Move your contracted selection 2 pixels down and to the right using the Arrow keys. Then press Delete. This creates a sharp-edged highlight.

Now all we have to do is add a darker shade to our letters. Create yet another layer and call it Shade. Load your text selection, contract it by 2 pixels, and then fill it with RGB 54, 0, 0 (dark brown). With the Lasso Tool selected, move your selection 2 pixels up and to the left using the Arrow keys, and press Delete. Go to Filter > Blur and blur once. Adjust layer opacity to 48 percent and set Blending mode to Overlay. You should now have something similar to what's in Figure 10.35.

Figure 10.35
This is the result after adding a darker contour to the letters.

To make the letters look 3D, paint extra shading on them where they overlap in strokes. Load the text selection on a new layer for this, but make sure you use the Lasso Tool and deselect the areas that you don't want paint in. Use the dark brown color we used previously for shading with a 27 brush. See Figure 10.36.

Figure 10.36
Brush in darker areas to add depth to the letters.

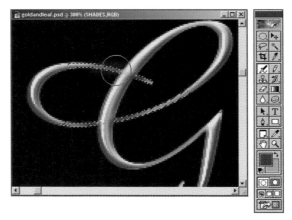

Industrial Objects

To make a cool interface for your Web site, you'll need to do more than just use filters to create brushed metal patterns. You'll have to add some objects as well. Let's take a look at some of the most common objects.

Metal Shapes

To create a quick and easy metal shape, use this simple trick: Type an S—or another suitable letter that resembles the shape you want—in black in a sans-serif font like Gill Sans Bold. Use Distort or Text Warp to change its shape. Render the letter when you're happy with it. On the Filter menu, choose Blur > Gaussian Blur with settings of approximately 17 pixels, depending on how big your letter is. See Figure 10.37.

Figure 10.37
The fastest way to create metal shapes is to use type and Gaussian Blur.

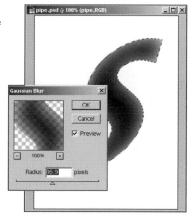

Go to the Filter menu and choose Stylize > Emboss. Apply with an angle of 165 degrees and a height of 10 pixels with the amount set to 340 percent. The angle may vary depending on your letter. See Figure 10.38.

Figure 10.38
Use Emboss filters to achieve shadow and light in a jiffy.

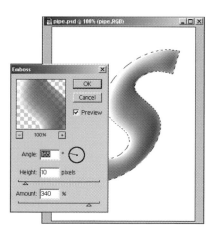

With the selection still active, choose Select > Modify and contract the selection by 4 pixels. Inverse, and then press Delete. This looks good on a white background, but when you change the background to black, you lose some detail, as seen to the left in Figure 10.39. To correct this, simply duplicate the object layer, lock transparency, fill with white, and merge the two layers. You'll soon have an object looking like the example on the right.

NOTE

You can easily create the popular metallic pipes used so often on the Web. Use the letter "l" in a sans-serif font if you want a straight pipe. You'll find several tutorials on the Internet to help you create metallic pipes, of course, but this method is far quicker.

Figure 10.39
You should duplicate layers and fill the copy with white when changing your background color to black or dark colors.

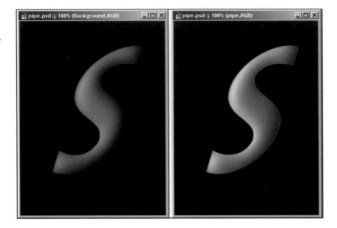

You can add highlights to your object by loading the selection on a new layer, contracting it by 10 pixels or more (depending on the width), and filling it with white. With the Lasso Tool selected, move 4 pixels down and to the right, hit Delete, and then deselect. Move your highlight almost to the edge of your letter. See Figure 10.40. Create shadows the same way or paint them in by hand using the Airbrush Tool.

Figure 10.40
Add highlights and
shadows by contracting
selections.

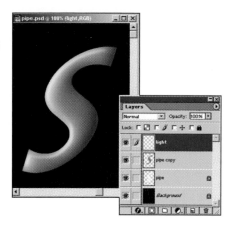

To make segmented pipes, create a rectangle and fill it with the steel texture displayed in Figure 10.28. Add light and shading by loading it as a selection and using the Linear Gradient Tool with black and white, respectively. See Figure 10.41.

Figure 10.41
Add highlights and
shadows with the
Linear Gradient Tool.

Duplicate this rectangle repeatedly and merge layers as you go along to make several at a time. When you have one layer with twelve rectangles or more with proper spacing, duplicate that layer to create the shadowed part of the pipe. Move them so they overlap. Fill the copy with 50 percent black and merge afterwards. Copy this as much as you like to get the size you need. Resize if necessary. Use linear gradients to create light and shading, plus draw a white glowing light almost at the top of the pipe. You can do this quickly by contracting the selection, filling with white, and moving it to where it looks good. You can adjust layer opacity if necessary. See Figure 10.42.

Figure 10.42
A fast way to create a
segmented pipe is to
adjust the color balance
to get a blue shine after
converting to RGB
mode.

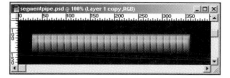

Nuts and Bolts

Let's take a look at some small objects that can perfect a metallic interface or illustration. We'll start with connectors, which connect wires and other objects to each other.

Start with a rectangle twice as big as you'd like the connector to be. Fill it with white, use black for the color, and then Airbrush it. Remember to hold Shift down while you draw to constrain lines. I also recommend a size 65 brush. See Figure 10.43.

Figure 10.43
Airbrushing a white
rectangle with black
will create shading.

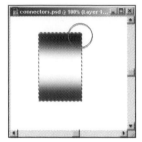

Duplicate the layer and hide the first one. Distort it by dragging the left handles while holding down the Shift key. See Figure 10.44.

Figure 10.44
Use Transform > Distort
and drag the handles.

View the first layer and move it so the two shapes together look like the tip of a crayon. Now we need a pattern for the rectangle. Create a new file, only 4 pixels high and 1 pixel wide, with white as the background. Zoom in and fill the two upper pixels with black color. Use Ctrl+A (Command+A) to select all pixels, and on the Edit menu, select Define Pattern. Name it Squares. Close the file.

Go back to our crayon-like connector and create a new layer. Load the rectangle selection on it. Choose Edit > Fill, and select Pattern from the contents menu in the Fill dialog box. Choose Multiply in Blending mode. Make sure the Blending mode is set to Multiply in the Layer palette as well. You will now have a connector that looks like Figure 10.45.

Figure 10.45
This object was filled
with a pattern that
simulates grip lines.

Another trick I discovered on the Internet, is to create grip lines that use the same pattern but look different. Instead of making a selection for the pattern, fill the whole (new) layer with the pattern. Then rotate the pattern approximately 10 degrees to the left and copy it using Ctrl+A (Command+A). Hide this layer. Load the rectangle selection, and use Edit > Paste Into. Apply the layer mask. Select Preserve Transparency and create shading like we did in Figure 10.43, using the Airbrush Tool. Create light the same way. Hold Shift down to constrain the lines while you draw. Resize the connector to 50 percent, and then you're done. See Figure 10.46.

Figure 10.46
This is the same connector and same pattern but with a twist to the Pattern layer.

Rounded Screws

Start with a file of 200 × 200 pixels with a white background. On a new layer, create a circle with the Ellipse Tool, holding Shift down. Paste our previously made brushed metal structure into the circle and choose the Gradient Tool. Set black as your background color and use RGB 240, 241, 230 as your foreground color. Set Opacity to 47 percent. Drag from the top right—just a bit outside the center—and down to the left. The metal structure should be barely visible. Apply the layer mask.

Create a new layer called Lines. Zoom to 200 percent and draw a thin rectangle horizontally over the exact middle of the circle to create the slot on the head of the screw. Use the Airbrush with black color, and fill the rectangle carefully at first with a large brush, and then add darker areas at the edges with a size 21 brush. See Figure 10.47.

Figure 10.47
Paint in shading with the Airbrush Tool.

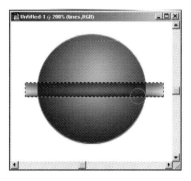

Deselect, load the circle as a selection, and select Inverse. Make sure you're on the Lines layer and press Delete. This removes the paint outside the circle. Merge the two layers and Scale to use on your interface. Add shadow and light around it for depth by painting it in with the airbrush. See Figure 10.48.

Figure 10.48
Resize your screw to fit
your artwork.

Rusted and Worn

Sometimes you'll want your metal to look torn and worn instead of buffed and brushed. You
can easily apply a texture from a photo to achieve that effect.

Let's make some rusty chains. Create two black letters on separate layers, an "O" and an "l." Fill
them in with our brushed metal pattern, and apply the layer masks. Paint in light and shading
by hand or with the nifty Selection trick of contraction that we just read about. Merge layers of
light and objects when you're satisfied with the results. Duplicate them and place them, rotate
and so on, to create a chain. Merge all layers except the background when you have them placed
right. See Figure 10.49.

Figure 10.49
Create chains by
using text.

Duplicate your layer before working on the rust effect. On the copied layer, use Filter > Artistic
and the Smudge Stick. Use a Stroke length of 1, a highlight of 0, and an Intensity of 1. Click OK.
Change to RGB mode if you've been working in grayscale, but don't flatten the layers. Create a
pattern like we did before, but make it 20 or 30 pixels wide. Fill these pixels with various
shades of blue and gray or pick a pattern from a picture. Use this pattern to fill the chain. Find a
photo that has well oxidized appearance. Paste this into the chain selection. On the layer mask,
remove areas with the brush so the original chain is visible in some areas. Finish with some

shadows on a separate layer, and you're done. See Figure 10.50. The finished Photoshop 6 file with three layers for Figure 10.50 is available for download at **www.iril.no,** so you can view how the effects are applied to each layer.

Figure 10.50
Use photos or patterns in your artwork for quick results.

Metallic Buttons

You can use the screw as a button, of course, but creating buttons with a varied surface is more fun.

Open your file with the brushed metal. Create a circle selection on a new layer in an image that measures approximately 150 × 150 pixels. Paste our metal structure into it. Duplicate it and cut an arrow out of the top layer using the Selection tools. Hide it temporarily. Create a new channel and name it Round Button. While on the channel, load your selection and hit Delete. Deselect. Copy this channel and name it Blur. Go to Filter > Blur and use Gaussian Blur > 12 pixel radius. Still on the Blur channel, choose Select > Modify > Contract and contract by 10 pixels. Feather the selection with 5 pixels and fill it with a gray color like RGB 184, 184, 184. Select the Round Button channel and click the Load Channel as Selection icon. Choose your layer with the button on and select Filter > Render > Lighting Effects. Use the settings as in Figure 10.51, where the texture channel is set to Blur. Click OK.

Figure 10.51
Use lighting effects and your Blur channel.

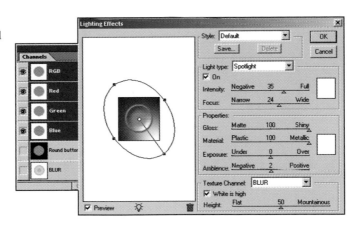

Now view your Arrow layer. Go to Layer > Layer Style > Bevel and Emboss. Use the settings as in Figure 10.52. Set Style to Pillow Emboss, set Technique to Smooth, set Depth to 271 percent, set Size to 5 pixels, and so on. Your button is ready in Figure 10.53.

Figure 10.52
Pillow Emboss adds a nice effect to objects that you want pushed down on the surface.

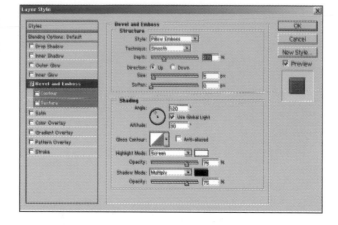

Figure 10.53
The button is ready to be pushed.

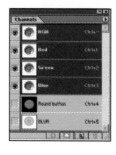 

Finally, you can put what we've gone through in this chapter to good use by using the various examples and creating an illustration like Figure 10.54. Duplicate the steel background to create a larger one, add all the other elements, and scale them as needed.

Figure 10.54
This is an example of how our objects can be used.

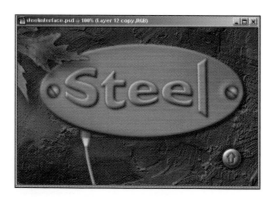

11

Drawing Weather and Nature

Mother Nature and her weather are fascinating to capture on paper and screen. Nature is very difficult to draw, however, especially water effects. In this chapter, we'll draw water effects, lightning, and other challenging work. We'll look at how subtle nature's colors are. We'll use Painter and Photoshop, but you can easily follow the tutorials with any program that has layers. We'll also look at how you can create your own brushes. This chapter teaches you:

▶ How to draw clouds and stormy weather, including lightning

▶ Basic techniques for creating water reflections

▶ How to create rain and snow effects in a few easy steps

▶ How you can draw a beautiful rose

Weather Effects

Drawing weather effects means anything from clouds, haze, and rain to snow and water reflection. Weather is really exciting to draw, but also tough to get just right. It doesn't help that everyone knows what a blue sky with clouds looks like. In this section, you'll learn the basic techniques behind water reflection and how to simulate snow and rain.

To begin with, we'll look at a few clouds. We'll also throw in a thundercloud with some lightning and combine our examples to create stormy weather. The following examples are created in Photoshop 6, but you can use other programs with layers, such as Painter or Photoshop Elements, instead.

Clouds

We'll begin with a soft, hardly visible cloud, the kind often seen in a blue sky on a hot summer day. Imagine some sand between your toes, feel the sun warming your back, and visualize what the sky would look like. Start with a canvas that measures 400 × 400 pixels with a resolution of 72 dpi. Fill the background with a linear gradient of two blue colors with the darker of the two at the top, as shown in Figure 11.1. The darker blue can be RGB 67, 117, 213, and the lighter blue can be RGB 74, 155, 213. You can choose darker blues and greyish-blue colors for a more dramatic sky like in fall, or lighter blues for early spring, but right now, let's stick to summer.

Create a new layer called Soft cloud. Use the Elliptical Selection Tool to draw a selection of three ovals that overlap. Then fill them with a pale blue color (RGB 205, 231, 239). Apply the Motion Blur filter as shown in Figure 11.1. (In Painter, look under Effects > Focus > Motion Blur; in Photoshop, look under Filter > Blur > Motion Blur.) This is a quick and easy way to create a soft cloud, as shown in the small preview window.

Figure 11.1
A soft cloud created with Motion Blur in Painter.

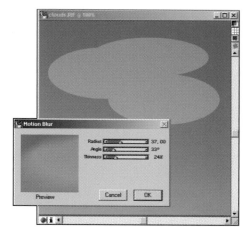

Clouds are as varied as grains of sand are numerous, and most of us don't know their differences or characteristics. Clouds are classified according to altitude, appearance, and origin, so here's a Web page called the Cloud Boutique at **http://vortex.plymouth.edu/clouds.html.** You can use this site to increase your "cloud knowledge base" before incorporating clouds in your artwork. The Web page is full of inspirational cloud descriptions and pictures. Here, we'll touch on how to create two different types of clouds, stratus and cumulonimbus.

Stratus Clouds

Stratus clouds are usually the lowest clouds you see, often appearing as an overcast deck. They can also be scattered, however. They have very soft, diffuse edges compared to other clouds.

Use the blurred cloud shape we previously created, and move the cloud to the right so you'll see only about half of it, sticking out from the right edge of the canvas. Duplicate this layer and flip the cloud horizontally so the two clouds overlap in the middle of the canvas. Scale the left cloud so it is a little larger than the right one. Create a new layer called Clouds. Now choose a large brush and the Airbrush Tool in Photoshop (in Painter, use the Digital Airbrush). In a few short dabs, paint with RGB 233, 244, 247 to make some areas of the clouds whiter and create more depth and texture in the cloud. Think of almost flat cotton balls when doing this, and make sure the cloud is as even as possible without turning into a flat area of color. Use very little pressure; only small amounts of color are necessary. Switch to a smaller brush at size 20 or so and paint soft "forks" of color highlights in the clouds, but not at the edges. The result should look similar to Figure 11.2. You can also use the Smudge tool and drag color around to create the "forks."

Figure 11.2
How to paint stratus clouds with the Airbrush Tool in Painter.

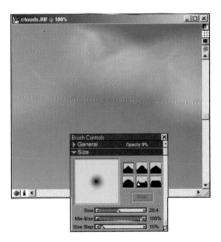

Cumulonimbus Clouds

Now let's look at some bad weather. Cumulonimbus clouds can produce lightning, thunder, heavy rains, strong winds, and tornadoes. They are the tallest of all clouds and can span all cloud layers, extending above 60,000 feet. They can be visible against clear blue sky—but not for long, because they are a sign of weather change.

Let's change our background. Use the Linear Gradient Tool and draw a gradient from top to bottom using two dark blue colors: RGB 32, 48, 82 and RGB 64, 90, 127. Create a copy of the left cloud and scale it down to approximately 100 pixels in width. Then use Motion Blur at an angle of 20 degrees and at a distance of 620 pixels. This will create a soft, "stripy" area below our clouds.

Now, hide the Clouds layer. Duplicate the Clouds layer with the "right side" clouds, to make it more dense, and then merge the two layers. Set layer opacity on the left cloud down to 35 percent. Move your clouds, as shown in Figure 11.3.

Figure 11.3
This image shows how to paint cumulonimbus clouds in Photoshop.

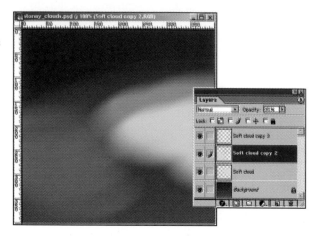

On a new layer above the background, paint stripes horizontally by hand. Do *not* use Shift to constrain your strokes; this will look unnatural. Use a size 21 brush and a soft, round size 13 brush. Create denser dots and thicker areas on the stripes as you go along. Use a pale, grayish color (RGB 252, 247, 231). Set layer opacity to 59 percent when you're done.

Now for the rough cloud shapes. Work on a new layer using the same color, and switch to a large brush using the aforementioned color plus this grayish hue: RGB 211, 208, 204. Use smaller brushes for details and for an *almost* white color. Use dull blue (RGB 87, 98, 135) for "shades" in the clouds. See Figure 11.4.

Figure 11.4
A dull blue color creates "shades" in these clouds. The next step is to draw out shapes and rough contours with three or four colors. Note that we have not used white color yet.

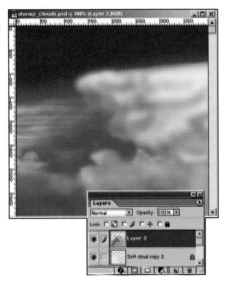

Paint in small circles at the details using the 13-pixel brush. Set pressure down to 12 percent if you have trouble with strokes and turn off Pressure in Brush Dynamics. Use the Smudge Tool to even out crisp edges and to add extra pressure on the tablet to create areas of more dense color. Work in circular movements with the Smudge Tool and follow your brush strokes. This way you can drag them out and create softer "endings" for them. Another trick is to draw at a layer set to 60 or 70 percent opacity right away if you find it hard to get the strokes soft enough. We'll leave our cloud for now, but we'll look at it again when we're drawing stormy weather later in this section. See Figure 11.5.

Figure 11.5
Some of the details have been painted, and we're now halfway there.

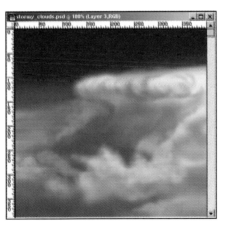

Snow

Snow can add great atmosphere to a winter landscape. To create a snowy hill, copy the big cloud shapes on the bottom right side of your image, or draw a hill shape at the bottom of a new file. The background color should be a dark blue, for example, RGB 41, 54, 86.

Remember how we created snow by drawing it in Chapter 7? Here's another trick where you don't have to draw *anything at all*. Fill a new layer with black color and go to Filter > Noise > Add Noise. Select as your settings 25 percent, Monochromatic, and Gaussian. Now go to Filters > Blur > Gaussian Blur. Use a radius of 1 pixel. This doesn't look snowy yet, so go to Image > Adjust > Threshold. Use 45 or so in value, or simply drag the slider to the left to see how many snowflakes you want. See Figure 11.6.

Figure 11.6
You can set the desired amount of snowflakes in Threshold.

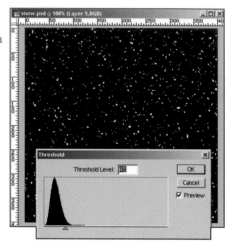

Now, these flakes look horrible—they are just pixilated white dots. Use Filter > Blur and choose Motion Blur. Set the angle slightly askew, depending on whether this should be a small amount of snow falling softly to the ground or a severe blizzard. In this filter, I set the angle at –80 and the distance at 7 pixels. See Figure 11.7.

Figure 11.7
Soften the flakes and set the angle at which they're falling by using the Motion Blur filter.

Now it's time to view our lovely winter picture. On the Layers Palette, set Blending mode to Screen, and there you have it—snow! (I probably shouldn't have shown you this trick, because you'll never draw snowflakes by hand again.) Look at Figures 11.8 and 11.9 to spot the differences in the Motion Blur settings. The blizzard version has two layers, one of which is set to 24 percent opacity. This makes some snow seem farther away and creates depth. Paint a few large snowflakes in the foreground by airbrushing them in by hand to add even more depth.

Figure 11.8
Motion Blur settings determine if you have a blizzard or softly falling snow.

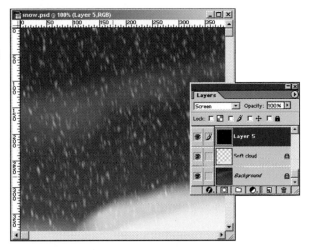

Figure 11.9
This blizzard uses layers to create depth.

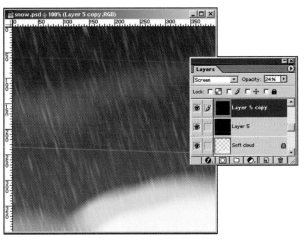

Simple Lightning

There are many filters to create lightning. But if you're getting comfortable with your tablet, you can draw lightning yourself in the same time as it takes you to find the filter. (Well, almost the same amount of time.) Start with a canvas of 300 × 300 pixels, fill it with black and a dark blue/purple linear gradient (RGB 78, 1, 104). Create a new layer; use white color and the Paintbrush Tool with a size 3 brush. Draw a jagged line to create the thickest fork of the lightning. Switch to a size 2 brush. This size doesn't exist in Photoshop, so create it! (See the last section in this chapter for a how-to.) Paint the smaller forks and side forks. Be careful to release the pressure when ending the strokes; start at the main fork and draw away from it. If you're not happy with the way your strokes end, flip your stylus around and use the eraser carefully at the ends (or use an eraser tool). See Figure 11.10.

Figure 11.10
Use a size 2 brush with the Airbrush or Paintbrush Tool for the smaller forks.

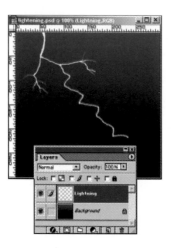

When you're done drawing forks, duplicate the layer and add Gaussian Blur at a radius of 6 pixels. The blurred layer should be the lower layer for best effect. See Figure 11.11.

Figure 11.11
Gaussian Blur creates a "highlighted" look on your lightning.

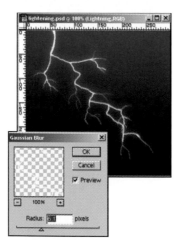

Now, create a new layer (or work on the lightning layer without the blur). With brushes of 9 and 13 pixels, create soft "dots" of white where these forks divide, plus at the very beginning of the lightning. See Figure 11.12.

Figure 11.12
Add dots of white to highlight the areas where the forks divide.

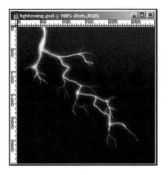

TIP

Use the technique of two layers, one layer with Gaussian Blur, to achieve highlighted effects. This is a great technique for lightning, and for neon lights and other brightly lit objects as well.

Stormy Weather

If you already have drawn the clouds in the previous examples, there's no reason not to recycle this artwork. Open the artwork we created previously in the Clouds section. Create a new canvas measuring 500 × 400 pixels and fill it with the same dark blue color from the clouds background. Delete the Stripes layer from the Clouds artwork. Link the other layers except the background and drag them onto the new canvas. You should have three layers above the background, one with cloud details, one with the "main cloud," and one called Soft cloud. The latter should be as it is, and the other two should be set to Multiply in Blending mode. Remove any hard edges with a layer mask or the Stylus eraser. Your artwork should look like Figure 11.13.

Figure 11.13
Blending modes is a
great tool for instantly
making your clouds
more stormlike.

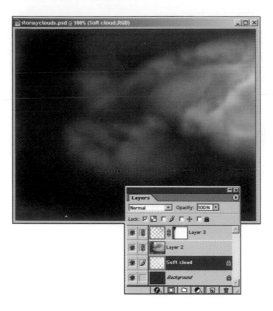

Go back to your lightning artwork. Merge the three lightning layers and drag the new, merged layer to the top of the new artwork. Place the lightning over the brightest area of the clouds. Use the Eraser Tool or a layer mask to remove the beginning of the lightning so that it looks like it's coming from the clouds. Add a layer above the clouds to add light to the cloud where the lightning appears. I've used very little highlight, simply because this is a small streak of lightning that doesn't light up the sky very much. Now copy the snow layer from the snow tutorial and scale it to fit so that it looks more like rain. Set layer opacity on the rain layer to approximately 35 percent. You really don't want to go outside if the sky looks like Figure 11.14.

Figure 11.14
Rain and lightning—
you can almost hear
the sound of thunder.

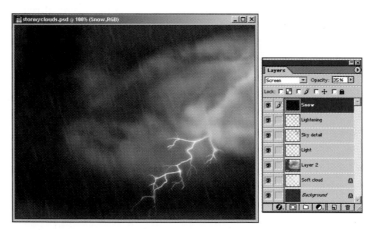

TIP

Study photographs of nature when you're creating artwork. These photos can be great references when working, especially for selecting colors. Zoom in on details to see what colors these scenes are made of, and use the same colors when drawing.

Filters for Weather Effects

There are plenty of filters available that create sunsets or weather effects in a snap. They can be very useful for creating weather effects in large areas such as backgrounds and so on for your artwork. We'll take a longer look at filters and plug-ins in Appendix B, but worth mentioning here in the "weather department" are the following filters:

► **Four Seasons/KPT Sky Effects (www.corel.com)**—Rayflect created an excellent filter called Four Seasons some time ago. Four Seasons was then made part of Kai's Power Tools 6.0 and was called KPT SkyEffects. This was subsequently bought by Corel and is now part of a filter package called KPT6. It has numerous presets where you can choose different cloud types, night or day scenes, and so on. You can create beautiful sunsets, choose Alien Skies for incredibly colored landscapes, or use the Special Effects setting for just adding glares and bursts of light. See Figure 11.15.

Figure 11.15

Four Seasons is a great filter package for skies, clouds, and complete night and day scenes.

▶ **Flood**—Flaming Pear (**www.flamingpear.com**) has several good filters, and some are excellent for weather and other natural effects. Flood is a filter that lets you create very realistic 3D-style water effects. You can control how the waves look, how the water ripples, and, most importantly, perspective. This product is great for creating quick water backgrounds and surfaces. See Figure 11.16.

Figure 11.16
"Flood" from Flaming Pear lets you create all kinds of water surfaces.

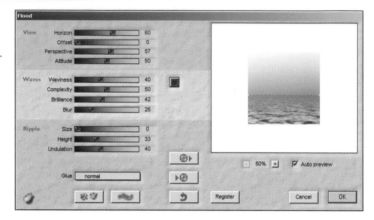

▶ **Solar Cell and Lunar Cell**—Solar Cell from Flaming Pear lets you design your own sun. This product has nothing to do with a regular sun in blue skies, but it's cool for special effects images like eclipses and close-ups of a burning orb. You can also use it to create other objects that don't simulate the sun at all. See Figure 11.17.

Figure 11.17
Use Solar Cell from Flaming Pear if you want to create your own sun. And, why not create a burning globe on the ground?

Lunar Cell, also from Flaming Pear, is an excellent filter with a lot of settings for everything in the world, from Climate, planetary details, and Air to other neat items. Add clouds, cities, or desertscapes to your heart's desire. This thing is unbeatable for creating sci-fi illustrations. You can combine this software with Glitterato, which creates nebulas and stars. Beam me up, Scotty. See Figure 11.18.

Figure 11.18
Lunar Cell is a great filter for all those who want to create a world of their own.

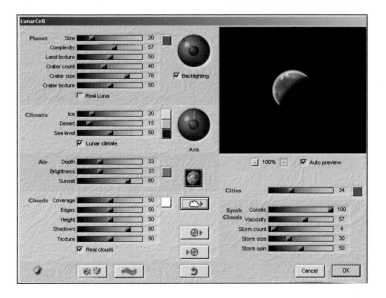

Drawing Nature

Drawing nature scenes is extremely difficult. Everyone knows—or can check—what an object from nature looks like, which contrasts with science fiction in that viewers simply must accept green men from Mars and other made-up stuff. In this section, we'll take a look at some basic techniques to help you simulate nature and its beauty in your tablet artwork.

Water

Water has to be the Number One headache for graphic artists, and this probably explains why filters simulating water are so popular. If you flip back to Chapter 7, you'll see examples of how to draw a sea with waves. In this chapter, we'll focus on creating other water images, including waves on a beach and rain drops.

At the Beach

You can easily imitate a beach with water reflection by using multiple layers in Painter or Photoshop. Follow this tutorial for your own private hideaway:

1. Start with a background fill at the lower half of the canvas, using a pale beige color for the sand (RGB 199, 194, 162). Now, add some Noise to it.

2. Create a layer above the background and paste in the Clouds we created in the previous section on the upper half of the canvas.

3. On a third layer, add a rough shape for the sea cliff and fill it a greenish-brown color such as RGB 121,125,91.

4. Create yet another new layer and make a darker brown oval shape for the sand with the Selection Tool. Set the feather at 2 pixels and fill it with brown color, RGB 167, 156, 100. Add Noise to this fill in the amount of 2 percent, Gaussian, and Monochromatic. Duplicate this layer, lock transparency, and move it 30 pixels or so to the right. Fill with RGB 144, 124, 74. Load the selection, switch to the Lasso Tool, and move sideways. Press Delete so you're left with just a thin brown shape. See Figure 11.19.

Figure 11.19
We're making a beach.
Start with the sand and
background.

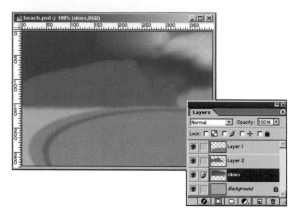

5. Duplicate the oval sand shape again. Now fill it with green (RGB 96, 119, 77). Add a layer mask and use the Linear Gradient Tool at 30 percent opacity. Draw from the left to the right, removing the fill on the left side so you can see the sand. Set Blending mode to Multiply and layer opacity to 70 percent. Duplicate this layer *twice* and fill with two paler greens (try RGB 99, 145, 134 or brighter). Cut away areas of the brightest green, as we did on the sand.

6. Work on the sea cliff a bit, using broad strokes and finishing off with the Noise filter. Take advantage of the textured brushes in Photoshop and "dot" areas of light on the rock, using the sand color plus RGB 229, 229, 195 for this. Use the Smudge Tool to create distance.

7. Add a layer called Black Shadow and create a rough selection with the Lasso Tool at the rock edges and into the water. Use a medium-sized brush with black color and add shade; paint from the cliff and towards the water. If you have the Intuos Airbush, this is a good time to use it. Use the layer mask to remove unwanted edges. See Figure 11.20.

Figure 11.20
Add depth by using black at the edges of the rocks.

Part IV Special Effects and Filters

8. Create a layer below the Black Shadow layer and name it Dark Blue. With a size 65 brush, carefully paint from right to left using a dark blue (RGB 42, 67, 111), moving your strokes towards the beach.

9. Above the Dark Blue layer, create a new layer called Pale Blue. Use the sand shape, load it as a selection (Ctrl+click / Command+click), and fill with this shade of bright blue: RGB 72, 133, 136. Remove parts of the selection so you're left with a horizontal "half-moon" shaped area. Use the layer mask to adjust the edges with a size 65 or 45 brush. Apply the layer mask. See Figure 11.21.

Figure 11.21
Use a bright blue to create the water shape.

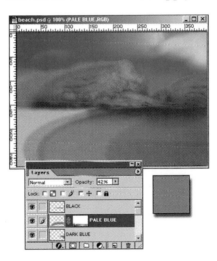

10. Copy your Black Shadow layer and fill it with blue RGB 104, 164, 167. Move it above the Black Shadow and adjust opacity to 44 percent or so.

11. Now copy your sky background and paste it on the top layer. Flip it vertically and add a layer mask. You want only some parts of it reflected in the water, so remove the areas where the black shade is and remove everything that covers the sand area. Use a size 35 brush for most areas and set the pressure as low as 10 percent. When you're finished, it should look like Figure 11.22.

Figure 11.22
Use the sky for reflection by copying it on a new layer, flipping it, and erasing areas.

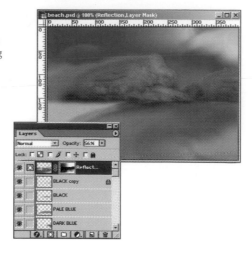

12. Repeat the sky duplication technique for the sea cliff. Copy, flip, and set layer opacity to 36 percent. Then create a mask and erase the areas overlapping the sand. Remember not to make the copies "perfect." (I erased some smaller areas so they'll look more natural.) Work some more on the details, but be careful to not create new details that aren't in the reflections. Make sure you're happy with the sky and the rocks before you flip them to create reflections. See Figure 11.23.

Figure 11.23
Be careful when using reflections—they may steal the show. Always remove parts of them using layer masks.

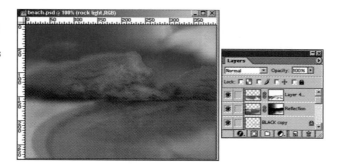

Rain and Raindrops

A quick way to create rain is to use the same technique as for snow that we discussed earlier in this chapter. This creates a rain effect as seen in the Stormy Weather example. To get your image just right, adjust the angles when you apply Motion Blur. Then duplicate your layer and scale the copy. Select Blending modes > Darken. This makes the image seem farther away. You can also try filling the layer with noise before applying the Motion Blur filter. Use the angles to fine-tune your image. The angle combined with distance determines whether your rain will be a soft drizzle or heavy rain.

Raindrops can be strong focal points for the eye and are used in many illustrations. Let's make a simple one ourselves.

1. On a green background, create a shape that simulates a leaf with a raindrop hanging from the edge.

2. On a new layer, create a circle and fill it with black from the edges and towards the middle using a medium-sized airbrush and very little pressure.

3. Keep the selection, but create a new layer and make a soft area of light blue color, as in Figure 11.24.

Figure 11.24
These are the first two steps towards a raindrop.

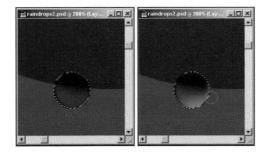

4. Create yet another layer for a reflection. Add a small white dot and drag it carefully in all directions using the Smudge Tool. Adjust your layers if necessary regarding opacity and link the raindrop layers together. Scale it vertically to get rid of the perfect circular shape.

5. This drop is hanging down, which means it's heavy and can fall any time. Add a picture to the background to view the transparency of the raindrop, and you're as good as done. See Figure 11.25. Add a small white highlighted area on the left side. Use a brush and then erase the edges, because this is supposed to be more of a reflection than a shine.

Figure 11.25
This raindrop, which appears ready to fall, adds a sense of anticipation to this illustration.

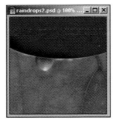

TIP

The secret behind creating wet surfaces is reflection. Just like the technique used on the beach scene that we created earlier, you can apply "wet surface" effects instantly by duplicating layers, flipping them, and adjusting them with layer masks and opacity.

Natural Objects

Drawing natural objects is a real challenge, and we'll look at some basic techniques to get you started. Textures will help you to give your artwork the natural surfaces you're trying to copy or create a quick background area of your object. Customized brushes, which can be used to create texture, come in handy when working with natural objects. Noise filters come in handy as well. To make our next illustration a real challenge, we'll use Photoshop and stay clear of Painter's wonderful brushes.

Leaves

 Leaves are not the easiest objects to draw, especially if you want to view them close up. If you do, you have to draw in their veins and other details. This level of detail takes a lot of work to get just right. When drawing natural objects, it can be a huge advantage if you work on a colored background instead of a white canvas. It's easier to get the colors right if you work with backgrounds of similar (or contrasting) colors to your motif, and not some "unnatural" shade. In the following tutorial, I've filled a background with green color (RGB 86, 112, 40) and added the Noise filter in Photoshop.

1. To begin, draw a leaf shape with the Lasso Tool and fill it with a moss green or dark green color (RGB 82, 102, 36). If you deselect it, reselect the shape by clicking inside it with the Magic Wand or Ctrl+click the layer. To Save the selection, go to Select > Save selection.

2. Use the Sponge filter and use the settings shown in Figure 11.26. Then, draw thin lines to sketch out the veins of the leaf. Use little pressure when doing this, because this is meant as an aid for your artwork.

Figure 11.26
Use the Sponge filter to get some pattern on your leaf.

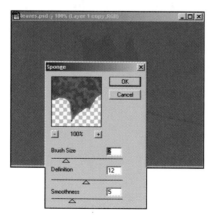

3. Now you're ready to move to the next phase of this illustration. Lock transparency, use the Smudge Tool to remove any darker areas, and apply Gaussian Blur at a maximum radius of 1 pixel.

4. Load your saved selection on a new layer called Yellow. Work with a warm yellow color, like RGB 220, 180, 46, and brush in rough areas.

5. On a new layer, use red (RGB 181, 75, 25) and a textured brush. (I used one from the default brush set in Photoshop, number 27.) Just dab the color on, using a darker red color at the edges. Create a new layer called Green and repeat the procedure. Dab carefully with the same brush using the darkest green color (RGB 82, 102, 36) from the sponged leaf layer. When you're done, change to a brighter green for highlights. See Figure 11.27.

Figure 11.27
Dab areas of color onto your leaf with a textured brush.

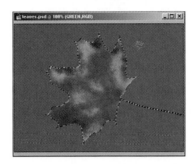

6. Finally, create selections with the Lasso Tool that *follow* the veins. Use the two green colors for this. Begin at the vein and paint outwards, creating sharper edges against the veins and smooth transitions towards the edges. Use a warm brown color at the darkest red areas as well.

7. Now, set the Yellow layer to Soft Light in Blending mode, then add a drop shadow on the bottom (sponged) leaf layer. You can also add an exciting background if you're not satisfied with the green color and noise filter background we began with. In the finished artwork, I have added some more leaves, and changed the background to something that resembles asphalt. See Figure 11.28.

Figure 11.28
This leaf was created by "dotting" on paint.

Grass

Grass, thankfully, is easy to draw compared to leaves, flowers, and other objects with lots of details. Use layers to duplicate your blades of grass and merge them. Then add light or shade and create vast areas of grass using layer duplication. You can draw grass much the same way as the pine twig in Chapter 7, but draw from the bottom of the blade to the tip to get a smooth end on each stroke.

When creating artwork that has large areas of flat color, and not an overall airbrushed look, you can use a different technique to simulate areas of grass or straw. Take a look at the sketch in Figure 11.29. This grass was created by selecting jagged shapes with the Lasso Tool and filling them with green. A brighter green was used here and there to create highlights and outlines in the grass. Varying the green color helped give life to the flat areas of color. Notice the layers: The grass areas were copied repeatedly to avoid drawing literally thousands of blades of grass.

Figure 11.29
Detail of sketch
with grass.

Flowers

Drawing a delicate flower, such as a pale rose, can be a challenge. The colors are very subtle and this subtlety gives the rose its depth. It's easy to make the mistake of creating hard shadows on natural objects, but if you study nature, you'll discover that the subtle changes are what it's all about. If you use the Color Picker on a photo of a flower, you'll be surprised when discovering the various shades and colors of it.

Let's begin by looking at how a rose is formed. First, draw a soft outline of a rose using a contrasting color, like bright green. This will be a sketch layer, and you will *not* paint anything else on it. Work with an almost black background to clearly see the subtle shades in this example, and use the smallest brush on your sketch layer. See Figure 11.30. Or, download the Photoshop 6 file for this tutorial, containing the sketch layer, from **www.iril.no**.

Figure 11.30

Start with a rough sketch in a contrasting color. Make sure your sketch lines connect so you can select the petals (areas) in your sketch layer. If not, you have to select small areas each time you want to paint them. Saving your selections is a good idea!

To start creating a rose based on your sketch, this is what you do:

1. Click on the transparent background with the Magic Wand and choose Inverse. On a new layer below the sketch, fill the selection with your base color (by this, I mean the primary color of the rose). In this case, use a soft pink color: RGB 237, 210, 197.

2. Make a new layer for highlights. Select a color that's slightly brighter than the base color, and use area selections from your sketch layer. Select areas with the Wand and swap to the highlight layer—but make sure you don't paint on the sketch layer. Use a size 45 Brush and paint with low pressure on your stylus at the edges of the petals. Do not use this color against the center of the rose petals. Don't mind any jagged edges of the selections; we'll fix them later. See Figure 11.31.

Figure 11.31
The sketch layer for our rose is hidden when we start painting the petals.

3. Pick a pink color that has a darker hue than the base color, such as RGB 227, 191, 174. On a new layer, repeat the procedure we just did, but paint at the bases of the petals and anywhere else you'd want darker areas. Use smaller brushes, like sizes 35 and 27.

4. Hide the sketch layer and use two new colors, one a reddish pink (RGB 224, 131, 115) and the other a brownish pink (RGB 135, 80, 69). Use the reddish pink at the center of the rose, and use the brownish pink for shades. See Figure 11.32. Create selections for the folds in the petals and fill them gently with brownish pink, using the larger brushes. Create small selections of 1-feather settings with the Lasso Tool, and make sure to cover any non-colored areas that the sketch lines created. Merge all rose layers—but do not merge the sketch and background layer.

Figure 11.32
Create small selections with the Lasso Tool and fill them with a reddish pink and a brownish pink.

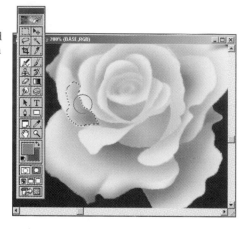

5. Now get your Smudge Tool going if the edges are jagged, with a 5-pixel brush (or smaller) and low pressure. Work along the edges of the petals for best results; this way, you won't drag the color everywhere. Finally, use a reddish brown color that goes well with your darkest pink to draw thin, darker lines along the petals and at the very center of the rose. Use a size 2 brush and use the Smudge Tool afterwards to soften your stroke.

6. For extra details on the petals, use a pale beige color or a darker beige if your petals are dark pink (RGB 199, 194, 162 or brighter) and the smallest brush to draw thin lines that follow the structure of the petals. The color you choose for these lines depends on the colors you've used on the petals—the strokes should barely be visible. Use a separate layer for this. (This work could easily take hours.) Use the Smudge Tool as you go along. Note that I have not drawn lines on all the petals, just a few for the sake of the effects. See Figure 11.33.

Figure 11.33
Details were added and areas were darkened using the smallest brushes and the Smudge Tool.

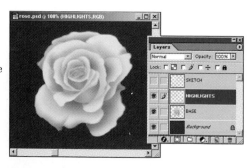

Make Your Own Brushes

Customized brushes are vital for drawing large textured areas in a few quick strokes. In this section, you'll learn to create, save, and use your own customized brushes in Painter 6 and Photoshop 6. If you have skipped ahead and are reading this *before* doing the tutorials earlier in this chapter, you'll be able to "cheat" by using textured brushes instead of painting everything by hand. Creating and saving your own brushes can be a time-saving tool that helps you create your artwork faster and with more consistency.

Creating Brushes in Photoshop 6 and Photoshop Elements

You can add and replace your brushes easily in Photoshop 6 and Elements, and, most importantly, you can delete the ones you don't want or even replace the full set of brushes. Deleting brushes one by one is helpful if you download huge brush collections from the Internet and you don't like some of them. To avoid cluttering your brush palette, name the brush collections using comprehensible names and load them one at a time. Working with the pop-up Brush palette is similar to working with Actions and Swatches palettes, so you'll know your way around it. Photoshop is, by definition, not a painter program, so you can't expect the amount of brushes you'll find in Painter. There are some options available to you, though, and if you can't find a brush you like for a specific task, simply create it yourself!

 To create a regular brush, choose New Brush from the pop-up palette menu and adjust the settings for brush angle, spacing, roundness, and so on. *Spacing* controls the distance between the brush marks (or dots) in your stroke. Type a value or use the slider to enter a value that is a percentage of the brush diameter. *Angle* means you can achieve a chiseled stroke with the brush. See Figure 11.34.

Figure 11.34
This is the New Brush Dialog box in Photoshop 6.

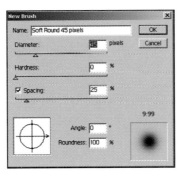

If you want to create a customized, textured brush, use the Rectangular marquee and select the area (pattern) you want. The other Selection tools can't be used to create a brush, and feathering cannot be used either—you have to use the Rectangular Marquee. You have to make your adjustments to the pattern itself before creating the brush. (Make sure feathering is set to 0 or you won't get access to the Define Brush command.) On the Edit menu, choose Define Brush and give your brush its name. See Figure 11.35. Use existing patterns in photos or draw a texture or symbol you are happy with and save it forever as a brush.

Figure 11.35
Create a new brush by selecting the required area.

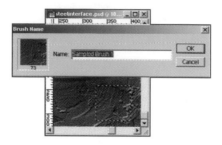

This brush that you've created is more than just a snapshot of a pattern. You can paint with it just like a regular brush, using any color you like. Manipulate your pattern by softening the edges and so on *before* you create a brush of it. If you don't, you'll get something just as boring as the brush I made in the previous figure.

NOTE

Here's how to edit a brush in Photoshop after you've created it. Click the Brush thumbnail on the Options bar and you can make the changes you want. "Edit Brush" is not an option on the pop-up menus, either on the Options bar next to the brush thumbnail or in the Brushes palette. See Figure 11.36.

Figure 11.36
This figure shows you where the Brush settings are.

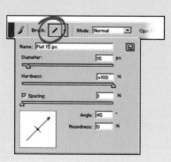

You can use an existing brush to create a new one based on its settings. This is handy if you want to make minor adjustments in size or spacing. Just click the small icon in the Brush Preferences dialog box; the icon looks like the standard Windows "document icon" with the folded corner. Switch to this new brush and make your adjustments by clicking the brush thumbnail. Right-click over the brush in the Brushes palette to rename it.

To create your own specialized set of brushes, *append* new brushes to your existing set and save under a new name. On the Brushes palette pop-up menu, choose Load to append. Choose replace to load just the new set. If you open sets separately, you can save them under different names after you've deleted and added brushes. You can then append each customized set to your liking. Note that when you append a new set to another, it ends up at the end of the first one. Think about the *order* you want your brushes in before appending. When you're working with your brushes and you're wondering where the original brushes went, don't panic. They're hidden under Reset Brushes. Choose OK or Append in the dialog box that pops up.

TIP

If you want to create natural-looking brush strokes that fade and to avoid crisp ends to your strokes, take advantage of the pressure-sensitivity features in Photoshop and Painter. Let the Stylus always control size and opacity when drawing with brushes in these programs. You can simulate soft lead pencils, watercolors, and similar items.

Creating Brushes in Painter

Painter has fifteen impressive brush collections to choose from. These collections range from Pencils to Airbrushes. The brushes have names describing their appearance, such as Dry Ink, Graphic Paintbrush, Round Camelhair, and Smeary Round.

All the brushes are pressure sensitive, and you can adjust Spacing, Bleed, and other settings for each brush in Brush Controls. You can go back to the original brushes by using the Restore Default Variant command. The Expression Settings give you numerous options for choosing settings for Pressure, Direction, and so on, to control everything from Size and Opacity to Angle, Grain, and Color.

Painter has a vast list of options for customizing your brush. One of them is especially cool: the ability to set Bristle. This creates the look of a real brush stroke, because it simulates the striations that hairs on a real-life brush make! You can use the Bristle controls to set how many individual bristles you want in a single brush dab. I'm sure we could use a whole chapter just going through all the options in Painter, so let's move on to the how-to example of creating a brush.

The brush icons in Painter are just symbols that hide several brushes of the same type in one collection for each icon. Start your own brush collection by doing this: Create a small icon for your new brush collection and select it by dragging the Rectangular Selection Tool around it. Remember to hold Shift down to constrain the selection. On the Brushes palette, choose Brushes menu > New Brush, as shown in Figure 11.37. Name the Brush and click OK.

Figure 11.37
Create a selection around your symbol to make an icon for your new brush collection. (Please work on your icon more than I did!)

If you want to create different collections, like one for watercolors, one for oil paints, and so on, it's wise to create representative icons for them as they will be added to your Brushes menu. You can create and save variants now. Draw something you'd like to save as a brush. Make sure you have your Brushes icon collection active in the Brushes menu palette. Create a selection around it, and on the Brushes menu, select Variant > Save Variant. Give it a clever name and tick off Save Current Colors if you want the exact colors you have drawn it with. See Figure 11.38.

Figure 11.38
Suddenly, you have your own icon!

And now for the fun part. Use Brush Controls to fine-tune your freshly made brush. Change its size, spacing, angle, and so on, and even use Impasto options. You could play around with this for *hours*. Add random jittering to the brushes that you create for irregular spattering all over the place. You can also copy a variant you're happy with and place it in one of the existing brush collections. This is handy, for example, when creating a new pen you want to be accessible under the Pens category. See Figure 11.39.

Figure 11.39
Choose Save Variant to
save your new brush in
your Brush collection.

Drawing with Brushes

When you use custom-made brushes, you have the option just to "dot" the pattern on your
artwork with the benefit of a pressure-sensitive tablet. Or you can draw continuous patterns,
depending on your brush preferences.

In Photoshop 6 or Elements, use Brush Dynamics to add some action to your brush. For
example, you can manipulate fade-out rates. Setting high values like 90 in steps on Pressure and
Color can also give you interesting effects. See Figure 11.40. Be careful with your choices for
background and foreground colors when playing around with this. It's easy to forget about the
options in Brush Dynamics when working with a tablet. Often, I just set pressure to be
controlled by the Stylus; sometimes I adjust color according to what I'm working on, but
generally I just leave the other settings alone.

When working with customized brushes, you need all the extra options you'll get, because you
won't get all the neat options of angle and so on as you would with regular brushes. On the
other hand, Photoshop 6 has a lot of brush collections for you to try—seven in all—from Drop
Shadow brushes to Natural brushes.

Figure 11.40
Don't forget the options
in Brush Dynamics!

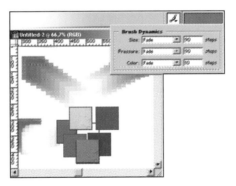

In Painter, the Brush Controls palette that I mentioned earlier holds the key to everything. This is the control palette where you can change every aspect of each brush by opening every option in this one place. Under General, you'll find settings for Dab type > Captured, Static Bristle, and so on, Stroke Type > Multi, Rake, and Hose. The next choices are for Size, Spacing, Bristle, and so on, with each holding multiple choices.

When you make changes to a brush, Painter "builds" the brush after your choices. When you have built a brush you're extremely happy with, go to the Brushes palette; choose Variant > Save Variant. The name of the existing brush (the one you've made changes to) comes up as the default. Name it "Purple Haze *Small*" for example, to separate it from the original Purple Haze brush, or "Purple Haze *Grainy*" if you made that change under the General options. Make many variants of the same brush, because it can be hard to remember your exact changes when you swap back and forth between brush collections. Spare yourself from trying to remember the exact settings of the brush you previously used and just save it right away.

There you have it. We've created weather effects with clouds, snow, and lightning. We've also drawn beach scenes and rain. Leaves, grass, and flowers were also covered. Then, we created the brushes that are quite useful for these projects. If you're looking for Photoshop brushes, there are a few links to Brush sets in Appendix B. You're now all set to put these items to use, and you can combine them with the Textures examples in the next chapter.

12

Textures and Patterns

Textures and patterns are quick and easy to create, either with filters or drawing techniques. We'll also edit and paint with patterns. We'll do all of this in Painter, Photoshop 6, and CorelDRAW. When you have finished this chapter, you'll have learned how to:

▶ Create your own textures

▶ Work and paint with patterns in Photoshop 6 and Elements

▶ Make seamless backgrounds

Working with Textures

All too often, flat backgrounds, bad fills, and poorly made gradients find their way into designs and illustrations. You, however, can avoid these problems if you know a few tricks for making cool and stunning textures and patterns yourself. Sure, you can cut and paste from photographs and images to get the right texture, or even use texture or pattern libraries, but there are plenty of advantages to creating your own. As an added bonus, creating textures is fun!

Using Filters

Programs like Photoshop and Painter are loaded with filters that make the creation of textures very easy. You have the option of fading the filter effect, and you can apply it several times to create variations. Or, you can put it on separate layers and use Blending modes or Layer effects to manipulate them. You can also combine various filters for exciting combinations.

The filters range from the weird to the useful, and many simulate various pens and brushes so you can add them to strokes or areas of your artwork. If you combine the filters with your Pen Tool and use hand-painted masks and so on, you can achieve even more nifty effects. *You control the filters; don't let them control you.*

Remember the vector illustration that we worked on in Photoshop 6 in Chapter 8? The trousers are a great example of how important a cool texture or pattern can be for good results. An eye-catching texture adds depth and interest to an otherwise flat surface, so let's analyze it more closely. In Figure 12.1, you can see the trousers as a flat green color to the left. Next to it is the same pair of trousers with filters added to create texture.

To create this texture, I first removed some of the left trouser leg with a mask. (This is also visible in the left image.) Then I added a Sponge filter to the right trouser leg and a new layer with light on the left leg. I painted with the Airbrush Tool afterwards, using a brighter green for highlights and a darker green for shadows. You'll discover that working with filters—or hand-painting textures—often will give you a great "background" to work on, making it easier to draw additional effects and details!

Figure 12.1
A close-up of trousers with and without texture. Notice the difference in substance and depth.

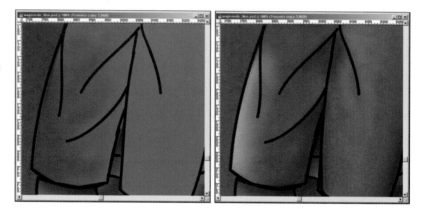

This example also brings up another important point when working with textures: Just as a flat-colored area can be boring, so also can a texture seem wrong or misplaced when created by using just a filter. The result is simply too perfect. You'll need to work on the texture afterwards with an Airbrush or another tool to add depth and life to it.

TIP

The texture can easily be destroyed when you edit it, so remember the trick of duplicating and hiding the layer with your texture on it. This way, you can try out different techniques without being afraid of losing your cool texture altogether. Yes, I know there's a History palette in programs like Photoshop, but many artists' heads will nod in agreement when I say that often you'll be so far into experimenting that your History palette is used up. In Photoshop 6, you now have the option to save States, so here's another way to be rescued from disaster.

Combining Filters

You can achieve enticing textures by combining two or more filters in your artwork. For a rough look, you could use pixilated filters first, Sponge filters next, and then finish off with a Blur or Noise filter, for example. In Painter, you have the option of applying a Surface texture, which is a good filter when you want to add depth and structure to a surface. (The "noisier" the surface is beforehand, the better the effect, in my opinion.) This filter has lots of controls regarding light and depth. Play around with the Shine and Reflection settings to get the surface you want. See Figure 12.2.

Figure 12.2
Use Painter's Surface Texture filter for quick results.

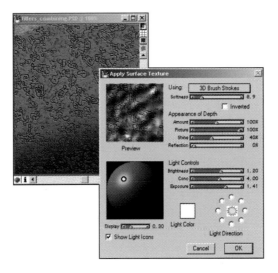

NOTE

Painter has several Paper textures to choose from. Paper textures are applied to the entire surface or canvas, and not to single items or areas in your artwork. The Brushes in Painter interact with the texture, or paper grain. (This interaction does not apply to Photoshop, where, on the other hand, you can apply textures to any item or area on any layer.) A good tip is to start out in Painter and apply the texture there, then work with it until you're nearly finished. Open it in Photoshop to apply effects in smaller areas and on various layers.

Let's take a look at some filters that look good together. Fill the canvas with a color, (in this example I've used a dark, maroon red (RGB 139, 47, 8). It's important that you start with filters that add structure to a flat color; many filters demand selections or variations in color to work properly. In Photoshop, add the Smudge Stick filter first. On the menu, choose Filter > Artistic > Smudge Stick. Then add a Plastic Wrap, but with low settings in Highlight strength and high settings in smoothness. (It's not a plastic *look* we're after.) Finish off with the Noise filter. Use the Uniform setting with an amount of about 4. See Figures 12.3a, 12.3b, and 12.3c. And voilà! You have depth, light, and texture all rolled into one. Just imagine the possibilities!

Figures 12.3a, 12.3b, and 12.3c
Use various filters for cool results. Here we have the Smudge Stick (a), Plastic Wrap (b), and Noise filters (c).

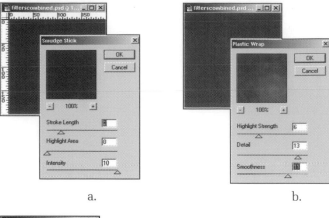

a.   b.

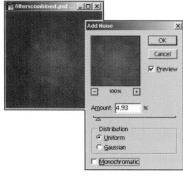

c.

And don't forget all the things you can do with Blending options as well. Copy the layer in Figure 12.3c and add another filter—the Fresco filter, for example—to the top layer. In Figure 12.4, you'll see it in Normal mode to the left. You'll get instant effects just by changing Blending modes. Note how the brighter areas come forward in the middle image, which is the Screen mode.

Figure 12.4
Blending modes make all the difference. From left to right: Normal, Screen, and Exclusion.

You can also combine several filters for reasons other than just cool effects. Flip back to the snow and rain examples in Chapter 11 and look at the filter combinations there.

Part IV Special Effects and Filters

Drawing Textures

Sometimes not even the coolest filter package will do the trick, so you have to create your own textures. I have no intention of convincing you that drawing textures by hand on a 600 × 800-pixel canvas is a *good idea*. I do recommend, however, painting a texture you're happy with in an area measuring some 100 or 200 pixels and then making a brush of it. (For the full scoop on making your own brushes, turn to "Make Your Own Brushes," in Chapter 11. If your program doesn't give you that option, you have to go down the familiar road of duplication once more. Take a look at the upcoming "Working with Patterns" section too, because it provides an easier way to paint large areas of texture and patterns. Patterns are also saved in color. See Figure 12.5.

Figure 12.5
Save your texture as a "Texture Brush." Notice that a colored texture is used, and not black and white, because I want lots of nuances in the texture.

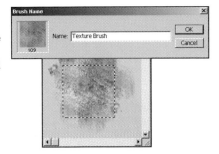

Play around with the spacing of your brush, or just "dab" the texture where you want it. A light touch on your tool combined with different colors "stamped" over each other can achieve texture effects you that can use to simulate fabrics. See my test canvas in Figure 12.6.

Figure 12.6
Use your Texture brush with various spacing and pressure settings.

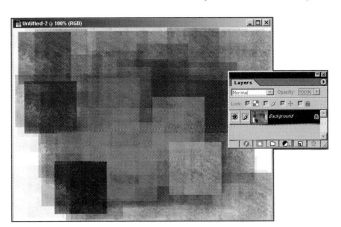

Working with Patterns

In this section, we'll take a look at Patterns and how you can save your own and paint with them in Photoshop 6 or Elements.

A pattern can be as simple as horizontal lines drawn with your Pen and a Brush Tool or a more complex design of several shapes that fit snugly to each other. You can make simple patterns just by using a distortion filter or two, like the Twirl filter in Photoshop, which we're going to try here: Create two vertical rectangles side by side, in the same size. Select All (Ctrl+A; Command+A) and choose Filter > Distort > Twirl. Use an Angle setting of 300 or more (like 305). See Figure 12.7.

Figure 12.7

Patterns are as easy as can be with the Distortion filters in Photoshop.

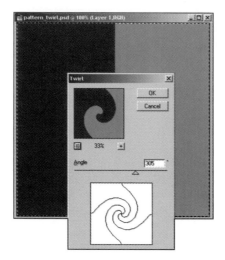

By duplicating this pattern and rotating it 180 degrees, you can paste the copies next to each other to create a larger, more complex pattern. This type of pattern can be used in your illustrations for curtain backdrops, carpets, and furniture. They can even be wrapped around other objects. You can add effects endlessly by using other filters with your simple patterns. See Figure 12.8. Our pattern was duplicated, then all the layers were merged, and the Ripple filter was added. Use your Pen and a Brush or other tool to go over any unwanted areas or irregularities in the pattern.

TIP

You can create patterns out of existing images or drawings by duplication. Use a photo of your pet, family, a flower, or anything you'd like. You can add effects to the photo, convert it to greyscale or add duotones, and then create a pattern when you're pleased with the result. This could be fun for personal Web page backgrounds and so on.

Figure 12.8
You can add other filters to your patterns. This is our pattern before and after the Ripple filter in Photoshop.

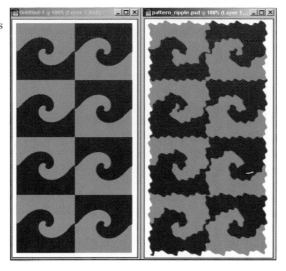

Painting with Patterns

Nowadays, Photoshop lets you save a pattern just as easily as a texture brush. Photoshop comes with a library of patterns you can use, or you can create your own. To begin, create a rectangular selection around the area you want for your pattern, and choose Edit > Define Pattern. Give the pattern a name and click OK. You can now use the pattern to fill, for example, the background of a new image; simply choose Pattern in the Fill dialog box. See Figure 12.9. Note that just as with brushes, you can't use feathered selections to create areas for patterns.

Figure 12.9
Select the area and give your pattern a name.

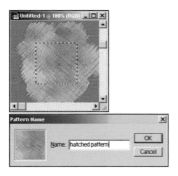

You can use the Pattern Stamp Tool to paint with a pattern. Choose your brush size and select the Pattern from the Options bar. If you select Aligned on the Options bar, you can paint the pattern as seamless, uniform tiles in whatever brush size you wish. Use Brush options as usual for controlling pressure. As you can see from Figure 12.10, a Pattern is saved as is, colors and all. So when you want to fill large areas, Pattern, not Brush, is the way to go.

Figure 12.10
Paint areas as large as
your brush allows you
to with a Pattern.

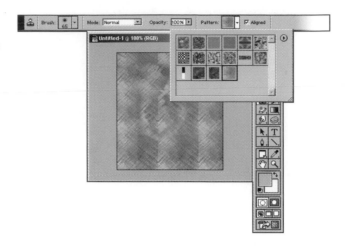

TIP

You can paint with a picture as well, and not just with the textures and
patterns you have created. Make a rectangular selection of your picture and
save it as a Pattern if you want it as is. (Or you can save it as a Brush.) Load
the Pattern from the Options bar. With the Pattern Stamp Tool selected, you
can paint away.

Creating Seamless Backgrounds

To create a seamless background, you can simply paint it using your own pattern as mentioned
previously. Check off Aligned and start painting. In all places you draw, Photoshop will recreate
the pattern for you, nicely aligned. There are, indeed, other methods to create seamless
backgrounds if you don't want to create a pattern for it. Note that the Pattern Stamp Tool,
although seamless, will create unwanted seams if your pattern selection isn't precise enough at
the edges.

The Clone Stamp Tool can help you create seamless backgrounds. If you are unfamiliar with the
Clone Stamp Tool in Photoshop, you'll soon discover why this tool could be your new best
friend. Let's say you have a small pattern you'd like to make much bigger so you can create a
large background, perhaps for an illustration or a Web page. Open your pattern or favorite
texture and crop to the area you'd like to convert to a bigger background. (Make sure your image
is square, 72 dpi, and in RGB mode.) In this example, our image is just 150 × 150 pixels.
Choose Filter > Other > Offset and enter values for both Horizontal and Vertical that are exactly
half of your image size, in this case, 75 pixels. Select Wrap Around in the dialog box, as shown
in Figure 12.11.

Figure 12.11
Create quick backgrounds for Web pages with the Offset filter.

You now have an image consisting of four small squares with a clear seam dividing them in the middle. This is where your new friend, the Clone Stamp Tool, will rush to your aid. Zoom to 200 percent and select the Clone Stamp Tool. Set Opacity to Off in Brush Dynamics. "Erase" or edit the seams by selecting an area in the pattern next to the seam. Click Alt where you want the source to be, and when you paint, you'll see that this tool keeps the distance between your source area and where you paint. In this example, a brush size of 9 should do the trick. (Brush size depends on the details in your pattern.) Stay away from the edges of the image, because these will get next to each other. Use a soft brush when editing details in patterns unless your pattern is very pixilated and has clear-cut areas in it. You can also use the Smudge Tool for this kind of work. See Figure 12.12.

Figure 12.12
In this image, the tool is a circle and the clone source is the cross in our pattern image.

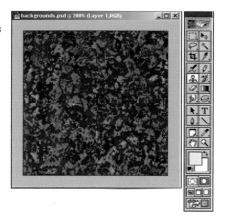

When you're happy with the seams, you can duplicate what you've made to create a background in an image. You can also export it as a GIF to use on a Web page. To use on the Web, choose Save For Web, select GIF from the drop-down menu, and click OK. In your favorite HTML editor, use the GIF as a background, where it tiles automatically. This is the exciting part, because you can see whether the image will tile nicely or not. In some situations, you may discover unwanted areas in your pattern that you didn't see until you tiled it as a background. These could be areas of a specific color, or a small area that repeats itself so that you'll notice it and nothing else. This depends on your original selection and its size. The smaller the size, the more repetitive the effects are. At the same time, you don't want heavy graphics to take forever to load in your browser, so don't overdo the size—keep it between 150 and 200 pixels and in as few colors as possible. See Figure 12.13. Go back to your pattern image and make the necessary adjustments, and save as a GIF again. Remember, you can now save your work as a Pattern to use later on!

Figure 12.13
You can tile your GIF as a background for a Web page.

TIP

So you don't have an offset filter? No problem! Simply copy your pattern on a canvas twice as big as the pattern and flip the copy horizontally or vertically, so the two edges "match." Merge the two layers. Duplicate this new layer and flip in the other direction, merge layers, and use the Clone Stamp Tool on any irregularities. See Figure 12.14 to visualize how it's done.

Figure 12.14
Copy and flip horizontally. Then merge and flip vertically. Easy!

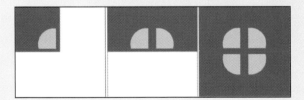

Painting Patterns as Straight Lines

To paint patterns as straight lines, choose your brush size and pattern plus the Pattern Stamp Tool. Select Aligned on the Options bar. Place the Brush where you want the pattern to start and hold Shift down while dragging the Tool horizontally. I've used a large brush, size 65, which creates the rounded edges at the beginning and the end of the line. See Figure 12.15.

Figure 12.15
Click and drag while holding Shift down to create a pattern as a straight line.

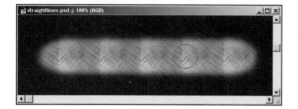

Editing Patterns in Painter

You can edit the Patterns in Painter 6 by choosing Windows > Show Art Materials. Click the Patterns section menu to view the controls. A small drop-down menu is hidden on the right as well; choose Check Out Pattern, as shown in Figure 12.16. The pattern opens up in a separate window, where you can edit it just like any other image. Now, see Figure 12.17.

Figure 12.16
Choose Check Out Pattern to edit your patterns.

Part IV Special Effects and Filters

Figure 12.17
Edit, draw, and do whatever you want, including adding a surface texture to the pattern.

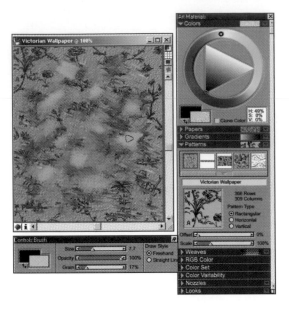

When you're done editing the pattern, you have to save it to the pattern library. From the drop-down menu, choose Add Image To Library, as shown in Figure 12.18. Give it a unique name, because the name that automatically comes up is simply "Default." If you don't give it another name, you replace the existing pattern. Click OK and see that the pattern you created is now present on the Pattern menu. If you want to create a pattern from scratch and not from an existing one, you'll follow the same steps as described above. If you want to keep the Pattern you used to create a new one from, just select No when the dialog for Save pops up when you close the pattern.

Figure 12.18
Save your pattern for eternity by using the Add Image to Library choice.

Creating Tiled Patterns in Painter

You can create tiled patterns easily with the Capture Pattern command. I have opened the Vines pattern that comes with Painter. I want a new pattern with a close-up of the lavender-blue flowers, so I chose Check Out Pattern as before. With the rectangular selection tool, I selected one of the flowers. See Figure 12.19.

Figure 12.19
Use the Rectangular
Selection Tool to select
the area you want as a
pattern.

From the drop-down menu in the Patterns section, select Capture Pattern. In the dialog box, you can choose Rectangular Tile, Horizontal Shift, or Vertical Shift. Rectangular Tile places your selection in a grid for fills, Horizontal Shift sets the tiles in rows, and Vertical Shift sets the tiles in columns. The Bias slider controls the amount of offset. This feature is cool for setting patterns on top of each other in rows or columns like bricks. Use a setting of 50 percent for neat patterns, like the example you see in the left corner of Figure 12.20. Give the pattern a name and click OK. Try out your new pattern by creating a new document and filling it with the pattern: Effects > Fill > Pattern. Choose the opacity you want and click OK.

Figure 12.20
You can create new
layers and fill them
with other patterns
as well.

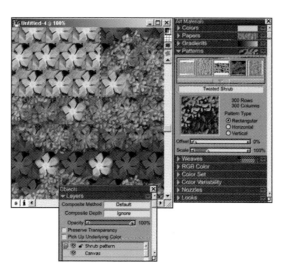

You can, of course, combine several patterns for fun effects. In Figure 12.22 above, the pattern of captured flowers is filled on the canvas. You can see the pattern in the upper left corner selection. A new layer was created above it and filled with another pattern called Twisted Shrub. With the Eraser Tool, you can remove areas of this pattern, which has already been done on some of the flowers. The pattern fill was set to 70 percent so you can see some of the flower pattern on the canvas as well.

Creating Custom Pattern and Texture Fills in CorelDRAW

You can change a pattern or texture to create a custom fill in CorelDRAW 9. You can adjust the pattern or texture fill using the so-called *fill tiling vector*. You can also transform an object and fill it simultaneously with the Transform Fill With Object option or just add a texture fill—CorelDRAW is loaded with them.

Click the Fill Tool flyout and click the Texture Fill dialog icon (the blue-patterned icon). In Figure 12.21, you can see the dialog box for Texture Fills. Select one of the libraries in the drop-down menu at top left, and then select the texture from the scrollable list below. Shown is the Leopard texture fill. Note that you have lots of options for the texture fill, including Softness, Brightness, and the option to replace any color the texture is made of. These options vary depending on which texture you have selected.

Figure 12.21
This is the Texture Fill dialog box in CorelDRAW. Replace any color with one of your liking.

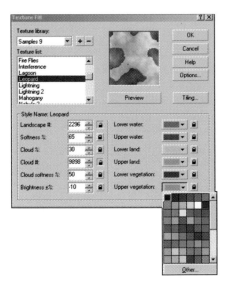

In the dialog box, you have a Tiling button. Click this to access the Tiling dialog box, which lets you set Skew angles and Row/Column offsets for the texture fill. You can draw strokes and fill them. In Figure 12.22, you see a drawn shape. Keep the shape selected and open the Texture Fill dialog box. Select the fill you want and make the necessary adjustments. I've chosen the Wood Grain fill. Note the options for Grain, Rainbow grain, minerals, and so on.

Figure 12.22
Add texture fills to
objects or strokes.

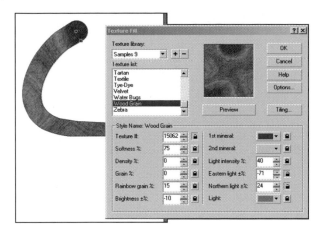

The Pattern fill in CorelDRAW also provides a few options. Create an object such as a circle.
Click the Pattern Fill icon (the blue-and-pink patterned icon) from the Fills flyout menu to get
the dialog box. Choose 2-color, Full color, or Bitmap pattern fill; plus size, offset, and so on.
Clicking the previewed Fill opens up a drop-down menu of Pattern fills, where the gradients are
hidden as well. The Load button as marked in Figure 12.23 opens up a dialog box where you
can access the huge library of patterns included in CorelDRAW.

Figure 12.23
Access the Patterns
library included in
CorelDRAW by clicking
the Load button.

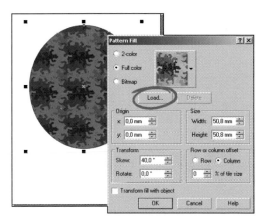

Textures and patterns can add the details that keep eyes on your artwork. These textures and
patterns can be created from scratch or simply altered from existing elements. Before you know
it, this type of eye candy will find its way into your print pieces, Web pages, and everything else
you do.

Part V
Appendices

Appendix A
Filters and Plug-ins

The following pages are meant to give you an overview of the most important tablet software, plus filters and plug-ins. The software includes Wacom's PenTools and PenOffice, as well as Sensiva's clever "draw-a-command" software. Filters and plug-ins discussed here are for Adobe Photoshop and Corel's Painter and include KPT 6, Xenofex, Eye Candy 4000, Deep Paint, Squizz, and "Flood" from Flaming Pear.

In the next section, I'll give you Web addresses for Wacom and Sensiva. These sites will supply more info about the software that you can use with Wacom's tablets. Also, the companion Web site I created for this book—**www.iril.no**—has tablet software updates, links to vendors, and so on. To get a better idea of what you'll see before you go out on the Web, read on.

Wacom Pen Tools

The people at Wacom have created some of the best tablet software themselves. The PenTools software package is free, works with programs such as Painter, PHOTO-PAINT, and Photoshop, and can be downloaded from Wacom's Web site at **www.wacom.com.**

After installation, select Photoshop's Filter Menu and PenTools. The effects open up in a new window where you can paint with them and apply after you're finished. (PenTools is available for both Mac and Windows.) Choose from among eight tools, including 3-D Chisel, Bit Blaster, Virtual Airbrush, and more. Brief descriptions of some of these effects follow:

- **3-D Chisel**—This effect adds a chiseled look to your artwork. Choose settings for Groove, Contrast, Depth, Light, and so on.
- **Bit Blaster**—You can choose from several textures with this one, from Bricks to Noise to Wood. It's pressure-sensitive. See Figure A.1.

Figure A.1
PenTools' Bit Blaster
effect lets you use
pressure sensitivity with
the textures in your
artwork.

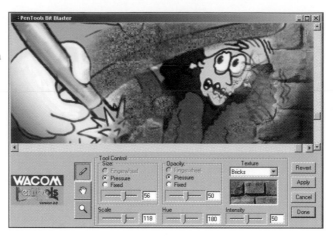

▶ **Brush-On Noise**—This effect is good for painting noise into areas that can be tough to select (otherwise, I recommend Photoshop's Noise filters for large areas).

▶ **Pen Duster** and **Despeckler**—The Pen Duster creates pixelated effects you rarely want on even-colored surfaces. It makes lines and color subdued and somewhat grayish. Despeckler can be used to smudge out areas or strokes in your artwork. You have settings for Amount and Size. This is a good tool for drawings with flat areas of color and when you want to soften lines and transitions quickly. If used with caution, you can also achieve a watercolor effect using Despeckler.

▶ **Metal Leafer**—Choose between silver and gold effects with this tool. Just pick one of the textures and paint away. Both tones create very pixelated effects; you'll have to blur the areas afterwards for a smoother result. (I found it hard to set a color range on the Gold effects that I was happy with. The colors mostly turned out yellow, especially with the Wal3B texture selected.)

▶ **Super Putty**—This product is the same as using the Smudge Tool in Photoshop, and you have options for Size and Distortion that work very well. Use this tool with caution when manipulating the shapes of objects, or smudge areas for that matter. This tool is great for fading out crisp lines, hair, and so on. The more you drag, the softer the lines will be, so be careful.

▶ **The Virtual Airbrush**—This is the last tool in the PenTools collection and it is the best. Its sensitivity is great, and I often use it instead of Photoshop's Airbrush Tool. You can control Size and Ink Flow, and you can also set the Splatter size if that's your fancy. The Splatter is pixelated, so don't use this for smooth work. (The only thing I really dislike about the Virtual Airbrush is the Color palette. I would prefer to pick color from the drawing and not just from the palette.) See Figure A.2.

Figure A.2
The Virtual Airbrush is
a good alternative to
Photoshop's Airbrush
Tool.

Sensiva

Sensiva is a program that lets you draw letters or symbols with your pen or mouse to launch commands or applications. Sensiva works with Windows 95, 98, 2000, and NT 4. (Mac and Linux versions are on the way and might be available by the time you read this.) Users can simply take their Wacom pens and draw symbols to control all their software and Internet applications. Sensiva is fully compatible with Wacom pens and understands your written commands even though you tilt the pen at different angles. You can launch applications, cut, copy, paste, zoom, and even play powerful macros in your favorite programs.

Sounds almost too good to be true, doesn't it? You can also use Sensiva for navigating the Internet. Let's take a closer look at how it works.

After installing Sensiva, open your favorite application—for example, Photoshop. Sensiva has a lot of standard commands, including Cut, Open, Copy, New, and so on. On the mouse or pen, just hold the right button pressed down, draw the symbol, and release. This action executes the command. For example, instead of using Ctrl+N or File > New to open a new document, you do this: Hold the right button on your pen (or mouse) down, draw an N and release—and there's the New document dialog box! It's amazing. An overview of what letters to draw (and how to draw them—it's important that you draw the strokes in the correct order) is available in Sensiva's window at all times. Note that you draw in the application you're working with; Sensiva is working in the background. See Figure A.3.

Figure A.3
Sensiva is the most
impressive and intuitive
application I've ever
seen.

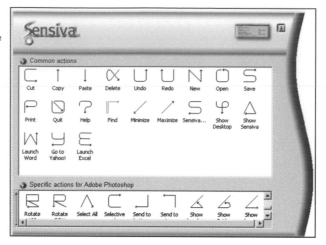

What *really* got me interested was that, when Photoshop was opened, a dialog box came on screen, telling me there might be special plug-ins available for Photoshop at Sensiva's Web site. After downloading the small 48 K plug-in file, I simply dragged it onto the Specific Actions area in Sensiva, as shown in Figure A.3. Now we're cookin'! Here you'll find actions like Rotate, Select All, Deselect, and so on. What really made me excited was that Sensiva automatically changes the actions for whatever program you have on top. So, if you swap between programs a lot—I have a minimum of four going at all times—this is a very cool application indeed. Forget the keyboard shortcuts and use Sensiva instead. You can create your own plug-ins as well.

Another impressive feature is that if you try Sensiva with other programs it does not support by default (for example, Adobe Acrobat), a dialog box pops up with the message: "You are using Sensiva with an application it does not now…" and then asks you if you want to connect to its Internet site to search for a plug-in for that application. Really neat.

Did I mention that Sensiva is free? Go to Sensiva central to download plug-ins for almost any application under the sun. I guarantee that after a few days of learning the various symbols and letters for each application, you'll work much faster.

You can download this gem from **www.sensiva.com** or follow the link from Wacom's site. Make sure you download the Wacom edition if you have a Wacom tablet! Afterwards, download the Photoshop plug-in.

Other plug-ins available for download includes (among others) AutoCad 2000, ColdFusion Studio, CorelDRAW 8 and 9, Director, Dreamweaver, Excel 2000, Frontpage 2000, Flash 4, Outlook, Internet Explorer 5, and many more.

The Sensiva Professional Edition was scheduled to be released during summer 2001. If it's as good as the version we tried, we'll have something to look forward to!

PenOffice

PenOffice adds natural handwriting recognition capability to all Windows platforms. A 30-day trial version is available from Wacom's Web site, **www.wacom.com.** The small PenOffice program dialog box is seen in Figure A.4.

Figure A.4
The PenOffice program toolbox is a cute little thing, but powerful.

PenOffice analyzes pen strokes written in the application window. This program converts the strokes to text and sends the recognized text to the application. PenOffice works in three modes: Recognition mode, ScreenDraw mode, and Markup mode. You turn PenOffice modes on and off just by clicking the Mode icon in the taskbar. Let's take a look at the three modes:

Recognition Mode

This mode translates your handwriting into text and pastes it into the active window. (Double-clicking on icons or clicking dialog box buttons will work as usual.) The trial version made my screen go crazy a couple of times, but the Recognition mode worked smoothly in Microsoft Word. In Figure A.5, I am writing directly in a Word document (this book manuscript, actually); PenOffice recognizes my letters and, after a short delay, "pastes" them correctly in the spot where I began writing. Note that you have to draw clear, precise letters and not doctors' scribbles, or your sentences will be gibberish. PenOffice recognizes whole words and phrases. This program does have a correction mode for editing any mistakes, but the best thing is to write clearly, so that it understands your writing.

Figure A.5
This screenshot shows the toolbar for the PenOffice program while using it with Microsoft Word.

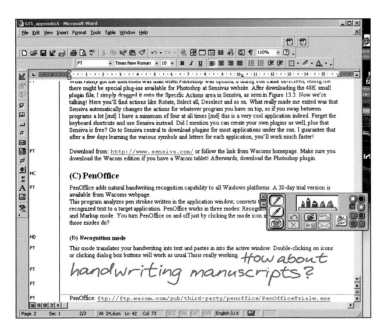

ScreenDraw Mode

This mode lets you draw on-screen sketches by defining an active area in the size you want. After you define the active area (by clicking and dragging across the screen), the cursor will change to the currently selected Pencil/Marker Tool. You can erase anything you've drawn if you have a Wacom Pen. You can then save and e-mail your doodles. (Only what you're drawing in the active area will be saved, however.) When you don't need to draw something above the whole screen, you can use PenOffice's ScratchPad and do your drawing there. Simply click the yellow scratch pad icon in the toolbar and draw stuff like directions to your house, for example, like I've done in Figure A.6.

Figure A.6
ScratchPad lets you doodle away, just like on a regular yellow pad.

Markup Mode

This mode works in Word only but is a great tool for editors and others who share documents and want to draw attention to certain paragraphs, create highlights, and so on. Just select this mode and start drawing in your Word document. PenOffice converts your scribbles to shapes and lines as shown in Figure A.7, and you can delete them afterwards by selecting them and hitting the Delete button. Amazing!

Figure A.7
In Markup mode, Word will never be the same again.

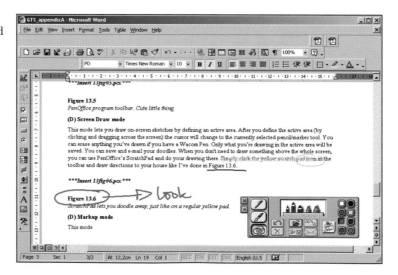

A PenOffice tryout is available directly at **ftp://ftp.wacom.com/pub/third-party/penoffice/ PenOfficeTrialw.exe.**

There are so many filters and plug-ins out there that this section could almost be a book of its own. We'll take a quick look at some of them and which ones you should invest in first. Most filters and plug-ins are reviewed thoroughly on the Internet, so we'll discuss them only briefly here. In Appendix B, you'll find the Web addresses for them and other filters as well.

Photoshop and Painter

Many filters and plug-ins work with both programs, so we've listed them simultaneously. The following filters and plug-ins should be on your "Most Wanted" list:

KPT 6

The KPT (Kai Power Tools) 6 plug-in package is outstanding. Previously a MetaCreations release, but now available from Corel, this package really is value for your money, because it contains hard-to-achieve or time-saving effects. And that's the whole point when considering a filter package: Find out what you need the most, and then decide whether you can create the effects yourself or whether you need a filter package to do it. When combined, glossy surfaces and textures, added light, and so on could save you a lot of work. See Figure A.8.

Figure A.8
KPT Materializer is one of the plug-ins in KPT 6. You can do weird stuff to photographs or artwork with this package's numerous options.

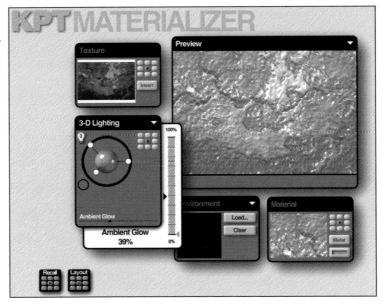

KPT 6 has ten plug-ins in all. One of these is called **Goo**. Goo is a distortion plug-in that performs like a hopped-up Smudge Tool. You can apply liquid distortion effects using various tools like Smear, Smooth, or Pinch. You can also control the effect with pressure-sensitive tools, brush size, and flow. The next one is **Equalizer,** which lets you sharpen or smooth effects, contrast amounts, and so on. With **Projector,** you can apply two- or three-dimensional transformations to an image or even tile them. **Turbulence** adds waves, ripples, and similar effects to an image by reacting to the movements of the pen. You can use the presets or create your own effects.

The **Scene Builder** plug-in is as close to 3D as you'll get without an actual 3D program. You can create realistic, three-dimensional scenes in a two-dimensional or three-dimensional view. You also have multiple preview modes, including Wireframe, Bounding Boxes, and Textured, to mention some. Add texture to, move, rotate, and resize objects.

The **Gel** plug-in is simply a three-dimensional gel lying on top of an image, similar to glass effects but jellyish. You'll apply it with brushes and modify it afterwards with various tools. You can control opacity, light, and refraction as well.

Materializer, as seen in Figure A.8, is a powerful texture plug-in. Create your own textures or use the presets and modify them. You can also control lighting, depth, reflectiveness, and so on. **Lens Flare** simulates the flare that appears in a photo, and its appearance can be controlled through adjustments to brightness, shape, glow, and more. **Reaction** is a plug-in for creating more organic-looking textures that tile seamlessly. You can choose from several options and apply modes to control the texture. The **Sky Effects** plug-in lets you create realistic or weird skyscapes with many options for controlling moon, sun, cloud density, and more. Surf to **www.corel.com** for more info.

Xenofex and Eye Candy 4000

Alien Skin has released two more filter packages after the all-time popular Eye Candy 3.0: Xenofex and Eye Candy 4000. The latter contains, among lots of other filters, the excellent Shadowlab, in which you can use numerous preset shadows like the Short Perspective shadow shown in Chapter 10, "Shadows, Depth, and Special Effects." Or you can create your own from scratch. You have options to set Opacity, Blur, Offset Distance, and so on. If you're looking to buy an overall good filter package, I can recommend Eye Candy 4000, because you get several other filters as well.

If you want a filter package mainly for shadows, I would recommend that you download a demo of Eye Candy 4000 and compare it with Shadow from Andromeda. The latter has more advanced features, such as adding a camera, rotating the objects, and—one I'm personally fond of—the ability to move the shadows around simply by dragging instead of entering values.

Demos are available at **www.alienskin.com** and **www.andromeda.com.**

Figure A.9
Andromeda's interface.

Deep Paint

Deep Paint from Right Hemisphere is both an excellent plug-in for Photoshop and a great stand-alone program. (I have tried the demo, and if you download it, do NOT try to run it from inside Photoshop, because it will cause Photoshop to hang. Instead, work within the Deep Paint program and export your work to Photoshop afterwards.) Deep Paint supports pressure-sensitive tools, including the Wacom Intuos Airbrush.

Deep Paint is not just another drawing program; it offers dynamic 3D lighting and texture control plus artistic cloning that transforms photos to media like oil or watercolor. The list of brushes and paints is huge, from Crayons to Pastels to Felt Pens. The Airbrush Tool behaves like a real airbrush, with a variable spray pattern based on the pressure, angle, and direction of the Pen. Because Deep Paint costs a few bucks, I would not buy it if I already owned Painter, but if I had Photoshop and was looking for those extra-artistic drawing effects, then Deep Paint it is. Take a closer look at Right Hemisphere's Web site at **www.us.righthemisphere.com.** See Figure A.10.

Figure A.10
Deep Paint is excellent for drawing. You can use it as an addition to Photoshop if you don't have Painter.

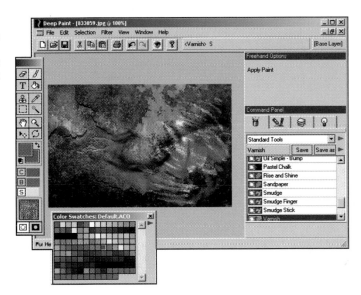

Squizz

Human Software (**www. Humansoftware.com**) has a really neat filter package called Squizz. Basically, it creates distortions using brushes, grids, and warping effects. It also lets you perform morphing effects and tweening inside Photoshop. Squizz handles the in-between tweening (transitions) of animation frames, so all you do is register the Key frame and leave the rest of the job to Squizz.

The brush lets you distort in any mode, from grayscale to CMYK or on a layer selection. The unique Grid Warping feature lets you move points of the overlay grid in any direction to expand, pinch, and distort. You can also save the effect and apply it to another piece of artwork. (See Figure A.11.) You should also take a look at Human Software's other filters: Textissimo (text effects), PhotoSpray (spray pictures on RGB photos and layers), MagicFrame (creates cool frames), and more.

Figure A.11
In this illustration, I'm distorting the Eiffel Tower using Squizz and its Grid Warping feature.

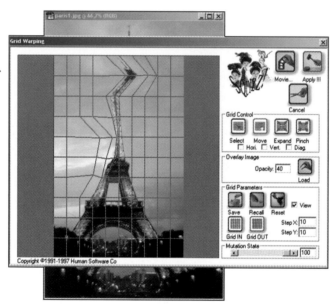

Flood

Flaming Pear (**www.flamingpear.com**) has several good filters, and some are excellent for weather and other natural effects. Flood is a filter that lets you create very realistic 3D-style water effects. You can control how the waves look, how water ripples, and, most importantly, you can control perspective. This filter is great for creating quick water backgrounds and surfaces. If you do a lot of work with watery illustrations, this is a filter you should consider. (If, however, you're looking for more than just water effects filters, you're better off with KPT 6 or some other package.)

Appendix B
Tablet Web Resources

This appendix will give you the best links to tablets and software, software plug-ins, tablet reviews, and other useful items mentioned in this book. This stuff would be great to add to your Favorites folder!

Tablet Manufacturers

Acecad • **www.acecad.com**
Acecad makes tablets for the PC platform (Windows, OS/2) and has products that range in size from 5 × 5 inches (127 × 127 mm) to 12 × 18 inches (304 × 457 mm).

Aiptek • **www.aiptek.com**
Aiptek has currently three small PC-tablets with 512 pressure levels.

Altek • **www.altek.com**
This site features Kurta tablets and digitizers.

Dynalink • **www.dynalink.com**
Dynalink has a graphics drawing pad you can read about here.

Fujitsu • **http://www.fpsi.fujitsu.com**
Hand-held pen tablets.

GTCO Calcomp • **www.gtcocalcomp.com**
Various tablets, from small consumer-priced tablets up to large digitizers for CAD professionals. They offer the "Learn'n'Sketch" for kids as well.

Genius/KYE • **www.genius-kye.com** (US)   **www.geniusnet.com.tw** (TW)
Read about the NewSketch and other small tablets.

Mitsubishi • **http://www.mitsubishi-mobile.com/**
Hand-held computer tablets. Read about the Amity CP and XP.

Sony VAIO Slimtop Pen Tablet • **www.sonystyle.com/vaio/pentablet/index.html**
PC and LCD tablet all in one.

UC-Logic • **www.uc-logic.com**
Small tablets or cordless keyboard plus tablet.

Wacom • **www.wacom.com**
> The industry leader. Choose from Web sites in the U.S., Europe, Japan, and Asia. You can buy tablets from industry leader WacomDirect (**www.wacom.com/wacomdirect**) or from one of their resellers.

Xploretech • **www.xploretech.com**
> See the heavy duty GeneSys system, the toughest tablet out there.

Resellers of Tablets and Digitizers

I've selected a few links so that you may compare prices on various tablets. However, use the links below at your own risk. We have not ordered from every company listed below, and therefore I can't guarantee their service or reliability. Use common sense if you consider ordering from the Internet. Make sure the e-shop gives you the necessary info, including telephone numbers, contact persons, and so on, so you can feel confident you're dealing with a safe company. Check delivery prices and security. Do not give out your credit card number if the shopping basket is not residing on a secure server. You should see a small yellow padlock (Explorer) or a key (Netscape) in your browser (bottom corner, right side) if the shopping basket is secure.

Advantage Outlet • **www.advantage-outlet.com**
> This site sells Kurta/Altek digitizers.

Amazon • **www.amazon.com** (US) **www.amazon.co.uk** (Europe)
> This site sells tablets from Wacom, GTCO Calcomp, Crayola Kids, and KB Gear.

Buy.com • **www.buy.com** (US) **www.gb.buy.com** (UK) **www.canada.buy.com** (CA)
> These sites sell GTCO Calcomp, Wacom, and KB Gear tablets from their online stores in the US, UK, Australia, and Canada.

CAD Warehouse • **www.cadwarehouse.com**
> This site sells GTCO Calcomp, Altek, and Summagraphics digitizers.

CDW • **www.cdw.com**
> This site sells Calcomp, Wacom, KB Gear, and Genius tablets and accessories, plus various cordless products.

Jungle • **www.jungle.com**
> This site sells Wacom and Natural Pen (Ivelltrade) tablets; ships outside the UK on request.

MicroWarehouse • **www.warehouse.com**
> This site sells Wacom tablets for PC, SGI, and Mac; U.S. deliveries only.

NecX Direct • **www.necxdirect.com**
> This site sells Wacom tablets; U.S. deliveries only.

Outpost • **www.outpost.com**
> This site sells hardware and software for both the PC and the Mac. The company offers tablets from Wacom, KB Gear, and Micro Innovations.

Sony • **www.sonystyle.com**
> Sony's shopping site, where you can buy the VAIO Pen Tablet.

WacomDirect • **www.wacom.com/wacomdirect**
> Wacom's shopping site.

Tablet Reviews

Here's a selection of links to some online computer magazines. These e-publications have tablet reviews as well as software and filter reviews.

CNET • **www.cnet.com**

CreativePro • **www.creativepro.com**

Digital Media Designer • **www.digitalmediadesigner.com**

Electic Tech • **www.electic.com**

Futurelooks • **www.futurelooks.com**

IT Reviews • **www.itreviews.co.uk**

MacAddict • **www.macaddict.com**

MacCentral Consumer Reviews • **www.maccentral.epinions.com**

PC Artist • **www.pcartist.com**

PC Review • **www.pcreview.co.uk**

PC World • **www.pcworld.com**

Planet3Dart • **planet3dart.com**

ZDNet Computer Shopper • **www.zdnet.com/computershopper/**

Software

The breakdown of this section is as follows: Applications; Tablet Software, Filters, and Plug-ins; Third-party Plug-ins and Filters; Tutorials; and Links for Fonts and Typography.

Applications

The following applications can be found at their respective Web sites:

Painter, CorelDRAW, and KTP 6 • **www.corel.com**

Illustrator • **www.adobe.com/products/illustrator/main.html**

Paint Shop Pro • **www.jasc.com/**

Photoshop • **www.adobe.com/products/photoshop/main.html**

Photoshop Elements • **www.adobe.com/products/photoshopel/main.html**

Tablet Software Packages, Filters, and Plug-ins

The following software packages, filters, and plug-ins can be found at their respective Web sites:

PenOffice for Windows • **www.wacom.de/Download/penoffice/DoOthS04.htm**

Cybersign • **www.wacom.de/Download/DoOthS05.htm**

Netwriter • **www.paragraph.com**

Sensiva • **www.sensiva.com**

Wacom PenTools for Photoshop • **www.wacom.de/Download/dopt00.htm**

Third-party Plug-ins and Filters

Many plug-ins and filters are available in demo versions. Download them and try them out to see if they're worth the investment. The following third-party plug-ins and filters—which are but a sample of what's available—can be found at their respective Web sites:

Alien Skin • **www.alienskin.com**
  Plug-ins (such as Eye Candy 4000 and Xenofex) for Photoshop, ImageReady, Fireworks, Corel PHOTO-PAINT and Paint Shop Pro.

Altamira • **http://204.29.20.136/**
  Genuine Fractals, Genuine Fractals Print Pro.

Andromeda • **www.andromeda.com**
  Photoshop plug-ins such as Varifocus, LensDoc, Three-D, Shadow Filter.

Auto F/X • **www.autofx.com/homepage_media/homepage.html**
  Photoshop plug-ins such as Photo/Graphic Edges and AutoEye.

Chroma Graphics • **www.chromagraphics.com**
  Photoshop plug-ins such as MagicMask and EdgeWizard.

Cytopia Software • **www.cytopia.com**
  Photoshop color correction plug-in CSI PhotoOptics.

Intense Software • **www.creoscitex.com/products/workflow/intense/index.asp**
  Photoshop and Illustrator plug-ins like Powertone, Silvertone, and so on.

Right Hemisphere • **www.us.righthemisphere.com/dpaint/deep_paint_home.htm**
  Deep Paint (a Photoshop plug-in) and other software.

Human Software • **www.humansoftware.com**
  Squizz filter package and more.

Color Calibration Software

ViewOpen and ScanOpen • **www.heidelberg-cps.com**

Pantone ColorSuite and Pantone Personal Color Calibrator • **www.pantone.com**
  Read a review on PCC at:
  http://www.zdnet.com/pcmag/stories/reviews/0,6755,2455887,00.html.

Corel Premium Color Edition • **www.corel.com**

Kodak Colorflow Custom Color Software ICC • **www.kodak.com** or
www.kodak.com/global/en/professional/products/software/colorFlow/customColor/customColor.shtml

Other Color Calibration Tools and Plug-ins

Test Strip • **www.vividdetails.com**
  From Vivid Details, this is a Photoshop plug-in for color correction. It is available for Windows with a Mac version coming up. No demo.

Colorsync • **cfm.imation.com**
>   This is a color management module (CMM) software package from Imation for the Mac.

Colorific • **http://www.sonnetech.com/products/colorific/welcome.html**
>   This product from Sonnetech measures the colors that your monitor displays. This information is used by your computer's operating system to give you more accurate color. Colorific works with applications such as Photoshop, PageMaker, and CorelDRAW and runs on Windows and Mac operating systems.

Radius PressView SR Series • **www.radius.com**
>   This plug-in from Radius/Digital Origin is designed to be used as a step-by-step calibration software application. Included are the PressView SR Display, the PressView Display Management application, and the ProSense Display Calibrator. This software supports standard resolutions and timings for Macintosh and VESA. See also ProSense, which is the company's professional display calibration system for Mac.

EzColor • **www.monacosys.com**
>   This entry-level ICC profiling tool from Monaco is for both PC and Mac. A demo is available.

Tutorials

Adobe.com has lots of tutorials for Photoshop 6, Elements, Illustrator, and so on. Always check the company's Web page for information and tutorials for its software. The following tutorials can be found at their respective Web sites:

Apple Creative, Digital Imaging • **www.apple.com/creative/digitalimaging/**
>   Some good stories and a couple of tutorials on digital imaging on can be found on Apple's Web site. Take a look at the Web and Print sections also.

Desktoppublishing.com • **www.desktoppublishing.com**
>   This site has links to tutorials, reviews, and other resources.

Eclipse e-zine • **www.lunareclipse.net**
>   This site has some good tutorials for Photoshop (like Fun with Sepia) and other great stuff.

GraphixLand • **www.graphixland.com**
>   This has some tutorials for CorelDRAW, Photoshop (these are basics but still good), and Paint Shop Pro, as well as for CSS, HTML, Flash, and more.

Saturation in Photoshop 6 • **www.digitalmediadesigner.com/2000/12/tutorial/ photoshop12_00a/photoshop12_00-page1.htm**
>   Here you'll find a video tutorial by Deke McClelland, plus more tutorials on the Digital Media Designer's Web site, including ones on layers and effects.

Thinkdan • **www.thinkdan.com**
>   Dan has some good Photoshop, Illustrator, and Macromedia Freehand tutorials.

The Author's Page • **www.iril.no**
>   Here are links to even more tutorials and neat things.

Brushes for Photoshop

Photoshop 5.5 and 6.0 Brushes

Note that many of these Web sites also have other Photoshop goodies, not only brushes!

Cybia • **www.cybia.co.uk/brushes.htm**
Some excellent texture brushes.

Webbuilder101 • **www.webbuilder101.com/downloads/graphics/brushes/kms/brushes.asp**
Hosts numerous brush sets from various authors.

About.com • **graphicssoft.about.com/compute/graphicssoft/library/free/blfree_psbr.htm**
Four sets of decorative brushes the last time we counted, with illustrations so you'll know what they look like before downloading.

Comp.graphics.apps.photoshop • **www.geocities.com/SoHo/Coffeehouse/8144/eqstras/brushes.html**
Many brush sets are available from this newsgroups Web site.

Deepspaceweb • **www.deepspaceweb.com/brushes.shtml**
Various brush collections with themes like "winter brushes" and so on.

Ritual Myth • **www.ritualmyth.com/photoshop_brushes.html**
This has a couple of brushes.

Graphics Galore • **http://people.delphi.com/ekerley/brush/brush.ht**
Several sets of brushes, many Dingbats-style

Links to Fonts and Typography

Try the following links for understanding fonts and typography:

TYPOlis • **privat.schlund.de/t/typolis/engl/klas.htm**
Get information about type classifications.

Graphion's Online Type Museum • **www.slip.net/~graphion/museum.html**
Take a look at the section Glossary of Typographic terms at **www.slip.net/~graphion/gloss.html**.

Planet Typography • **www.planet-typography.com/**

TrueType resource archive • **www.typesource.com/Archive/Index.html**
Download fonts.

EyeWire • **www.eyewire.com/magazine/columns/robin/**
Type columns by R. Williams.

A Graphic Designer's Guide to the Galaxy • **www.icenter.net/~huebs/gdlinks/**

Index

Index

Index

Index

PowerPoint (presentation software),
    editing icons from, 198
PPI (pixels per inch), *207*
Premium Color Edition (color editing software), 143
Pressure feature (of 4D mouse), 45
pressure-sensitivity, *8*, 9
    in Adobe Illustrator 9, 56–57
    compatibility, 18
    in Corel Painter 6, 53–56
    in PhotoShop, 47–52
    setting, 36–37
print, creating graphics for, 207–8
Profile Viewer Tool, 143
Projector (effect plug-in), 310
Proportional setting, 39, 44
proportion, of cartoons, 160–61
Pucker Tool, 111
pucks, 8

Q

quadtones, 140
QuickPoint Mode, 40

R

rasterizing
    fonts, 209, *210*
    layers, 111
    shapes, 174
Reaction (effect plug-in), 310
Red Eye Brush, *48*, *94*
reflections, 192–93
removing
    applications, 47
    background, 51
    fringe pixels, 69–70
    pixels, 63–64
    unwanted objects, 97–98
renaming tools, *45*
replacing colors, 130–31
resizing objects, 243
resolution, graphic, 207
retouching images
    with Painter 6, *100*
    with Paint Shop Pro 7, *100*
    photographs, 50
reviews of tablets. *See* tablets
RGB (red, green, blue) mode, 117, 137, 207–8
Right Hemisphere Deep Paint (filter package), 311
Ripple filter, 291
RM graphics tablets, *19*
rotating images, 95
Rugged GeneSys System series pen tablets, 15
rusted effect, 254–55

S

sand, creating, 269–72
sans serif font, 210, 216
saturation
    adjusting, 96, 105
    explanation of, 118–21
ScanOpen ICC (color rendering tool), 142
scan quality, 95
Scene Builder (effect plug-in), 310
ScratchPad, 308
screws, creating, 253–54
seamless backgrounds, 292–94
Secrets of Color Management, The (book), *144*
segments, 176
selecting objects, 62–65, 72, 73
Sensiva (command/application launching
    program), 305–6
serial port connections, installing tablets with
    on Macs, 24–25
    under Windows, 22–23
serif font, 210
settings
    copying from one application to another, 46
    copying from one tool to another, *42*
sevenet font, *211*
Shadow (filter package), 237
Shadowlab (filter package), 236, 310
shadows, *77*, *78*
    adding, 106–8
    adding depth with, 239–42
    cast, 228–31
    drawing by hand, 233–34
    drop, 233–34
    filters for, 236–37, 310
    real versus filter-produced, 227–28
    using layers, 231–32
shapes
    See also vector graphics
    of cartoons, 160
    creating, 171–73
    of objects, adjusting, 110–11
    rasterizing, 174
    using effects with, 174–75
using filters with, 173
sharpening, 52, 93
shortcuts
    adding, 40, *41*
    for Intuos Lens Cursor, 31
    and keyboard placement, 32
    pre-programmed, 17
    for selecting, 73
silver effects, 245, 304

U

UC-Logic graphics tablets, 11, *19*
UltraPad series graphics tablets, *19*
unsharp masking, 93
USB ports, 17, 23–24, 25

V

VAIO Slimtop PCV-LX900 (pen tablet computer), 15
vector brushes, *179*
vector fonts, 209–10
vector graphics, 167
    See also shapes
    combining with bitmap images, 169–70
    composition with, 183–93
        in Illustrator 9, 183–87
        in PhotoShop, 188–93
    converting to bitmaps, 174
    creating, 171–82
        paths, 176–79
        shapes, 171–73
        strokes, 180–82
ViewOpen ICC (color calibration tool), 142
Virtual Airbrush effect, 304–5

W

Wacky Kids Pad (graphics tablet), *19*
Wacom graphics tablets, 12
    See also names of specific Wacom tools
    compatibility, *19*
    Graphire series, *19*
    Intuos series, 9, 12
        DualTrack feature, *31*
        tools for, 27–32
    LCD tablets, 13
    PL series, *19*
    UltraPad series, *19*
Wacom PenTools, 303–5, 316
warp effects, *111*, 214

watercolor, creating strokes like, 49–50
water effects, 268, 269–72, 312
weather effects, 257–69
    clouds, 258–61
    filters for, 267–69
    lightning, 264–65
    snow, 262–63
    stormy, 265–67
Web graphics, 201–24
    also creating for print, 207–8
    color information and file size, 218
    color palette for, 208
    compression techniques, 219
    creating and exporting buttons, 220–23
    dithering, 204–5
    exporting, 219–20
    file formats for, 201–4
    text as, 217
    transparent, 205–7
Web Painter (graphics tablet), 10
Web palette setting, 218
Wet Edges option, 49
wet paint effects, 94
Windows (operating system)
    creating icons for, 195–96
    installing tablets
        with serial port connection, 22–23
        with USB port connection, 23–24
worn effect, 254–55

X

Xenofex (filter package), 310
XGT (graphics tablet), 10, *19*
Xplore Technologies hand-held pen tablets, 15
X-Rite ColorShop (color editing software), 143–44
X-Rite's *Color Guide* (booklet), *143*

Y

YTG graphics tablets, *19*

Order Form

Postal Orders:
Muska & Lipman Publishing
P.O. Box 8225
Cincinnati, Ohio 45208

Online Orders or more information:
http://www.muskalipman.com
Fax Orders:
(513) 924-9333

Title/ISBN	Price/Cost
Scanner Solutions 0-9662889-7-1	
Quantity _____	× $29.95
Total Cost _____	
Digital Camera Solutions 0-9662889-6-3	
Quantity _____	× $29.95
Total Cost _____	
PhotoImpact Solutions 1-929685-12-2	
Quantity _____	× $34.95
Total Cost _____	

Title/ISBN	Price/Cost
Paint Shop Pro Web Graphics 1-929685-13-0	
Quantity _____	× $39.95
Total Cost _____	

Subtotal _____

Sales Tax _____
(please add 6% for books
shipped to Ohio addresses)

Shipping _____
($6.00 for US and Canada
$12.00 other countries)

TOTAL PAYMENT ENCLOSED _____

Ship to:

Company _____

Name _____

Address _____

City _____ State _____ Zip _____ Country _____

E-mail _____

Educational facilities, companies, and organizations interested in multiple copies of these books should contact the publisher for quantity discount information. Training manuals, CD-ROMs, electronic versions, and portions of these books are also available individually or can be tailored for specific needs.

Thank you for your order.